# Coaching
# Track and Field
# Techniques

# About the Author

Ken Foreman has been a successful track and field coach for 35 years. During his tenure as track and field coach at Seattle Pacific College, members of his men's team earned 20 all-American awards and his female athletes set more than 25 American and world records. He is a member of the Sports Medicine Committee, the Athletic Congress. Coaching accomplishments include:

1. Head coach, the U.S. International Track and Field Team . . . U.S.A. versus the British Commonwealth, 1967
2. Head coach, the U.S. International Cross Country Team . . . Barry, Wales, 1967
3. High elevation coach, the U.S. Olympic Team . . . Los Alamos, New Mexico, Mexico City, 1968
4. Head coach, the U.S. International Cross Country Team . . . San Sebastian, Spain, 1970
5. Coach, Pacific Cup Cross Country Team . . . Victoria, B.C., 1973
6. Head coach, United States World University Games Track and Field Team . . . Moscow, U.S.S.R., 1973
7. Coach, U.S. Women's Pentathlon Team . . . Winnipeg, Canada, 1974
8. Head coach, U.S. International Cross Country Team . . . Milan, Italy, 1974
9. Assistant coach, PanAmerican Team . . . Mexico City, Mexico, 1975
10. Head coach, U.S. International Track and Field Team . . . Pacific Conference Game . . . Canberra, Australia, 1977
11. Coordinator, United States versus Canada, Pentathlon, 1978
12. Consultant, The PanAmerican Team . . . Puerto Rico, 1979
13. Head coach, U.S. Women's Olympic Track and Field Team, 1980
14. Women's head coach, U.S. World Cup Team . . . Rome, Italy, 1981

# Coaching
# Track and Field
# Techniques fourth edition

## Ken Foreman
The Sports Medicine Clinic
Seattle, Washington

**wcb**
Wm. C. Brown Company Publishers
Dubuque, Iowa

Former editions of this textbook were titled *Track and Field Techniques for Girls and Women* and were coauthored by Virginia Husted.

Consulting Editor

*Aileene Lockhart*
*Texas Woman's University*

Printed in the United States of America
10  9  8  7  6  5  4  3

# Contents

# Preface

The new title, *Coaching Track and Field Techniques,* is indicative of the transition that has occurred since the first edition of this book was written. At that time, well over a decade ago, girls and women were being given their first opportunities to participate in sport and athletics. They were doing so without the benefit of coaching during their formative years, and they did not have the long term conditioning which has traditionally prepared sport minded boys. The first edition was, therefore, an attempt to meet the needs of girls and women at that time. It was a sort of primer on track and field, technically sound, though written for the unsophisticated performer.

In subsequent editions an effort was made to inject new ideas and to meet the needs of both the beginner and the maturing performer. This edition goes even further. With Title IX bringing parity into school athletic programs, many female athletes now have a sports history similar to the male athlete. In recognition of this fact the fourth edition has been revised to meet the needs of both male and female track and field athletes.

Those who are familiar with earlier editions will note that the chapter dealing with the "lost art of running" has been eliminated. This was done because it now appears that most boys and girls are learning the fundamentals of running, jumping and throwing in their school physical education programs. In place of the general material about running, a chapter has been added concerning the art and science of talent selection. To my knowledge this is the first serious attempt to identify and analyze those factors which seem to be essential to high achievement in track and field. The identification of performance factors, the suggestion of tools for testing these factors, and the establishment of criterion scores for the selection of track and field athletes give this chapter relevance to both the physical education teacher and the coach.

The brief historical information about female track and field performers which formerly was found at the beginning of each chapter also has been eliminated. This was done because such information about men and women would require more space than its value seemed to warrant. In place of the specific information about women, there now is a general statement in the sections concerned with running, jumping, and throwing, which describes the success of the American athletes in these events on an international basis. This opening statement also includes general information relevant to the specific events covered in each section.

Most of the photographs in this edition are new. Many of these were taken by the writer during his tenure as head Olympic coach. In every instance the photographs show America's top track and field athletes in action. Technical information throughout the book has been updated and in some instances chapters have been completely re-written. All of the information reflects the best thinking of coaches from around the world. This is noted both to acknowledge the author's indebtedness to fellow coaches and to assure the reader that all of the material reflects the ideas most frequently espoused by authorities on track and field.

Undoubtedly the most significant change in this fourth edition has been the addition of material concerning the steeplechase, the triple jump, long distance running, the pole vault, and multi-event participation. The book now covers all the track and field events in which both men and women engage, except the walks and the hammer throw. The decision not to include the latter stems from the fact that few schools and universities include these events in their competitive schedules.

Throughout the revision of this manuscript the question of relevance has been continually raised. What are essentials where each track and field event is concerned? What kinds of questions does the coach ask on a day to day basis? How does one teach a skill or give advice that will help the mature performer? It is my belief that these questions have been addressed in a straight forward manner. There is pertinent material here for the beginning coach as well as for the young and inexperienced athlete. There also are tips for the highly skilled performer. Indeed, the clear explanation of teaching procedures and the insights into performance evaluation represent a unique and important dimension of this book.

The latest thinking on the holistic training of the track and field athlete is to be found throughout the book. This includes suggested single week work loads for the off season, pre-season, and competitive season. The representative training schedules for beginners and mature athletes also are a reflection of the holistic perspective. This is to be noted in the expanded chapter on conditioning and weight training as well.

In the final analysis this is a book for teachers and coaches that has been written by a coach having more than thirty years of active experience in track and field. The latter includes experience working with athletes of all ages and abilities. The book also relfects more than a dozen international assignments as coach of U.S. cross country and track and field teams. Indeed, I would be remiss if I did not thank all of the athletes and coaches with whom it has been my privilege to work. They have taught me about coaching, about the art of working with people, and the science of understanding the technique of sound athletic performance. It is my sincere hope that this book does justice to all of them.

As always the writer must take full responsibility for all of the ideas that have been expressed in a work of this kind. There are, however, those who have made completion of the book a reality. I give thanks to my family and friends for their support and concern. And special thanks must go to Dwight Cottrill who so painstakingly produced black and white prints from hundreds of colored slides taken around the world.

part 1

# Principles
Teaching–Coaching–Performing

# 1 Get Set!

It would be foolish to argue which of the commands initiated by a starter is more important, that is, "On your marks," "Get set," or a gun shot signaling the runners to "Go." The command "Get set," however, assumes a readiness to go—a readiness stemming from appropriate perparation prior to the call to the marks. At the risk of pushing an analogy too far, this chapter is entitled "Get Set" because it deals with material deemed by the author essential to getting ready to teach, coach, or perform effectively. In so doing I have chosen to identify practices that are employed by successful coaches and which consistently yield effective results.

## Holistic Planning

**Get Set by Careful Planning and Thorough Organization**

Effective coaches plan "holistically," a concept first expressed by Doherty in his excellent book *Modern Training for Running*.[1] Holistic planning is comprehensive, covering as well as possible the whole person and the whole season. A first step in planning is the development of a general schedule encompassing time commitments for an entire year, such as the schedule provided here.

September 1 to November 30
Cross-country running for middle distance and distance runners, including hills, Fartlek, marathon, and interval training. General conditioning activities.

Cross-country running. Form striding. General and specific conditioning activities for sprinters, hurdlers, and jumpers.

Extensive weight training, conditioning, sprint, and technique work for throwers.

---

1. Kenneth J. Doherty, *Modern Training For Running* (Englewood Cliffs, N. J.: Prentice-Hall, Inc., 1964).

*December*

Active rest. Participation in a variety of activities for the purpose of maintaining gains accrued during fall training.

*January 1 to March 30*

Overdistance running, including Fartlek and road racing. Interval training for middle distance and distance performers. Specific conditioning activities.

Interval running. Acceleration runs. Form-endurance training and specific conditioning for sprinters and hurdlers.

Sprint work. Special conditioning and technique work for jumpers.

Sprint work. Special conditioning and technique work for throwers.

*April 1 to July 30*

Overdistance running, Fartlek, and speed-endurance interval training for distance runners.

Fartlek and speed-oriented interval training for middle distance runners.

Sprints and relays, starts, and technique training for sprinters and hurdlers. Specific conditioning.

Sprints, special conditioning, and technique work for jumpers.

Sprints, special conditioning, and technique work for throwers.

*August*

Active rest for all performers.

Another dimension of holistic planning and organization is the preparation of individual training schedules. This is a time-consuming task and often represents the difference between ineffective and successful coaches. Over the years the author has developed a training schedule format, with slight variations for different events. Since these will be used extensively hereafter, the reader is urged to study them carefully and either adopt them or develop a comparable form for personal use. In either instance, it is helpful to have training schedules prepared on prepunched paper and enclosed in a sturdy binder so they can be used on the field.

Next, one must determine the emphasis to be given to the elements of each program throughout the year. Time commitments recommended by the author are shown in the accompanying graphic illustrations.

It is to be noted that each of the schedule forms utilize key terms for which code letters are given. These were developed through trial and

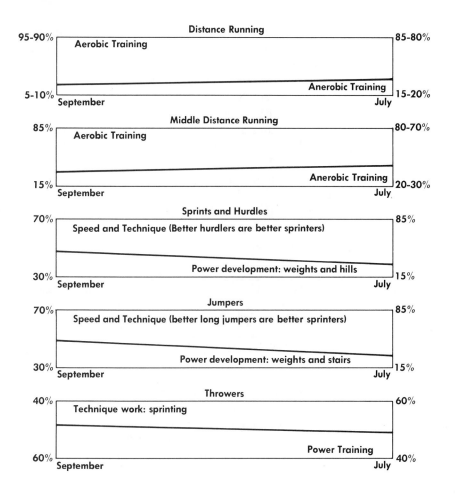

Distance Running

95-90% Aerobic Training — 85-80%
5-10% September ——— Anerobic Training ——— July 15-20%

Middle Distance Running

85% Aerobic Training — 80-70%
15% September ——— Anerobic Training ——— July 20-30%

Sprints and Hurdles

70% Speed and Technique (Better hurdlers are better sprinters) — 85%
30% September ——— Power development: weights and hills ——— July 15%

Jumpers

70% Speed and Technique (better long jumpers are better sprinters) — 85%
30% September ——— Power development: weights and stairs ——— July 15%

Throwers

40% Technique work: sprinting — 60%
60% September ——— Power Training ——— July 40%

error and represent the elements most commonly found in the training programs for runners, jumpers, and throwers. It should also be noted that the key terms have meanings which are specific to the person for whom the schedule has been prepared. This specificity of meaning is further delineated in the training schedule provided here.

| Code | J | Jog | ( ⅓ speed ) | YD | Yards |
|------|-----|-------------|---------------------|-----|---------|
| | ST | Stride | ( ⅔ speed ) | MI | Miles |
| | FS | Fast Stride | ( Relaxed sprint ) | M | Minutes |
| | BU | Build Up | ( Jog to fast stride ) | S | Seconds |

**Middle Distance and Distance Training Schedule**

| Date | Warm Up | Distance | Time | Reps | Recovery | Other |
|------|---------|----------|------|------|----------|-------|
| | | 440 | 65 S | 8 | 440 J | |

Is is assumed that the terms *yards, miles, minutes,* and *seconds* need no explanation. However, since the training of runners often necessitates the careful control of such elements as distance, pace time, recovery time, and the like, it is essential that these terms have a specific meaning. In the example just mentioned the performer is expected to repeat 440-yard runs in the time of 65 seconds each. The recovery after each would be a 440 jog in 3 minutes and 15 seconds. Since a jog is, by definition, one-third speed, the jog time is determined by multiplying 3 times pace time ($3 \times 65 = 3$ M 15 S).

The rational for determining stride time is the same as for a jog. The code terms for fast stride and build up are relative to individuals. A fast stride is the fastest cadence that an individual can achieve without pressing or trying too hard. A buildup is an acceleration run, beginning at a jog and finishing at a fast stride.

## Sprint and Hurdle Training Schedule

| Code | J | Jog | ( ⅓ speed ) | AD | Acceleration-Deceleration |
| | ST | Stride | ( ⅔ speed ) | B | Block Work |
| | FS | Fast Stride | ( Relaxed sprint ) | M | Minutes |
| | BU | Build Up | ( Jog to fast stride ) | S | Seconds |

| Date | Warm Up | Distance | Time | Reps | Recovery | Other |
| --- | --- | --- | --- | --- | --- | --- |

On the schedule for sprinters and hurdlers are two special terms. The first is *block work* which means starting practice from blocks. The other is *acceleration-deceleration* running, often referred to as "in-and-out" running. This involves a series of buildups with letups, buildups with letups, a drill used by sprinters to facilitate the development of relaxed control.

## Jump Training Schedule

| Code | J | Jog | ( ⅓ speed ) | SA | Short Approach |
| | ST | Stride | ( ⅔ speed ) | FA | Full Approach |
| | FS | Fast Stride | ( Relaxed sprint ) | M | Minutes |
| | BU | Build Up | ( Jog to fast stride ) | S | Seconds |

| Date | Warm Up | Running | Jumping | Recovery | Other |
| --- | --- | --- | --- | --- | --- |

A term having specific meaning for jumpers is the *short approach,* or "pop-up" jump. Short-approach jumping is done to conserve energy and permits the performer to concentrate on the jump, rather than on the approach. In the long jump, a short approach would be from fifty to sixty feet and accurately measured. In the high jump five to seven strides would be considered short-approach jumping. A full approach for most long jumpers is between one hundred five and one hundred twenty feet and in the high jump between ten and thirteen strides.

| Code | J | Jog | ( ⅓ speed ) | SA | Short Approach- ½ circle |
| | ST | Stride | ( ⅔ speed ) | FA | Full Approach |
| | FS | Fast Stride | ( Relaxed sprint ) | WT | Weight Training |
| | BU | Build Up | ( Jog to fast stride ) | | |

| Date | Warm Up | Running | Throwing | Recovery | Other |
| --- | --- | --- | --- | --- | --- |

Short-approach throwing in the javelin usually involves from three to seven strides. Most of a javelin thrower's training in the fall is from a short approach. Half-circle work in both the shot and discus events is aimed at refining the explosive action out of the power position.

The preparation of individual schedules is the final step in holistic planning. Since each schedule should reflect both current status and future expectations, one begins by carefully reviewing the record of the athlete for whom the schedule is being prepared. Armed with specific information, the coach makes a judgment as to where he or she expects an athlete to be at the end of the forthcoming season. Once such a judgment has been made, goals are set, and the training program for that athlete is developed accordingly. (When dealing with a first-year performer, the coach could conduct a series of time trials to obtain relevant information.)

An example of this approach is a hypothetical middle distance runner with current best times of 62 and 2:17 for the 440 and 880, respectively. If a review of records revealed that this runner had best times the previous year of 65 and 2:28, these times and the improvement made over the year would be cause to believe that this performer has excellent potential. Accordingly, a coach might set 2:10 as a reasonable goal for the year ahead. This time would then be the basis for the development of subsequent training schedules, going from where the performer is to where she is expected to be by late spring.

Advocating a training cycle which involves ten months of specialized activity and two months of active rest, we plan to have our athletes hit their target times by the end of May. Since there are eight training months between September and May, I recommend that training times for September be set eight seconds above the target times for May, with a reduction of one second each training month.

Referring back to our hypothetical middle distance runner, repeat 440s run in September would be at seventy-three-second pace, or eight seconds above the target time of sixty-five seconds for May (assuming that sixty-five seconds is even pace for a 2:10, 880). The training pace for October would be seventy-two seconds, for November, seventy-one seconds, and so on, as the performer is patiently prepared to reach the goal set for the current season.

The reader will readily recognize that it is not possible to accurately predict what any individual might ultimately do. Thus all goals are tentative and stated in such a way that they neither discourage nor limit athletes in their development. As the season progresses, new information is used as a basis for revising both short-term goals and the more speculative long-term goal for the season.

**Get Set by Improving Communication**

Planning and organizing are one thing; communicating information and ideas, another. Steps identified with effective communication are delineated by such terms as *explanation, demonstration, exploration, supervision,* and *evaluation.* These terms, it will be noted, clearly depict the teaching-training-testing loop so essential to improved performance. The manner in which each step can be a facilitator of communication is briefly outlined.

Research findings seem to indicate that poor communicators tend to talk too much; they flood the learner with too much information and confuse rather than clarify the situation. Thus, explanation should be brief and clear. The giving of succinct cues, the use of key words, is all important. Following verbal communication the effective teacher clearly and accurately demonstrates the skill, or part thereof, to be practiced (explored) by the learner. Two or three demonstrations are enough, with such factors as speed, force, rhythm, and timing being precisely shown.

Exploration ought to be a time of self-communication. That is, the performer tries out the skill, seeking both intrinsic and extrinsic feedback in terms of errors in technique. As the performer explores a skill, the effective teacher or coach continues to clarify the specific task at hand. At this point the temptation to add more and more information must be thwarted.

The final step in the communication process is evaluation. This means that the performer is required to "put it on the line," as it were. The common practice in track and field is to conduct time trials or engage in competition to determine where each athlete is in terms of preparation. While some coaches and athletes do not believe time trials are essential, it is our opinion they constitute an indispensable part of the teaching-training-testing loop. An authority of unequivocable stature who agrees with this position is Ed Temple of Tennessee State University. Mr. Temple stated in a recent conversation with the author that "sprinters have to sprint against other sprinters if they are going to attain their real potential." In like manner, distance runners, throwers, and jumpers have to "put it on the line" if they are going to exceed mediocrity.

A sorely neglected facet of effective communication is the selection and use of words that are appropriate to the situation at hand. Use of the word *throw* is a classic example. The discus throw, for example, is not a throw at all, but more appropriately should be called a *fling* (a term perhaps first used by Paul Ward in his excellent discussion of this complicated and technical event).[2]

Other examples of words which may facilitate the learning process are given in the paragraphs that follow. These are intended to be illustrative, rather than comprehensive, as the reader is urged to develop a descriptive vocabulary of his or her own.

Cue words in the shot put are *shift* and *lift*, or *drive* and *lift*, which are far more suggestive of the explosive power essential to this event than the frequently used words *glide*, or *hop* and *reverse*. In like manner the "put" is not really a "put," but more appropriately a "thrust" or a "slap" at the instant of release.

Words having special meaning to the javelin event are *hip punch* and *whip* or *flail* which denote whole-body action terminating in a balistic release.

The five-step drill between hurdles is appropriately called a *quick step* drill. Lead-leg action is a *sprint off* the hurdle rather than a *step down*. The effective hurdler *punches* the trail leg through, thus negating any tendency to *lay out* over the hurdle or *sit on* the hurdle, as the beginner is likely to do.

The long jumper does not deliberately *slow down* during the final approach, or *lengthen* the last few strides, but rather the athlete "settles into a sprint off" the takeoff board. In like manner the high jumper *drives up* from the takeoff foot rather than *gather* for a spring.

Appropriate cue terms for runners might be *power runs*, denoting the purpose of a particular session, and *step downs* or *funnels* depicting a specific focus or commitment of energies. The term *lift* is an important cue to sprinters whose arms and knees tend to *drop* at the end of a race.

Throughout the remainder of this book every effort has been made to reflect careful planning, thorough organization, and clear communication. Chapter 2 assumes that an understanding of selected mechanical principles is the starting point for understanding how a specific skill ought to be performed. For the coach working with highly skilled athletes, knowledge of mechanics is absolutely essential to an analysis of performance during practice and during a subsequent study of action movies. The development of chapter 3 stems from the acquisition of data over a period of more than three decades. It is the purpose of this chapter to

---

2. Paul Ward, "Discus Slinging," Unpublished material presented to participants in the United States Olympic Development Clinic, Eugene, Oregon, 15-17 June, 1975.

help the teacher and the coach more effectively select athletes for specific track and field events. It should be recognized that while it is possible to identify many of the factors that contribute to successful performance, the factor of ultimate significance, the human will, cannot be quantified in any known way.

In subsequent chapters each event is introduced holistically. There then follows a part-by-part analysis of the event, with tried-and-proved teaching procedures discussed in detail. Comprehensive training schedules complete each chapter.

# 2 Mechanical Principles

A perusal of track field records will reveal that the improvement of performance over the last fifty years has been no less than dramatic. Performance records for men still exceed those for women in all events, though women are now improving at a more rapid rate than men. Although the difference between world records for men and women was thirty percent or more in 1930, in all comparable events the difference now is less than ten percent. There seems to be evidence that in the middle distance and distance events the difference between performance marks for men and women will be less than three percent by 1990.

Factors contributing to improved performance by both men and women include greater opportunity for women to compete, increased size, greater strength, superior skills, better facilities and equipment, better genetic selection, better nutrition, better medical care, and better understanding of the principles of performance.

This chapter is an attempt to show how an understanding of basic physics can contribute to improved teaching and performance in track and field. While the materials have been purposely simplified, the principles are valid and hopefully will be applied in ways that have relevance for the reader. Those persons desiring fuller understanding of the mechanics of track and field are encouraged to review the selected references given at the end of this chapter.

## Newton's Laws

The human body might appropriately be described as an intricate mechanism capable of unlimited movement combinations within the dimensions of time and space. Like other mechanisms, the human body is subject to the laws of nature. The effects of these laws in operation may be positive or negative, depending upon man's adaptability. An understanding of the laws of motion and the means of coping with them is therefore essential to effective teaching and performance.

It will be recalled from courses in physics and kinesiology that force is a predictable phenomenon. Newton noted this consistency in his experimentation and was led to formulate certain laws of motion. These include the laws of inertia, momentum, and interaction.

Figure 2.1                              Figure 2.2

**Figure 2.1.** When starting, the sprinter assumes a preliminary position with the weight distributed between all four points of support.

**Figure 2.2.** In the set position, the center of gravity is moved forward slightly so that the pull of gravity will help to overcome resting inertia.

Simply stated, the law of inertia tells us that a body at rest remains at rest and a body in motion tends to continue in motion with constant speed in a straight line unless acted upon by some outside force. This law has significance for track and field in numerous situations. Two examples are the sprint start and the shot-put shift and lift. The sprinter starts from a crouch. In the set position the center of gravity is moved forward over the hands so the action of the legs will drive the body forward out of the blocks. In this instance, both gravity and muscle power are used to overcome inertia. When putting the shot, the participant assumes a preliminary standing posture, dips and then drives forward across the ring. Gravity initiates the first action while muscles of the legs and hips keep the body moving forward.

Inertia also has an effect on running form and energy expenditure. Once the participant has overcome the resting inertia of the body and has begun to move, the energy expenditure for continued movement is less than the initial cost of getting under way. A constant rate of speed is, therefore, less fatiguing than a pace that is variable. On the ends of the track runners tend to fall away from the curve (centrifugal force) and must compensate for this tendency by leaning and swinging their arms to the inside of the track (centripetal force). Efficient running form thus involves a relaxed, steady pace and compensatory postural adjustments when the participant runs on the curve.

**Figure 2.3.** The power position permits the discus thrower to impart all available forces to the discus at the instant of release.

A second phenomenon was noted by Newton: namely, when a body is acted upon by a force, that body is changed in the direction of the force and in proportion to the amount or duration of the force. This is called the law of momentum, a law which describes force quantitatively as the product of mass or weight and velocity.

Momentum has an effect on all track and field events, but it is particularly significant in the shot put, discus, and javelin throws. Momentum, like inertia, may affect performance positively or negatively. Other things being equal, the performer having the fastest approach has the greatest potential for achieving maximum throwing distance. Too much speed, on the other hand, increases the performer's momentum to a point where it cannot be adequately controlled.

To overcome inertia and acquire the desired momentum, movement is started along lines of low resistance. In the throwing events, especially the shot and discus, preliminary postures cause the largest and strongest muscles to act as prime movers. Subsequent action is aimed at producing greater speed and a balanced position for applying force. Proper technique places the working muscles on stretch and permits them to contract explosively through their most effective working range.

The third law of motion involves interaction. This law states that for every force in nature there must be two bodies, one to exert the force and the other to receive it. Or, stated in other terms, the law says that for every action there is an equal and opposite reaction.

In track and field, interaction affects performance in numerous ways. The sprinter drives from the blocks, alternately thrusting the arms forward and backward in oppossition to the movement of the legs. The high jumper "pushes" against the takeoff surface to get vertical lift. The shot-putter shifts and lifts to apply force out through the shot. Thus each performer drives against a firm surface to attain maximum results from the expended energies. (The drive and the firm surface are essential.)

## Rotary Motion

Rotary or angular motion is a very special problem in all athletic activities. In track and field this is particularly true as the performer seeks to produce great torquing force for an event such as the discus throw or to skillfully control this force in the jumping events and the hurdles.

The laws that applied to linear motion also apply to angular motion, with certain modifications. Perhaps the most important modification is to be noted in the application of Newton's second law dealing with acceleration. In linear motion, acceleration—or the change of speed of an object—is proportional to the force imparted to the object and inversely proportional to its mass. Accordingly, when great force is applied to a light object, it accelerates markedly, though the same force might have little effect on a much heavier object.

In angular motion, acceleration is determined by the force applied and the relationship of the mass to the rotational axis of the object in question. Thus an object turns more rapidly when acted upon by a force if the mass is near to the axis of rotation than if the mass is distributed at a distance from the axis of rotation. This is easily demonstrated on a free-spinning turntable where merely raising the arms sideward reduces the turning speed.

The significance of this principle is obvious. The discus thrower who needs to increase turning speed must keep all body parts as close to the central axis as possible during the spin across the circle, whereas the long jumper who chooses to control rotary motion lengthens the body in flight to reduce forward or rearward turning speed.

The sprinter faces a somewhat different, though important, problem concerning rotation. As the athlete runs, each arm and each leg establishes its own center of rotation. These individual rotational forces may complement each other, or they may seriously limit the stride length and subsequent speed of the runner. Flexing the free leg during the forward swing permits rapid recovery, and when accompanied by vigorous arm action, it tends to increase stride length and running speed.

Since rotary motion is so important in track and field, it behooves the teacher to understand how this motion can be produced. *First,* it can be produced by checking a linear motion. An example is the final stride in the javelin approach wherein the forward leg acts as a break and fulcrum. (In kinesiology this is referred to as the "hinged principle" and is applicable to those activities in which the sudden fixing of one end of a lever system contributes to the turning speed of the other end.)

**Figure 2.4.** The completely extended takeoff leg indicates that the jumper has expended her force explosively against the firm takeoff surface.

A *second* means of producing rotary motion is the transference of angular momentum from a part of the body to the entire body. Perhaps the most important illustration of transference in track and field occurs in the high jump. In both the straddle and the flop the free leg is driven upward at takeoff. This kicking force is thus transferred to (added to) other forces produced at takeoff, helping to drive the body mass to its maximum height.

A *third* means of producing rotation is by application of what some choose to call "eccentric thrust." Closely associated with the principles of checking and transference, this principle is nevertheless an important one to comprehend. If a coiled spring were depressed so that all downward forces were perpendicular to the supporting surface, theoretically it would spring straight upward when released. If, on the other hand, the forces depressing the spring were at a tangent to the supporting surface, the energy within the spring would be expended back through a similar tangent upon release. In like manner, the jumper who leans into the bar at takeoff expends part of the force horizontally. If the lean is greater than is necessary to produce rotation around the crossbar, force is dissipated inefficiently.

**Figure 2.5.** A forward lean during hurdle clearance minimizes the tendency of the trunk to straighten up (reaction) as a consequence of the sprinting action (action) of the lead leg.

**Action-Reaction**

Implications of the third law of motion already have been discussed with respect to the impulse effect when movements from a firm surface are initiated. The results are *actions* of running, jumping, and throwing which are consequences of *reactions* to the firm surface. Movements occurring in space are unique, however, for the body, rather than the performance surface, absorbs the forces imposed and tends to *react* in different ways. At times the reaction is positive; at times it is negative.

Indeed, the finer points of performance technique often concern themselves with the maximum utilization or control of the force effect on airborne bodies. While these are discussed in detail in later chapters, comments pertinent to the hurdle event are made here to emphasize the importance of the principle in question.

There are three instances in the hurdle event when performance is seriously affected by the action-reaction phenomena. The first involves the takeoff, a point when the hurdler is still in contact with the ground. To utilize the action-reaction principle positively, one bucks or pikes forward to facilitate thigh lift and negate any tendency to rotate rearward away from the hurdle.

The second instance of action-reaction occurs during the sprint down of the lead foot beyond the hurdle barrier. The tendency here is for the head and chest to rotate up and rearward (reaction) toward the heel

**Figure 2.6.** The hurdler reaches across the body to negate the tendency to rotate around the long axis as the trail knee is punched through in preparation for the following stride.

of the lead foot which is driving downward and rearward (action). This negative force opens, or extends, the body, producing a breaking rather than a driving action and thus reducing the length of the important first stride after the hurdle step.

In the case of both examples thus far noted, the rotational effect is forward or rearward around the transverse axis of the body. In this third example of action-reaction, rotation occurs around the longitudinal axis of the body. The trail leg initiates this force as the knee is punched forward and upward in preparation for the next stride. The knee punch thus is the action, with inward rotation or displacement of the opposite shoulder constituting the reaction. If not compensated for, this force produces rotation away from the desired line of progress, shortening the stride and negating forward speed. The technical components of hurdling described in chapter 6, namely, the slight buck at takeoff and the action of the arms, constitute means of utilizing or compensating for the action-reaction phenomenon.

## Summation of Forces

Motor skills represent a complex pattern of interrelated movements. In skilled performance, parts or segments of the total pattern are discernible only to the trained observer. Skilled performance seems to flow from beginning to end. The pattern of events is a model of perfect timing, a summation of all related forces.

Each track and field technique is a unique combination of movements. To appropriately apply each technique for its intended use the teacher must sense the relationship of the parts to the whole. An effort must then be made to help the performer integrate all movements efficiently, adding force to force at the proper instant in order to attain the maximum expenditure of energy. Only by achieving a perfectly coordinated summation of forces will the performer realize the highest degree of proficiency.

It is for this reason that the javelin thrower approaches the throw from eightly to one hundred feet, gradually increasing speed until the point of release where all possible force is applied to the implement in an explosive, though coordinated, manner. The approach speed is transferred to the body an instant before delivery; the legs drive against the ground, ankles, knees, and hips lifting. The trunk is flexed, the arm is flailed forward, and a final ballistic action occurs. Success in all events is dependent upon a similar coordinated summation of all available forces.

## Center of Gravity and Balance

Gravity is a constant force acting on the body. A body is said to be balanced when the force of gravity falls within the base of support. When the force, or center of gravity, falls outside the base of support, the body is said to be off-balance, and a new base of support must be established in order to regain stability. These and other important properties of gravity and balance have numerous implications in the skillful performance of track and field events.

When starting, the athlete utilizes gravity by leaning forward. When stopping or changing direction, the center of gravity is shifted rearward, or in the direction of the turn as the situation might dictate. This latter point is especially important to the javelin thrower, the discus thrower, and the shot-putter, for these performers must learn to explode into their implements with abandon and then control their momentum in an instant of time. They do this with a follow-through which broadens their base and lowers their center of gravity.

In hurdle races, control of the center of gravity is extremely important. It is costly in terms of both time and energy when the body mass is moved up and down during the course of the race. The skilled performer thus lowers the trunk while hurdling, keeping the center of gravity as nearly constant as possible.

Jumpers must also deal with gravity, for the instant one leaves the ground, gravity pulls the body earthward at a predictable rate of speed. Ground release velocity at the time of takeoff will determine how well one is able to negate the downward pull of gravity. This is to say that takeoff speed is imperative to achieve both linear distance and vertical height.

**Figure 2.7.** The long jumper seeks to achieve maximum takeoff speed so that the downward pull of gravity can be negated for the greatest possible time.

**Trajectory**

All airborne bodies, within certain limits, adhere to the physical laws governing trajectory. According to these laws, the center of gravity of every missile follows a symmetrical path (a parabola) from the point of release to the point of landing—when these two points are equal in height. These laws thus govern the flight of all objects thrown by track and field performers as well as the flight of those who jump for either height or distance.

It is easy to calculate how far a given body will travel when its velocity and angles of release are known and when either its resistance to **movement** or its tendency to fly can be determined. In the case of the shot, there is little tendency to fly and minimal loss of velocity due to friction. The distance a shot will travel is thus a straightforward matter of imparting maximum velocity to the implement whose angle of release is between the optimum point of forty to fifty degrees. Since velocity is more important than trajectory, modifications in technique that are compensatory to individual differences should, if possible, affect the release angle rather than the release speed.

While the discus and javelin are also projectiles, these implements possess special aerodynamic properties that necessitate some marked modification of the angle of release. Modern javelins have been constructed to sail. When released at too steep an angle, they tend to rise abruptly, then die, and eventually fall far short of the distance they might go with an appropriate expenditure of energy. Indeed, recent research has shown that an aerodynamically sound (distance-rated) javelin attains its greatest distance when the release angle is between thirty and thirty-five degrees and the attack angle (difference between tip and center of gravity) is from three to five degrees.

The discus also tends to sail and, like the javelin, is vulnerable to the direction and force of the wind. When the discus is thrown into the wind, the release angle should be from twenty-five to thirty degrees, with an attack angle of one to two degrees. When it is thrown with the wind, the angle of release should be several degrees greater so that the implement may ride the air currents as far as possible. Within limits, both the javelin and the discus tend to travel farther into the wind than when thrown with a following wind.

**Mechanical Principles That May Influence Track and Field Performance**

The reader should be aware that human differences make it impossible to apply these mechanical principles to all individuals and all events without some reservation. Anatomical and physiological variations in individuals do not permit exact prediction. Individuals differ in temperament, body type, strength, and other factors that influence performance. Then, too, the skill and the ability to use force effectively are often matters of disciplined attention to the task at hand. The best teacher is one who recognizes that individuals are different, who understands that physical laws do not exactly fit human performance, but who applies those principles that seem to work.

1. When the inertia of a resting body is being overcome, force should be applied by the most powerful muscles in the direction of the intended line of flight. This principle applies to the sprint start and to those events that involve throwing and jumping as well.
2. To counteract centrifugal force the runner should lean into the curve, swinging the arms vigorously across the body. Since a body moving twice as fast requires four times as much centripetal force to maintain its curved path, the sprinter's inward lean must be more pronounced than that of the distance runner.
3. Although it is much simpler to increase one's mass than it is to increase one's velocity, the lighter performer in the throwing events can compensate for a weight disadvantage by learning to move with greater speed (Momentum = Mass × Velocity).
4. The force effect is greatest when applied through the longest possible range of motion—and when it is applied in the shortest possible time. (When throwing and jumping, the performer should learn to apply force explosively.)

5. To be of maximal effect a force must be applied in the direction of the intended flight of the body or of an implement propelled by the body. For this reason a high jumper seeks to maximize the expenditure of vertical forces at takeoff, while shot, discus, and javelin throwers expend their respective forces through the intended trajectory at the instant of release, and the hurdler sprints forward when clearing the hurdle barrier.

6. The acceleration (rate of speed increase) of a body is proportional to the force causing it and inversely related to its mass. For this reason, strength is an important factor in successful performance, while any excess weight is a liability.

7. The effect of interacting forces is greatest when applied to a firm surface. The shot-putter and the discus and javelin throwers should release their implements while in contact with the ground.

8. All moving bodies are influenced by the effects of rotation. To cope with these effects the performer must apply a counterforce. The long jumper runs in the air. The sprinter shortens the radius of the legs for greater leg speed, coordinates the arm swing with the stride pattern, and thus utilizes the rotary effect in a positive manner.

9. The successful performance of a complex skill will be determined in part by an effective summation of forces. All available forces should be utilized, each new force being added to the peak of the previous one, with the final force expended explosively. (When two forces are applied simultaneously, the weaker force prevails.)

10. Whenever possible, gravity should be used to overcome the force of inertia. This can be done by leaning forward in the starting blocks, quickly lowering the center of gravity to initiate the shift in the shot event and so forth.

11. To effectively control momentum in the javelin, shot put, or discus, the performer follows through by widening the base of support and lowering the center of gravity.

**Selected References**

Dyson, Geoffrey H. G. *The Mechanics of Athletics*. 6th ed. London: University of London Press, 1973.

Ecker, Tom. *Track and Field Dynamics*. Los Altos, Calif.: Book Division, Track and Field News, Inc., 1971.

Kelly, David L. *Kinesiology: Fundamentals of Motion Description*. Englewood Cliffs, N.J.: Prentice Hall, Inc., 1971.

Northrip, John W.; Logan, Gene A.; and McKinney, Wayne, E. *Introduction to Biomechanic Analysis of Sport*. Dubuque, Iowa: Wm. C. Brown Co., 1974.

Wilt, Fred. "Track Technique." *Journal of Technical Track and Field Athletics*.

# 3

# The Search for Talent

While it is recognized that the single most important factor in all of human performance is the strength of the individual performers will, it likewise should be recognized that there are specific and identifiable factors that contribute to success or failure in every track and field event. This chapter has been written to provide the coach with tools that can be used to assist in the process of talent identification. The key word here is assist, for if used wisely the criteria suggested will do just that and nothing more. Even so, more than thirty years of coaching have taught me that if we can short cut the process of trial and error, and if we can suggest to potential track and field performers where they might expect to find the greatest success, we have dramatically improved the art and science of coaching.

From the standpoint of the performer, the use of selective criteria also has great value. Like it or not there is at loose in our society both a cultural and racial bias that often determines the event which one might choose. Black children are subtly tugged toward the explosive events: the sprints, hurdles, and jumps. And while many perform there with exceptional ability, others do not. White children, on the other hand, are made to believe they cannot sprint well so they move toward distance running and the throwing events.

Where girls are concerned the large, displastic youngsters are pushed into the shot put and discus, events which demand power and strength, not just size. Then too, youngsters are frequently put in an event out of necessity where the team is concerned, or they choose an event because a friend is performing there. I have known more than a dozen outstanding athletes who spent one to several years in frustration because they were in the wrong event. Three of these went on to be Olympic performers and/or world record holders when they finally arrived at the event for which they were genetically and emotionally predisposed.

Actually, the use of prediction factors in the selection of track and field athletes has been a matter of discussion for more than three decades. In 1948 T. K. Cureton found that athletes in different sports and in different events within the same sport manifest specific event related characteristics. Correnti and Zauli reported in 1960 that athletes tended to manifest a wide range of heights and weights, as well as age variability between events, but that they had similar body shapes within the same event.

In 1964 Tanner reported a relationship between race and selected track and field events. He also noted that athletes can be separated according to body dimension where specific events are concerned. According to de Garay, body size and type are factors of importance to successful achievement in track and field. He noted that "one ought to look at the grandparents when selecting young athletes."

More recently (1972, 1976) Wilmore, et al stated that the higher the percentage of body fat the poorer the performance in athletic activities. This is particularly true in those events in which one moves his or her body through space. During the same year the writer studied the top 120 female athletes in the world to determine if there were distinguishing characteristics where event specificity was concerned. It was found that the age range among these performers was sixteen to forty, with seventy-nine athletes being older than twenty-five. An additional twenty-six were older than thirty, with three being over thirty-five. These data revealed a relationship between age and the event in which one participated, with the mature athletes to be found in the technical throwing events and the younger performers in the sprints, hurdles, and jumps. It also was noted that the explosive performers, that is, sprinters, hurdlers and jumpers, were naturally leaner than those athletes who participated in other events. In like manner the throwers were significantly taller and heavier than all other track and field performers.

Ryan and Allman stated in the text "Sports Medicine" that "size is a factor in all types of sports involving acceleration, that is, moving ones body over a distance, lifting it, turning it, and using it to exert maximum force." It also was noted that taller persons have a greater strength potential in proportion to their size, they have greater respiratory capacity, are slower to accelerate than shorter persons, and they are at a disadvantage in lifting their own body weight.

In delineating those factors, which lead to superior performance in track and field, Burke and Tait identified the following: increased size, greater strength, superior skills, better facilities and equipment, more facilities for more athletes, better genetic selection, better nutrition, a more competitive environment, and better medical care.

One additional study effecting the selection of track and field athletes is the long term study of Medford School children conducted by Harrison Clark of the University of Oregon. In the latter study it was shown that the standing long jump and the jump reach correlate highly with future success in athletics, generally, and the sprints and jumping events, specifically.

With the advent of the Sports Medicine Laboratory the identification of selection criteria has become even more sophisticated. This is to be seen in such activities as the monitoring of lactic acid as a means of evaluating stress, the calculation of oxygen uptake values to determine aerobic capacity, and the accurate appraisal of muscle strength and power.

All across the world today, efforts are being made to delineate those factors that seem to contribute to success in various athletic activities. In track and field the trend has been toward the teaching of a variety of skills during the growing years, with specific testing of performance factors occurring during the early teens. Perhaps the best of these programs is to be found in West Germany where the DLV coaches and trainers have devised a series of test batteries for the selection of potential candidates for each track and field event.

An analysis of the West German tests, as is true of those to be found in most of the Eastern Block countries, reveals that the factors being tested are speed, power, strength, aerobic capacity, and anaerobic potential. Specific tests that are used to measure these factors include such items as: (1) the 30 meter sprint (2) the jump reach and standing long jump, (3) a variety of single leg and double leg bounds, (4) throwing ability using various weighted objects, (5) distance runs of 2000-5000 meters, (6) power runs for time or at distances of 300-600 meters, and (7) specific event skill evaluation.

In attempting to devise so-called predictive measures the writer has drawn heavily on the West German Talent Search program. The writer also has drawn upon more than thirty years of coaching experience working with athletes at every level of skill and maturity, as well as data accrued at the USOC Training centers at both Squaw Valley, California, and Colorado Springs, Colorado.

A first step in the development of selection criteria is the identification and ranking of general performance factors. These have been delineated and ranked according to the writer's experience in the table below.

**Factors of Importance in the Performance of Specific Track and Field Events**

| Sprints-Hurdles | Jumps | Throws | Middle Distance-Distance |
|---|---|---|---|
| Natural speed | Power | Power | Aerobic capacity (distance) |
| Power (W÷T) | Strength | Strength | Anaerobic strength (middle distance) |
| Stride cadence | Natural speed | Body morphology factors | Natural speed |
| Strength | Body morphology factors | Coordination | % Body fat |
| Movement time | Coordination | Natural speed | Strength |
| Naturally high lean to fat ratio | % Body fat | | |

While most authorities on track and field would agree with the identification of performance factors as listed above, not all would agree to their relative importance. Agreement to the importance of each fatcor is not as critical, however, as finding simple tests for evaluating speeds, strengths, aerobic capacity, etc. Tests that one might explore for this purpose are to be found below:

Tests to Be Used in the Evaluation of Specific Performance Factors

| Factor | Test |
| --- | --- |
| Speed | 50 yard sprint from a stand |
| Power (explosive strength) | Jump reach, standing long jump, standing triple jump, bounding for time or distance, the Margaria-Kalaman test |
| Foot speed | Time a runner over ten yards when fully accelerating. (Perhaps between 40-50 yards). Count the strides and determine strides/second. |
| Reaction or movement time | By using any of a variety of response timers. |
| Body morphology | Height, weight, body build, leg length to trunk length ratio, arm span and the like |
| General strength | Push ups, sit ups, chin ups, bench press, lat pulls, full squat to sit, as well as determination of ratio of strength to body weight |
| % Body fat | Skin calipers, hydrostatic weighing |
| Coordination | Soft ball throw for distance, bounding with combinations, performance evaluation using primary sports skill |
| Aerobic "strength" | Maximum stress test with gas analysis, Astrands nomograms using bicycle ergometer, 15 minute run, harvard step test, timed 5000 |
| Anaerobic "power" | 45 second, 60 second power run, timed 300, exact distance covered in 2 x 60 second runs with 3 minutes recovery between each, calculation of percent drop off in time between best 200 and best 400. Best 400 and best 800, etc. |
| Competitive spirit | Run 800 meters for time |
| Self image | Observe athlete in social and competitive situations. |

It is to be recognized that there are at least four factors that will effect the scores derived by the tests suggested above. These are: (1) the motivation of the persons involved, (2) previous experience, (3) level of expectation, and (4) the accuracy of test administration. (See appendixes) It also should be recognized that the writer does not yet have sufficient data to set objective criteria for elementary and junior high school youngsters. Where high school or potential elite performers are concerned, however, the following guidelines seem to represent reliable criteria for talent identification.

| Factor (Power) | Jumpers | Throwers | Sprinters | Runners |
|---|---|---|---|---|
| Jump reach | 20" women<br>30" men | 18" women<br>26" men | 20" women<br>26" men | 14" women<br>20" men |
| Standing LJ | 8' women<br>9' men | 7' women<br>8' men | 7'6" women<br>8'6" men | 6'6" women<br>7'6" men |
| Overhead shot two hand throw | | 4 K 38"<br>12# 43" | | |
| 5 double leg bounds | 36' women<br>40' men | 36' women<br>40' men | 34' women<br>38' men | |
| Standing triple jump | 25' women<br>29' men | 24' women<br>27' men | 24' women<br>27' men | 20' women<br>24' men |

| Factor (Strength) | | | | |
|---|---|---|---|---|
| Bench press | Body weight W<br>1.5 body wt M | 1.25 body wt W<br>2.0 body wt M | body wt W<br>1.5 body wt M | body wt-M.D. W<br>body wt-M.D. M<br>.75 body wt. D W<br>.85 body wt D M |
| Squat | 1.5 body wt W<br>1.75 body wt M | 1.75 body wt W<br>2.0 body wt M | 1.5 body wt W<br>1.75 body wt M | 1.25 body wt W<br>1.50 body wt M |
| Snatch | .65 body wt W<br>.75 body wt M | .85 body wt W<br>1.0 body wt M | | |

| Factor (Anthropometric) | | | | |
|---|---|---|---|---|
| Height | (H.J.) 5'10" W<br>6'2" M | 5'8"-5'10" W<br>6'-6'5" M | | Slightly built for distance<br>Meso-ecto for middle distance |
| Weight | | 160-190 W<br>200-250 M | | 110-125 W<br>140-160 M |
| % body fat | 10-13% W<br>6.5-9% M | 15-21% W<br>12-15% M | 11-14% W<br>5-8% M | 5-9% W<br>1-5% M |

| Other Factors | | | | |
|---|---|---|---|---|
| Motor Coordination | Ability to transfer force to vertical lift | Softball throw 200' W 250' M | Stride cadence 4.2-4.5/second | |
| Speed | 6.4 50 yds W<br>5.8 50 yds M<br>30'/sec W<br>31.5'/sec M | 6.9 50 yds W<br>6.2 50 yds M | 6.3 50 yds W<br>5.6 50 yds M<br>30'/sec W<br>31.5'/sec M | 7.0 50 yds W<br>6.2 50 yds M<br>27'/sec 800W<br>30'/sec 800M<br>26'/sec 1500 W<br>29'/sec 1500 M |
| Aerobic Strength | | | 6 min/mile (55 ml/kg/min) men and women | 60 ml/kg/min W<br>64 ml/kg/min M |
| Anaerobic Power | | | Recommend 2 x 40 second power run . . . no norms as yet | 2 x 60 sec with 3 min recovery 820 yards W 930 yards M |
| Self Image | Strong support from parents and friends. . . . Coach should observe athlete's ability to deal with social situations, note reactions to peer pressure, etc. . . . especially with female athletes. | | | |

**Selection Factors for Elite Track and Field Athletes**

Perhaps it needs to be reiterated that coaching is an art and a science. The wise coach seeks to understand the science and to learn the art of its application. The wise coach also recognizes that we work with whole people, sees them as whole people, listens to them as whole people, and attempts to stretch them as tall as it is possible for them to be.

**Selected References**

Clarke, H. Harrison. *Physical and Motor Tests in the Medford Boys' Growth Study.* Englewood Cliffs, N.J.: Prentice-Hall, Inc., 1971.

Correnti, V., and Zauli, B. *Olimpionici 1960.* Rome: Marves, 1964.

Cureton, T. K., Jr. *Physical Fitness of Champion Athletes.* Urbana, Illinois: University of Illinois Press, 1951.

DeGaray, A. L.; Levine, L.; and Carter, J.E.L. eds. *Genetic and Anthropological Studies of Olympic Athletes.* New York: Academic Press, 1974.

Komarova, A. and Raschimshanova, K. "Ideal Characteristics of Female Discus Throwers," *Legkaya Athletika, No. 5,* 1975.

Ryan, Allan J., and Allman, Fred L., eds. *Sports Medicine.* New York: Academic Press, 1974.

Tanner, J. M. *The Physique of the Olympic Athlete.* London: George Allen and Unwin, 1964.

Wilmore, J. H. *Athletic Training and Physical Fitness.* Boston, London, Sydney: Allyn and Bacon, 1976.

# part 2

# Running Events
## Sprints–Relays–Hurdles–Middle Distance–Distance

There are four general categories of running events. These are the sprints (100-200-400 meters), the hurdles (100-110-400 meters), the middle distance races (800-1500-3000-meters), and the distance races (5000-10,000-marathon). Classification of the running events stems from tradition, performer speed or velocity, what one does during the race, and its length or duration. The factor of tradition, our historic classification of an event, likely has its greatest influence on the mental preparation of the athlete. That is, how one perceives what it is that one is doing, sprinting, running distances, etc. On the other hand, running speed and participation time are problems of primary concern where the physical conditioning of the athlete comes into question.

Historically American athletes have been world leaders in the sprints and hurdles. They have had from moderate to good success in the middle distance events, but have not consistently ranked among the world leaders in the distance races. This fact is likely a reflection of the outstanding talent base in our country, as well as the nature of a society that does not honor or support the commitment to long term, disciplined training which is so essential to the long distance events.

From the standpoint of basic mechanics there isn't much difference between sprinting and the gait of the distance runner. At every rate of speed there are periods of single support and nonsupport. All runners assume an essentially erect posture, the limbs are relaxed and in alignment. A basic principle here is the longer the race the shorter the stride and the shorter the race the longer the stride. In every instance, foot placement is natural, with initial weight bearing tending to shift from the forefoot to the full foot as the velocity of the performer decrease. Even hurdling can be viewed as a modification of the sprint stride as the performer modifies the running gait to accommodate barriers of varying height.

A key factor in the training of runners is understanding and applying the mechanisms of energy production. The reader is reminded that all muscular work stems from the chemical breakdown of a substance known as ATP (Adenosine triphosphate). This breakdown results in the formation of ADP (Adenosine diphosphate), a free phosphate ion and energy. The energy produced is used to power the muscle cells and thus "drive the human machine."

There are three mechanisms whereby the process of energy production involving ATP can occur. The first of these is known as the ATP-CP system. This is an anaerobic system, operating without the need for oxygen, and providing energy for work lasting about ten seconds. The ATP-CP system is used primarily for explosive activity such as sprinting and jumping, and has little to do with the middle distance or distance events.

A second system, which also in anaerobic, is the lactic acid system. The latter involves a complicated chemical process whereby carbohydrates are converted to glucose, and glucose to ATP through glycolysis. A by-product of this process is the production of lactic acid. The continued production of lactic acid becomes self-limiting. The muscle cell is poisoned by its own metabolic product, begins to function inefficiently and when no relief is provided, ceases working all together. This is what happens when a runner begins to gasp for air, suffers intense physical pain, loses coordination, and finally ties up in a demanding race. The lactic acid system is capable of providing energy for as long as three minutes. While the system is operative one goes into oxygen debt and must repay this debt during a period of recovery. When the debt has been repaid and the performer is breathing normally again, he or she is said to be operating aerobically (with the presence of oxygen).

It is generally assumed that participants in the sprint races (100-400) derive about 100 percent of their fuel from the anaerobic fuel systems. As the length of the race increases to 800 meters the energy distribution is thought to be about 50 percent anaerobic and 50 percent aerobic. The shift from anaerobic to aerobic continues as the athletes runs further and further with the marathon runner operating about 100 percent aerobically.

The aerobic system is also very complicated as the performer utilizes a combination of carbohydrates and fat as a primary fuel source. Indeed, one of the advantages of the aerobic system is the availability of fuel in quantities sufficient to provide energy for protracted periods of time.

It is to be noted that the training schedules provided for each of the running events are based on the problem of energy production. This is to say that the stress loads designed for sprinters-hurdlers, middle distance and distance runners have been carefully equated to maximize the energy source for each specific event. It also must be recognized that all of the training schedules to be found in this book are representative and should not be followed indiscriminately. Coaching is both an art and a science. The science is knowing the principles of performance; the art comes in applying these to meet the needs of individual performers.

# 4 Sprinting

Sprinters are naturally gifted athletes. While they come in all sizes, they share a common ability to start explosively, accelerate rapidly, and run with a cedence of about 4.5 to 5.0 strides per second. Although not everyone can be a sprinter, everyone can improve on natural speed. This chapter has been written for those performers who just want to run faster, as well as those who have great sprint potential.

The basic problem of starting is to overcome the resting inertia of the body in the shortest possible time while placing the sprinter in the most effective position for the continued application of force. Since this is a technical problem, there have been numerous experimental efforts to determine the best starting form. These efforts have revealed certain fundamental principles about starting, though there is still considerable difference of opinion as to which sprint start is the best.

**Sprint Start**

Some teachers are intent upon producing maximum speed out of the starting blocks; others sacrifice initial explosive speed for balance during the transitional strides between the starting blocks and the all-out sprinting effort. A third group seeks the best of each, namely, initial velocity and balanced sprinting form. To a large extent the end or goal that the teacher is seeking will determine the starting technique that one chooses. Differences in individuals also may affect ones judgment.

Traditionally block placements were classified as bunch, medium, and elongated. More recently there was a tendency toward the use of the so-called bullet start. The latter involved the shifting of both pedals twenty inches or more from the starting line, with a spacing of three to six inches between the two pedals. Current research has shown that there is reason to believe that the semielongated block setting is most effective for the largest number of performers.

## Block Location and Spacing

One should begin by selecting starting blocks which are accurately calibrated and easy to adjust. Initially these are set with the front block fixed at a point between two and two and a half foot lengths from the starting

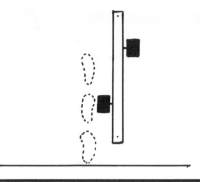

**Figure 4.1.** Placement of the starting blocks, showing the relative positions of the frame and the respective blocks in terms of foot lengths from the starting line.

line. The exact distance is determined by the structure and preference of the runner. The rear block is next moved to the extreme back end of the sliding frame. To locate the rear block, the sprinter assumes a four-point starting position with the preferred foot in the front block (whichever foot feels most comfortable). The sprinter then places the knee of the opposite leg parallel to the toe of the front foot and slides the rear block up to meet the rear foot. The distance between the two feet when this procedure has been completed will be about fifteen inches. Beginners usually find that their initial exploration of the sprint start is uncomfortable. They should be encouraged to experiment for themselves, to make minor adjustments which fit their particular needs, and to practice until they can start with poise and security.

## Starting Procedures

### 1. On Your Marks

This is the command given by the starter prior to the race. Upon receiving the command, the runners move to their starting blocks. Most sprinters step in front of the starting line, stretch, and back into the blocks. The hands are placed on the track, at shoulder width, just behind the starting line. The preferred foot is placed against the front block, part of the weight is shifted to the hands, and the opposite foot and leg are extended rearward to release muscular tension. This foot is next placed against the rear block, and the weight is shifted to the supporting knee. The runner assumes a relaxed position, lets the head hang naturally, and awaits the second command (figs. 4.2 through 4.5).

**Figure 4.2.** The sprinter should stretch well before working on starts.

**Figure 4.3.** By backing into the starting blocks, the performer can be certain that the feet are solidly against the foot supports.

**Figure 4.4.** Initially the weight is supported by the feet and the knee. This prevents the development of upper body tension prior to assuming the "on the marks position."

**Figure 4.5.** The preliminary position is relaxed, the weight being equally distributed between the hands, the knee, and the feet. The head is permitted to hang naturally.

## 2. Get Set

As this command is given, the sprinter takes a deep breath, rocks up and forward over straight arms, getting set for the starting signal. The weight is shifted to the hands as the shoulders move three to four inches ahead of the starting line. The feet are placed securely against the blocks, with the heels consciously pressed backward to produce the longest possible

**Figure 4.6.** In the set position the weight is shifted forward, placing the driving muscles in an optimum position for applying explosive force.

driving lever. The muscles are placed on stretch, the front leg assuming an angle of about eighty degrees, the rear leg an angle of about one hundred thirty degrees. The hips are elevated slightly above the shoulders, the back is straight, and the head is held comfortably in line with the body. The eyes are focused at a point that will permit the performer to hold the set position without strain for two or more seconds (fig. 4.6).

### 3. Go

Though there is some controversy over the focus of attention in the set position, the writer believes the sprinter should concentrate on exploding out of the blocks. The gun merely triggers the action which is perceived in the mind. The action sequence (for the sprinter with the right foot back) is left arm, right arm, right foot, and left foot. The left arm, counteropposing the right-leg drive and step, is up and out in a forceful thrusting action. The right arm is up and back. The first stride is quick, though not choppy, as the foot contacts the track about twenty-four inches ahead of the starting line. The left leg continues to drive against the front block throughout this sequence of action.

The sprinter must stay low during the acceleration period so that maximum force can be expended to drive the body forward. A good starter will relax, use the arms vigorously, and keep the knees high (figs. 4.7 and 4.8). Each stride will increase in length as the body gradually assumes a balanced runing posture. Maximum acceleration is attained at about fifty yards. Beyond this point, the sprinter's attention is focused on holding form.

**Figure 4.7.** During the initial strides, the sprinter stays low so that maximum force is expended forward, rather than upward.

**Figure 4.8.** Arm action is vigorous as the performer drives out of the blocks.

**Sprinting Stride**

The sprinting stride is long and powerful. The weight is caught and transferred by the toes as extensor muscles of the feet, legs, and hips react explosively to expend their force almost dirctly through the body. Arm action continues to be vigorous and perfectly coordinated with the driving legs. The forward leg action is out, down, and back in a pawing motion. Each new base of support is established directly beneath the body to avoid a breaking action and subsequent loss of speed. It is essential the sprinter continues to relax. Tension chokes off power and restricts the stride length. Because beginners frequently tense up, teachers must find ways to help them run with little effort. Some teachers constantly remind their sprinters with signs and verbal commands—"relax, relax, relax." More than one sprinter has discovered that taking a breath twenty or thirty yards before the finish of the 100-yard dash helps them to relax.

Races are frequently won and lost during the final two or three strides. For this reason a runner, and particularly a sprinter, should run to a point beyond the finish line. This will prevent a last instant letdown and ensure the maintenance of speed through the entire race. The actual finish of a sprint race may be negotiated in one of two acceptable ways. During the final driving surge for the tape, the sprinter may extend the torso in an attempt to move the chest beyond those of the opponents, or one shoulder may be turned toward the finish line in a final burst of energy. Both of these techniques make it appear that one sprinter has crossed the finish line ahead of the more erect opponents and may well constitute a margin of victory. While leaning and turning are acceptable finishing techniques, a runner never dives for the tape. A dive may result in injury and certainly is slower than sprinting through the tape.

**Finish**

## Starting Principles

**Principles to Remember When Teaching Students to Start and to Sprint**

1. When starting mechanics have been explored and the beginner is learning to drive out of the blocks, the commitment should be to a long, fast first stride. Any tendency to stumble should be compensated for by establishing a new base of support as quickly as possible.
2. Concentration in the set position should be on the motor response, not on the gun. Research has shown that listening for a sound does not produce a response equally as fast as concentration on the movement pattern itself.
3. Because beginners tend to step out of the blocks and run through their arms (which hang down like an inverted wishbone), it is important that the driving, explosive nature of the start be emphasized and that sprinters be encouraged to use their arms vigorously.

## Sprinting Principles

1. Running at all speeds involves a synchronous bilateral swinging of arms and legs. As leg speed is increased, arm speed must also increase to compensate for the added force of heavier legs. All movement is forward or backward to minimize torquing or twisting during the run.
2. Sprinting action involves high knees, a slight forward lean, and a straight back. The head is held so that a line of force extends from the foot through the leg, the body, and the head at the instant of push-off. This principle holds true for starting as well as for running.

3. The sprinter should learn to run through the finish line. One must not let up until reaching a spot five yards beyond the finish line. The practice of finishing strong will elimimnate many distressing losses at the tape.

4. The sprinter should avoid stopping suddenly. It is wise to drive through the finish line, letting up gradually after the race has been completed. Such a procedure will help to prevent injury to the working muscles and will help the sprinter to stay loose through the entire race.

5. Every runner must relax. This fact is so important that considerable time and effort should be given to this phase of running. Some release from tension is a natural consequence of learning how to run. The ability to relax while applying peak effort, however, stems from the conscious attention of the runner. Drills requiring the sprinter to overtake and pass an opponent during the practice session often help a sprinter to concentrate on running faster with little added effort. Breathing during a race also may help the sprinter relax. In the 100-yard dash, a single breath should be taken at about the 75-yard mark. In distance as long as the 220, several breaths should be taken as a natural part of the race. (This point is made because some sprinters attempt to hold their breath during an entire 100-yard dash, only to find that they tense up near the finish line.)

**Steps in Teaching Sprinting**

Although running is a natural skill there are a number of drills that can be used to improve the technique of performance. Some of these drills can be used on a daily basis even when working with the advanced performer. This is particularly true of those activities that improve the athletes strength and power.

Running a Line

The shuttle drill, with students sprinting back and forth across a football field along the yardage lines, teaches one to keep the body parts in alignment.

Tandem Push

An effective technique for teaching sprinters to drive against the ground, expending their forces through their bodies, is the tandem push. This drill involves working in pairs, one person standing facing the direction the pair will run. The other moving behind the first, grasps the waist with outstretched arms, inclines the body forward, and on a signal begins to push. The front person resists slightly as both runners accelerate down the track.

**Figure 4.9.** The start resister.

## Start Resister

This drill places the sprinter in a position that demands a powerful expenditure of force against the starting blocks if movement is to occur. The starter thus learns to drive forward and upward, applying force through the center of gravity. The sprinter also becomes aware of the importance of arm action to the maintenance of balance and stability.

## Sprint Buildup

This is an excellent technique for teaching the sprinter to increase and decrease speed with little or no obvious change in form or effort. The buildup may be run out of the starting blocks or from a standing start. The runner gradually increases speed to a peak and then lets up in a long, smooth period of deceleration. When the athlete has learned to change speed effortlessly, it is good to experiment with several buildups in a series. These may be run on the track or on grass, though grass is preferable. When several buildups are run consecutively, the sprinter is performing what many coaches call the in-and-out drill. To the observer, the performer appears to be prancing over a series of hot spots in an exaggerated or animated manner.

### Uphill-Downhill Running

There is some evidence that sprint speed can be improved by downhill training. When coupled with uphill training the performer is building power as well as learning to experience a different stride cadence. For best results this drill should be performed on a three to five percent grade, over distances of twenty-five to fifty yards.

### Reaction Drills

There are a variety of drills that can be used to quicken movement time. One of the most effective is to have the sprinter assume a four point stance with the feet at the individuals block spacing. Although the hands are touching the track, the legs are essentially straight as the performer assumes an inverted U position. With the coach giving starting signals the performer reacts by moving one hand, both hands, or running in place as directed.

**Training Schedules for the Beginning Sprinter**

The following schedule would be appropriate for students in physical education classes or for club performers who are just beginning. One should resist the urge to work too hard too soon. Enjoyment is important during this period when the performer is building the foundation for serious training later on.

**Training Schedules for the Mature Sprinter**

The reader is reminded that all schedules hereafter have been selected from the author's files. Thus each day's activity represents the work actually done by a highly successful performer. Note that each schedule covers a fourteen-day period corresponding to the normal high school or college program. Since each schedule is repeated twice to maximize the concept of individual containment, a given schedule actually covers a period of one month.

Schedules representing work completed during the fall, winter, and spring are provided for the reader's consideration.

## Training Activities Appropriate for the Beginning Sprinter

| Code | | | | AD | Acceleration-Deceleration |
|------|------|------------|-------------------|------|---------------------------|
| | J | Jog | ( ⅓ speed ) | AD | Acceleration-Deceleration |
| | ST | Stride | ( ⅔ speed ) | B | Block Work |
| | FS | Fast Stride | ( Relaxed sprint ) | M | Minutes |
| | BU | Build Up | ( Jog to fast stride ) | S | Seconds |

| Date | Warm Up | Distance | Time | Reps | Recovery | Other |
|------|---------|----------|------|------|----------|-------|
| 1 | 10 M J Stretch | 150 | AD | 4 | Walk back | 10 M J down |
| 2 | 10 M J Stretch | 1 mile | J | | | |
| 3 | 10 M J Stretch | 300 | ST | 2 | 440 walk | Wt. training |
| 4 | 10 M J Stretch | Freewheeling | 20 M | | | 10 M J down |
| 5 | 10 M J Stretch | Fartlek | 30 M | | | |
| 6 | 10 M J Stretch | 75 | BU | 6 | 220 walk | Wt. training |
| 7 | 10 M J Stretch | Active rest | | | | |
| 8 | 10 M J Stretch | 400 50 | ST FS | 1 5 | 5 M J | |
| 9 | 10 M J Stretch | 220 | AD | 3 | Walk back | 90 ST,  40 FS 90 ST |
| 10 | 10 M J Stretch | Sprint drills | 20 M | | | Grass |
| 11 | 10 M J Stretch | Fartlek | 20 M | | | Wt. training Depth jumping |
| 12 | 10 M J Stretch | 500 75 | ST BU | 1 5 | 10 M J Walk back | |
| 13 | 10 M J Stretch | Freewheeling | 30 M | | | |
| 14 | 10 M J Stretch | Active rest | | | | |

## Fall Training Schedule

| Code | | | | | | | |
|---|---|---|---|---|---|---|---|
| | J | Jog | ( ⅓ speed ) | | AD | Acceleration-Deceleration | |
| | ST | Stride | ( ⅔ speed ) | | B | Block Work | |
| | FS | Fast Stride | ( Relaxed sprint ) | | M | Minutes | |
| | BU | Build Up | ( Jog to fast stride ) | | S | Seconds | |

| Date | Warm Up | Distance | Time | Reps | Recovery | Other |
|---|---|---|---|---|---|---|
| 9/1 | 10 M J<br>Stretch | Fartlek | 30 M | | | Wt. training<br>Depth jumping |
| 9/2 | 15 M J<br>Stretch | 150 | ST | 8 | Walk back | 5 M J down |
| 9/3 | 15 M J<br>Stretch | 330<br>20 | AD<br>B | 3<br>6–8 | 440 walk<br>Walk back | 110 ST, 110 J,<br>110 ST |
| 9/4 | 15 M J<br>Stretch | Freewheeling | 20 M | | | Wt. training |
| 9/5 | | 5 miles | J | | | |
| 9/6 | 15 M J<br>Stretch | 550<br>70 | ST<br>BU | 2<br>4–6 | 5 M J<br>Walk back | |
| 9/7 | | Active rest | | | | |
| 9/8 | 15 M J<br>Stretch | 75<br>220 | BU<br>ST | 6–8<br>3–5 | Walk back<br>Walk back | Wt. training<br>Depth jumping |
| 9/9 | 15 M J<br>Stretch | Freewheeling | 20 M | | | 10 M Fartlek<br>to finish |
| 9/10 | 15 M J<br>Stretch | 110<br>220<br>330<br><br>20 | FS<br>ST<br>ST<br><br>B | 1<br>1<br>1<br><br>6–8 | 110 J<br>220 J<br>880 J<br>10 M J | Repeat 110,<br>220, 330 |
| 9/11 | 15 M J<br>Stretch | 110 | BU | 10 | Walk back | 440 ST to finish |
| 9/12 | 10 M J<br>Stretch | | 30 M | | | Hill J<br>Wt. training<br>to finish |
| 9/13 | | Active rest | | | | |
| 9/14 | 15 M J<br>Stretch | 500<br>300<br>150<br>75 | ST<br>ST<br>FS<br>BU | 1<br>1<br>1<br>3 | 880 J<br>880 J<br>880 J<br>220 J | J down |

# Winter Training Schedule

| Code | | | | AD | Acceleration-Deceleration |
|------|----|------|------------------------|----|---------------------------|
| | J | Jog | ( ⅓ speed ) | AD | Acceleration-Deceleration |
| | ST | Stride | ( ⅔ speed ) | B | Block Work |
| | FS | Fast Stride | ( Relaxed sprint ) | M | Minutes |
| | BU | Build Up | ( Jog to fast stride ) | S | Seconds |

| Date | Warm Up | Distance | Time | Reps | Recovery | Other |
|------|---------|----------|------|------|----------|-------|
| 1/1 | 15 M J | 150 | ST | 1 | 220 J | |
| | Stretch | 300 | ST | 1 | 880 J | |
| | | 550 | ST | 1 | 10 M J | |
| | | 75 | BU | 4–6 | Walk back | |
| 1/2 | 15 M J | Fartlek | 30 M | | | Wt. training |
| | Stretch | | | | | |
| 1/3 | 15 M J | 75 | FS | 3 | 440 walk | |
| | Stretch | 600 | ST | 1 | 10 M J | Relay work to finish |
| 1/4 | 15 M J | Sprint drills | 20 M | | 5 M walk | |
| | Stretch | 330 | AD | | | 110 ST, 110 FS, 110 J |
| 1/5 | 15 M J | 75 | BU | 5 | Walk back | |
| | Stretch | 40 | B | 6 | Walk back | |
| | | 330 | ST | 1 | | Wt. training |
| 1/6 | 15 M J | 150 | FS | 3 | Walk until rested | Relay work to finish |
| | Stretch | | | | | |
| 1/7 | | Active rest | | | | |
| 1/8 | | Fartlek | 35 M | | | |
| 1/9 | 15 M J | 30 | FS | 3 | Walk back | Flying start |
| | Stretch | 40 | FS | 3 | Walk back | Flying start |
| | | 50 | FS | 3 | Walk back 440 walk | Flying start |
| | | 600 | ST | 1 | | Wt. training |
| 1/10 | 15 M J | 220 | ST | 1 | 110 J | |
| | Stretch | 110 | FS | 1 | 440 J 880 walk | Repeat 5 sets Relay work to finish |
| 1/11 | 15 M J | 440 | ST | 1 | 440 walk | |
| | Stretch | 330 | ST | 1 | 440 walk | |
| | | 220 | ST | 1 | 440 walk | |
| | | 75 | BU | 3 | Walk back | Wt. training |
| 1/12 | 15 M J | 4 miles | J | | | |
| | Stretch | | | | | |
| 1/13 | 15 M J | 25 | B | 3 | Walk back | |
| | Stretch | 50 | B | 3 | Walk back | |
| | | 75 | B | 2 | 440 walk | Relay work to finish |
| 1/14 | | Active rest | | | | |

## Spring Training Schedule

| Code | | | | | | |
|------|---|---|---|---|---|---|
| **J** | Jog | ( ⅓ speed ) | | **AD** | Acceleration-Deceleration | |
| **ST** | Stride | ( ⅔ speed ) | | **B** | Block Work | |
| **FS** | Fast Stride | ( Relaxed sprint ) | | **M** | Minutes | |
| **BU** | Build Up | ( Jog to fast stride ) | | **S** | Seconds | |

| Date | Warm Up | Distance | Time | Reps | Recovery | Other |
|------|---------|----------|------|------|----------|-------|
| 3/1 | 15 M J<br>Stretch | 180 B | AD | 4–6 | 260 walk | 60 FS, 60 ST,<br>60 FS |
| | | 440 | ST | 1 | 10 M J | Relay work<br>to finish<br>20 M |
| 3/2 | 15 M J<br>Stretch | 40 | FS | 2–4 | Walk back | Flying start |
| | | 60 | FS | 2–4 | Walk back<br>440 J | Flying start |
| | | 75 | BU | 3–5 | | Start into the turn<br>on 75s;<br>wt. training |
| 3/3 | 15 M J<br>Stretch | 150 | 17-18 S | 3–5 | 290 walk | Relay work<br>to finish<br>20 M |
| 3/4 | 15 M J<br>Stretch | 75 B | Time<br>trial | 2 | 10 M J | |
| | | 330 | AD | 1 | 10 M J | 110 ST, 110 FS,<br>110 ST<br>Wt. training |
| 3/5 | 15 M J<br>Stretch | 20 | B | 8–10 | Walk back | Easy 440 to finish |
| 3/6 | | Competition | | | | |
| 3/7 | | Stretch and<br>rest | | | | |
| 3/8 | 15 M J<br>Stretch | 660 | ST | 1 | 5 M walk | |
| | | 220 | ST | 1 | 220 walk | |
| | | 150 | FS | 1 | 440 walk | |
| | | 75 B | FS | 1 | 5 M J | Wt. training |
| 3/9 | 15 M J<br>Stretch | Sprint drills | 15 M | | | Relay work<br>to finish<br>25 M |
| 3/10 | | Fartlek | 30 M | | | Some hill work |
| 3/11 | 15 M J<br>Stretch | 90 | AD | 3 | Walk back<br><br>10 M J | 30 FS, 30 ST,<br>30 FS |
| | | 25 | B | 5–8 | | |
| 3/12 | 20 M J<br>Stretch | 440 | ST | 1 | | Relay work<br>to finish<br>20 M |
| 3/13 | | Competition | | | | |
| 3/14 | | Stretch and<br>rest | | | | |

a.                       b.                       c.

**Figure 4.10.** This is a straight line event. All body parts are in alignment as the performer accelerates into the full sprint stride.

## The Side View

**Analysis of Performance**

Is the performer solidly in the blocks? Are the heels back while in the set position? Are the supporting arms straight? Are the shoulders slightly forward with respect to the hands? Are neck muscles relaxed? Is the head hanging? Are the hips higher than the shoulders and the back more nearly flat than rounded? If not, make appropriate corrections.

How long is the first stride? Does the sprinter hesitate at any point when coming out of the block? Uncertainty as to whether to pull the back leg or to drive off the back block will result in hesitation.

Watch the front leg. It is completely extended the instant the sprinter leaves the blocks? A short first stride or a bent front leg are signs of weakness. It is to be remembered that this is a strength event in which the performer must explosively overcome inertia. Weak extensor muscles and unnecessary weight markedly affect the sprinter's start.

## The Front View

Look at the sprinters eyes coming out of the blocks. If you can see them during the first five yards, the performer is likely coming up too soon. Look for any twist or torque in the trunk. If torque is perceived, does it stem from foot placement or from arms swinging across the body? Make appropriate corrections; get everything in alignment. This is a straight-line event (fig. 4.10 a-c).

## A View Farther Down the Track

Are there signs of tension, tight neck muscles, clenched fingers, head back? Do the arms swing loosely, hands moving from hip to eye? Are the knees up, and thighs parallel with the track? Does the sprinter appear to bound over the track, as opposed to bobbing up and down? Build strength, stretch, and relax; this will negate the negative and fortify the positive.

If possible, time the sprinter's cadence, that it, the number of strides taken each second. Also, measure stride length. The cadence for most sprinters is between 4.2 and 5.0 strides (steps) per second. Stride length will vary from five to eight feet or more. It is the combination of these two factors which determines the speed with which a sprinter can move. While both can be modified within limits, increasing stride length is the most effective means of improving sprint speed. The facts are that a sprinter with a best 100-yard time of 11.0 seconds and who covers six feet nine inches with each stride could be a 10.7 sprinter by merely increasing the length of the stride by three inches. (This is a simple mathematical fact and can easily be proved by multiplying yards per second by the number of strides in 100 yards.)

Measurement of a sprinter's stride during the middle of a race will likely reveal a variation in the distance between right-to-left and left-to-right foot placement. Usually, the strength of the preferred foot and leg are greater than that of the nonpreferred foot and leg, which accounts for this variation. Thus, improving the strength of the weaker limb well could change a ho-hum runner into a highly competitive sprinter. Improved flexibility in the hips also could play an important part in such a change.

## A View from the Finish Line

Does the performer sprint across the finish line or seem to let up an instant too soon? Does the sprinter lean toward the line at the instant of crossing? Races from the playground to the Olympic Games are lost because sprinters let up too soon or fail to lean at the tape. What color are your uniform tops? Light colors often are lost at the finish line. Wear something that catches the judges' eye?

Does your sprinter consistently get passed in the last fifteen to twenty yards? Some sprinters lose because of tension, others because they lack strength endurance. If the finish strides are appreciably shorter than they were during the middle of the race, you have your answer. Work on speed-endurance. (When sprinters of equal ability race, the one whose strength first begins to ebb will lose the race.)

Although the 440 is classified as a sprint race, performers in this event must have significantly better speed-endurance than those athletes who participate exclusively in the 100 and 220 yards events. Because of this coaches should select 440 candidates from those sprinters who are willing to work, are aggressive, and are able and willing to experience pain and fatigue.

Training of the quarter-mile performer must be viewed as a holistic, or year around process. As is true with all events, the overall program moves from quantity to quality with an aerobic base developed in the off-season to support an aggressive sprint program in the spring. A typical training program for the 440 sprinter would include endurance training, power runs, strength endurance, and speed-endurance. Examples of these are to be found below with suggested seasonal training programs for both the beginner and the mature performer to follow. The reader is again reminded that these programs are representative of what a 440 sprinter might do and should not be followed without modification on an individual basis.

## Endurance Training for the Quarter Mile Candidate

Steady state running from 15 to 20 minutes.

Fartlek runs of 20 to 25 minutes duration.

6 × 880 runs over cross-country terrain. Full recovery between each.

## Power Runs

All to be run in 15 seconds or less, i.e., full speed 50, 60, 75 or 130 yard sprints. Full speed rope skipping for 10 to 15 seconds. Continuous relays with 50 to 130 yard segments.

## Strength Endurance

6 × 150, 6 × 60, 6 × 15 second sprints, long hills, stadium steps and the like. The recovery time would be sufficient to bring the heart rate below 120 beats/minute.

## Speed-Endurance

In this type of training, which is the heart of the preparation of the 440 candidate, the volume of training on a given day would be about two and one half times race distance, or 1000 yards.

10 × 100 with 5-10 minutes of rest

5 × 220 with 10 minutes of rest

4 × 300 with 10 minutes of rest

2 × 450 with 10 minutes of rest

| Code | J | Jog | ( ⅓ speed ) | | AD | Acceleration-Deceleration |
|---|---|---|---|---|---|---|
| | ST | Stride | ( ⅔ speed ) | | B | Block Work |
| | FS | Fast Stride | (Relaxed sprint) | | M | Minutes |
| | BU | Build Up | (Jog to fast stride) | | S | Seconds |

| Date | Warm Up | Distance | Time | Reps | Recovery | Other |
|---|---|---|---|---|---|---|
| 1 | | Easy J | 20 M | | | |
| | | 75 | ST | 3 | 5 M walk | Do 75s up hill |
| 2 | 10 M J | 220 | ST | 5 | 440 J | |
| | Stretch | 50 | FS | 2–4 | Walk back | Do 50s out of turn |
| | | | | | | Wt. training |
| 3 | 10 M J | 100-200 | ST | 5–6 | 3 M J | |
| | Stretch | Grass | | | | |
| | | 50 | FS | 4 | Walk back | |
| 4 | 10 M J | 330 | ST | 2–3 | 5 M J | |
| | Stretch | | | | | |
| 5 | | Fartlek | 30 M | | | Include some hills |
| | | | | | | Wt. training |
| 6 | 10 M J | 550 | ST | 1 | 880 J | |
| | Stretch | 440 | ST | 1 | 880 J | |
| | | 330 | ST | 1 | 880 J | |
| | | 75 | FS | 1 | | |
| 7 | | Easy J | 30 M | | | |
| 8 | 10 M J | 150 | ST | 6 | Walk back | |
| | Stretch | | | | | |
| 9 | 10 M J | 180 | AD | 5 | Walk back | 60 ST, 60 FS, 60 J |
| | Stretch | | | | | Wt. training |
| 10 | 10 M J | 75-150 | | 5–6 | | Freewheeling |
| | Stretch | Hills | | | | |
| | | Easy J | 10 M | | | |
| 11 | 10 M J | 660 | ST | 1 | 10 M J | |
| | Stretch | 75 | BU | 6 | Walk back | |
| 12 | | Fartlek | 30 M | | | |
| 13 | 10 M J | 110 | FS | 1 | 330 walk | |
| | Stretch | 220 | ST | 1 | 440 J | |
| | | 330 | ST | 1 | 880 J | Repeat 110-220 |
| | | | | | | Wt. training |
| 14 | | Active rest | | | | |

## Fall Training Schedule

Training Schedules for the Mature Quarter-Miler

| Code | J | Jog | (⅓ speed) | | | AD | Acceleration-Deceleration |
|---|---|---|---|---|---|---|---|
| | ST | Stride | (⅔ speed) | | | B | Block Work |
| | FS | Fast Stride | (Relaxed sprint) | | | M | Minutes |
| | BU | Build Up | (Jog to fast stride) | | | S | Seconds |

| Date | Warm Up | Distance | Time | Reps | Recovery | Other |
|---|---|---|---|---|---|---|
| 9/1 | 15 M J | 440 | 70s | 4–6 | 440 J | |
| | Stretch | 75 | BU | 6 | Walk back | |
| 9/2 | 15 M J | Fartlek | 35 M | | | Include some hills |
| | Stretch | | | | | Wt. training |
| 9/3 | 15 M J | 150 | 20-21 | 8 | 290 walk | |
| | Stretch | 50 | BU | 5 | Walk back | |
| 9/4 | 15 M J | 330 | AD | 3 | 880 J | 110 FS, 110 ST, |
| | Stretch | 1 Mile | J | | | 110 FS |
| 9/5 | | 4–5 miles with cross-country runners | | | | Wt. training |
| 9/6 | 15 M J | 110 | FS | 1 | 220 J | |
| | Stretch | 220 | FS | 1 | 440 J | |
| | | 330 | ST | 1 | 880 J | |
| | | 220 | FS | 1 | 10 M J | |
| | | 75 | FS | 4–6 | | Out of the turn |
| 9/7 | | Active rest | | | | |
| 9/8 | 15 M J | 660 | ST | 2 | 10 M J | |
| | Stretch | 50 | FS | 6–8 | | Flying start |
| | | | | | | Wt. training |
| | | | | | | Depth jumping |
| 9/9 | 15 M J | 220 | 31-34 | 10 | Walk back | Run in two sets of |
| | Stretch | | | | | 5 with a 5M J |
| | | | | | | between sets |
| 9/10 | 15 M J | 100-150 | ST-FS | 6–8 | Walking | Finish with free- |
| | Stretch | | | | | wheeling work |
| 9/11 | 15 M J | Power runs | 20 S | | 40 J | |
| | Stretch | | 30 S | | 880 walk | |
| | | 550 | ST | | J down | |
| 9/12 | 15 M J | 440 | AD | 6 | 440 J | 220 ST, 110 J, |
| | Stretch | | | | | 110 FS |
| 9/13 | 15 M J | 330 | Time | 1 | 15 M walk | |
| | Stretch | | trial | | | |
| | | 75 | BU | 3–4 | Walk back | Run into the turn |
| 9/14 | Stretch | Easy J | 25 M | | | |

## Winter Training Schedule

| Code | J | Jog | ( ⅓ speed ) | | | AD | Acceleration-Deceleration | |
|---|---|---|---|---|---|---|---|---|
| | ST | Stride | ( ⅔ speed ) | | | B | Block Work | |
| | FS | Fast Stride | ( Relaxed sprint ) | | | M | Minutes | |
| | BU | Build Up | ( Jog to fast stride ) | | | S | Seconds | |

| Date | Warm Up | Distance | Time | Reps | Recovery | Other |
|---|---|---|---|---|---|---|
| 1/1 | 15 M J<br>Stretch | 220 | 30–33 | 9-12 | Jog back | Run in sets of 3<br>880 J between sets |
| 1/2 | 15 M J<br>Stretch | 150 | 20–21 | 10 | 290 walk | Run in sets of 5<br>880 J between sets |
| 1/3 | 15 M J<br>Stretch | 660<br>75 | ST<br>BU | 2<br>6-8 | 5 M J<br>220 walk | Wt. training |
| 1/4 | 15 M J<br>Stretch | 25-35 | B | 6-8 | Walk back | Relay work 30 M |
| 1/5 | 15 M J<br>Stretch | 330<br>550 | AD<br>ST | 3<br>1 | 10 M J | 110 FS, 110 ST,<br>110 FS |
| 1/6 | 15 M J<br>Stretch | 600<br>400<br>200<br>100 | ST<br>ST<br>FS<br>FS | 1<br>1<br>1<br>1 | 880 J<br>880 J<br>880 J<br>10 M J | Wt. training |
| 1/7 | | Easy J | 30 M | | | |
| 1/8 | 15 M J<br>Stretch | 440<br>50 | 66–68<br>FS | 5-6<br>4 | 440 J | Out of turns |
| 1/9 | 15 M J<br>Stretch | 220 | 33–31<br>29 | 1-1-1 | J back | Run 3 sets of 3<br>with 5 M J<br>between sets<br>Wt. training |
| 1/10 | 15 M J<br>Stretch | 180<br>660<br><br>75 | FS<br>AD<br><br>BU | 2<br>1<br><br>3-5 | Walk back<br>10 M J<br><br>Walk back | 220 FS, 220 J,<br>220 FS<br>Run out of turns |
| 1/11 | 15 M J<br>Stretch | | | | | Work with<br>sprinters<br>Relay practice |
| 1/12 | 15 M J<br>Stretch | 330<br>150<br>75 | ST<br>Pace<br>FS | 1<br>1<br>1 | 440 J<br>220 J<br>880 J | Repeat 4 sets 330,<br>150, 75<br>Wt. training |
| 1/13 | 15 M J<br>Stretch | 220 or<br>660<br>90 | Time<br>trial<br>AD | 1<br><br>3-5 | 15 M J<br><br>Walk back | 30 FS, 30 ST,<br>30 FS |
| 1/14 | | Active rest | | | | |

## Spring Training Schedule

| Code | | | | | | | |
|---|---|---|---|---|---|---|---|
| | **J** | Jog | ( ⅓ speed ) | | **AD** | Acceleration-Deceleration | |
| | **ST** | Stride | ( ⅔ speed ) | | **B** | Block Work | |
| | **FS** | Fast Stride | ( Relaxed sprint ) | | **M** | Minutes | |
| | **BU** | Build Up | ( Jog to fast stride ) | | **S** | Seconds | |

| Date | Warm Up | Distance | Time | Reps | Recovery | Other |
|---|---|---|---|---|---|---|
| 3/1 | 15 M J Stretch | 330 | 43-45 | 3-4 | 440 walk 10 M J | Wt. training |
| | | 110 | BU | 2 | Walk back | |
| | | 50 | FS | 2 | | Flying start |
| 3/2 | 15 M J Stretch | 150 | 17-18 | 4 | Walk until recovered | Finish simulators Sprint off the turn |
| | | 500 | ST | 1 | | |
| 3/3 | 15 M J Stretch | 440 | AD | 3 | 10 M J | 220 25.5, 26.5, 110 J 110 12-13 Run each out of blocks |
| 3/4 | | Fartlek | 25 M | | | Flat grass |
| 3/5 | 15 M J Stretch | 20-30 | B | 6–8 | | Work with sprinters on blind exchange |
| 3/6 | | Competition | | | | |
| 3/7 | | Rest | | | | |
| 3/8 | 15 M J Stretch | 660 | 1:45 range | 2 | 10 M J | |
| | | 50 | BU | 3-5 | | Run into turns |
| 3/9 | 15 M J Stretch | 220 | FS | 3-5 | Walk until recovered | |
| | | 20-30 | B | 6-8 | | Wt. training |
| 3/10 | 15 M J Stretch | 330 | AD | 3 | 880 J | 110 12-12.5, 110 J 110 13-13.5 |
| | | 440 ST | 1 | | | |
| 3/11 | 15 M J Stretch | Sprint drills 20-30 | 20 M B | 5-7 | Walk back | Relay work |
| 3/12 | 15 M J Stretch | Easy ST Grass | 20 M | | | |
| 3/13 | | Competition | | | | |
| 3/14 | | Rest | | | | |

**Strategy in the 440-Yard Race**

Perhaps more than any other race the 440 is a maximum accelration, minimum deceleration event. Experience has shown that the well-conditioned quarter miler can hold about 90 to 93 percent of the best velocity achieved at 220 yards, over the 440-yard distance. Another way of making this point is to say that for the elite performer there should not be more than a ten percent drop off in the best velocity for 220 yards and the best velocity for 440 yards. In the final paragraph of this section guidelines will be suggested for estimating what the potential is of those 440-yard sprinters with whom you might work.

In general there are two types of 440 sprinters; the short sprinter moving up and the middle distance runner moving down. Racing tactics vary according to the abilities that these two types of athletes bring to the event. For best results the sprinter does not start as fast as the more highly conditioned anaerobic type. The sprinter lays back, saving strength for the final kick. Thus, the time differential between the second and fourth 110s for the sprinter might be greater than that posted by the middle distance type.

The athlete having greater endurance, though less speed, usually will go out faster trying to pull the sprinter in over his or her head. If this can be done, it effectively neutralizes the sprinter's kick. If not, the sprint type likely will win the race.

If one had the luxury of working with a so-called pure quarter-mile type the following approach likely would produce the best results. Subsequent to the development of strength endurance the performer is trained to approach the race in segments. The first, or opening segment (50 to 60 yards) is run hard; near to top speed. During the next segment, the athlete settles into the race without working the upper body quite as aggressively as at the outset. The key is to maintain near peak velocity to the 300 to 330 mark from which the race will ultimately be won or lost. From that point victory will go to the athlete with the most courage and the ability to hold form in the face of undeniable pain.

**Tips for Estimating Performer Potential**

1. How do they respond to training? If they are mentally tough and thrive on work they likely will make it in the event.
2. Time the 440 candidate over 220 yards. For male performers the quarter-mile candidate must be able to cover this distance in the low 20s, i.e. 20.5 to 23.0 maximum. For female quarter-mile candidates comparable times would be 23.5 to 25.0.
3. To estimate potential simply double the best 220 time and add 3.5 seconds for experienced performers and 3.5 to 5.0 seconds for the novice. Thus if you were working with an athlete having 22.0 speed at 220 you would add 22.0 + 22.0 + 3.5 and have a 47.5 quarter mile candidate.

One last tip on the strategy of training. It has been my experience that it always is better to work down in terms of training distances than to work up. Thus during the preseason, training segments would be longer than they would be during the competitive season. It always is easier to go from 660 yards to 330 yards than it is to move in the other direction. A wise coaching strategy would be to run hard training sessions at 660 yards in February, cut these to 550 in early March, on down to 480 just before the opening meet of the year. Subsequently the 440 yard race will seem to be a sprint and the candidate will be far better prepared mentally to run a maximum acceleration, minimum deceleration race than had the over-distance work not been done.

# 5          Relay Races

Relay racing can be one of the most satisfying activities in the entire track and field program. The relay race involves speed, endurance, teamwork, and exciting competition. Indeed, the effortless coordination of the well-drilled relay team is a fitting tribute to the painstaking practice of its members.

This chapter includes a discussion of different types of relay events as well as an analysis of relay racing techniques and strategy.

**Types of Relay Races**

Relay racing includes pursuit and shuttle events. At the secondary school level, participants run both shuttle and pursuit relays up to distances of one mile. In open competition the mile relay, sprint medley, and 4 × 800 are a part of the championship schedule.

### Pursuit Relay

Nearly every relay race involves teams with four members. In the pursuit race, performer one starts and carries the baton to the second teammate. The second runner exchanges the baton with team member number three who passes it to the fourth and final runner. Each athlete runs a specified distance, the same direction around the track, and exchanges the baton in a fixed zone twenty meters in length. The most common pursuit relays are the 440-yard sprint and the 880-yard medley. In the 440 relay each team member sprints 110 yards. In the 880-yard medley the first runner runs 220 yards, the number two and three runners run 110 yards each, and the anchor runner covers a distance of 440 yards.

**Components of Relay Racing**

### Handling the Baton

Baton handling includes both general and specific characteristics. The general nature of the baton exchange is determined by the distance run, whereas the specific refinements of the exchange are largely a matter of coaching preference. In the shorter races, the exchange is nonvisual, with the incoming runner responsible for placing the baton in the hand of the outgoing runner. In races where fatigue is a factor ($4 \times 440$ or $4 \times 880$), the exchange is visual, with both participating members sharing the burden of accuracy.

## Nonvisual Exchange

Successful coaches and teams have used a variety of exchange techniques to advantage. The two methods most commonly seen in recent years are the left-to-right-hand underhand exchange and the alternate overhand exchange. Both of these exchanges have their strengths and weaknesses. These will be explored in the paragraph below.

In the left-to-right-hand exchange the leadoff runner starts with the baton in the left hand. At the point of exchange the baton is passed to the right hand of the outgoing runner who immediately moves the baton to the left hand. The second and third exchanges are made in a similar manner. The strength of this technique is that several different sprinters can be trained to run any position on the team. There are at least two weaknesses; (1) runners sometimes drop the baton as they move it between the right and left hands while trying to sprint, and (2) it is not possible to achieve as much free space (space between passing and receiving runners) as is the case with the overhand exchange.

In the alternate-hand, overhand pass the passer places the baton in the receiver's hand, which is held palm up. This way the receiver does not have to change hands and has the long end of the baton facing out to facilitate the pass to the next runner.

In the *alternate-hand technique,* the first and third exchanges are from right hand to left hand, with the second exchange being from left hand to right hand. Mechanics of the exchange involve a downward striking motion, with the baton being slapped into the upturned palm of the receiver's extended hand.

This technique has several advantages. One advantage concerns the second and fourth runners who receive the baton on the turn. With the right-to-left-hand exchange they are able to accelerate along the extreme outside border of their lane, then cut diagonally into the turn after receiving the baton. This latter maneuver provides space for three or four straight-line strides and offers an added margin for the attainment of speed.

A minimum of baton handling throughout the race is another advantage stemming from this technique. Each runner receives, carries, and exchanges the baton with either the right or the left hand. The chances of dropping the baton or forgetting to change the baton from the receiving to the passing hand are therefore minimized.

Perhaps the most important advantage of the alternate-hand technique is that it permits the acquisition of maximum free space between participating members of the relay team. This free space is the distance

Figure 5.1

Figure 5.2

Figure 5.3

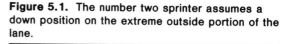

**Figure 5.1.** The number two sprinter assumes a down position on the extreme outside portion of the lane.

**Figure 5.2.** The incoming sprinter stays close to the inside border of the lane, accelerating through the point of baton exchange.

**Figure 5.3.** Relay runners think in terms of baton speed and seek to achieve maximum free space during each baton exchange. It has been our experience that working toward consistency with the baton exchanged at a point between five and ten yards inside the exchange zone, will produce the best results race after race.

gained during each exchange and is the hallmark of the championship team. Indeed, the principle of relay racing does not necessarily concern itself with participant speed, but rather with baton speed. The secret is to get the baton moving as fast as possible as quickly as possible and to maintain or increase that speed throughout the race. Every yard of free space attained thus contributes significantly to the speed with which the baton is moved.

Precision in baton handling, which is an important key to success in relay racing, constitutes the main disadvantage to using the alternate-hand technique. This stems from the fact that replacement of team personnel is almost impossible without a prolonged period of drill on the

**Figure 5.4.** In the visual exchange, the outgoing runner adjusts her speed to the incoming runner to achieve maximum free space, takes the baton and fights to maintain the advantage of the inside position going into the turn.

specific factors involved. Thus when four reliable sprinters are available, the use of the alternate-hand technique is strongly recommended. However, when team personnel is uncertain, it is likely that the similarity of the left-to-right-hand pattern would constitute the safest approach to the relay event.

## Visual Exchange

In the visual exchange the burden of responsibility is on the outgoing runner as the incoming runner often is very fatigued. The exchange advocated by the writer is right to left hand. The outgoing runner stands just inside the exchange zone, looking toward the incoming runner, the right side toward the curb. When the incoming runner is three or four strides away the outgoing runner turns, takes two strides, reaches back with the left hand, palm facing the teammate, thumb up and takes the baton.

It bears repeating that the key to success in relay racing is to move the baton with the utmost speed. To do this, a technique of baton exchange must be adopted that permits team members to accelerate quickly, to attain maximum free space at handoff, and to maintain peak velocity throughout the race. When these criteria have been met, four sprinters

**Strategy in the Relay Race**

with an average time of 11.0 seconds for 110 yards (or 44 seconds flat for 440 yards) can move the baton over this distance in from 42.5 to 43.0 seconds. This is possible because of free space, that distance which can be gained between teammates when each is in full stride and reaching as far as possible toward the other during the handoff.

Other, more specific, comments about the strategy of relay racing follow.

1. The placement of team personnel should follow a logical pattern.
    a. In sprint races held indoors it is wise to get the lead and force one's opponents to run wide around the turns. For this reason, the fastest starter should lead off with the hope that initial speed will attain running room for the teammates who follow.
    b. The distance which the baton is carried by a runner also must be considered. In a typical 4 × 110 relay race, each runner starts from the 10-meter shadow line, accelerates to a point 10 yards inside the exchange zone where the baton is exchanged and sprints to the next zone where the same circumstances eventuate. Diagramming such a race makes it obvious that the leadoff runner covers a distance of 115 to 118 yards with the baton. Runners two and three carry the baton approximately 110 yards, with runner number four carrying the baton from 102 to 105 yards. It is obvious that the leadoff runner must be a good starter who is strong enough to maintain his or her speed to the point of exchange.
    c. The second and fourth runners must be able to accelerate out of the turn. (Some sprinters cannot do this because of the length of their strides.) The second runner must also be a good baton handler since this team member both receives and passes off during this leg of the race.
    When using the alternate-hand exchange, the second and fourth runners assume a starting stance which permits them to look back along the left shoulder at their incoming teammate. Since this stance shifts the left foot rearward, it seems awkward to the athlete who normally places the right foot in the rear starting block. Occasionally a runner cannot make this adaptation. The coach should be aware of this when selecting and placing team personnel.
    d. The third runner also must be a good baton handler. Because this leg of the race begins on the straightaway, this is a good place for the long-striding performer who has trouble sprinting out of the turn.
    e. The fourth runner is known as the anchor runner. Traditionally, it has been the anchor runner's responsibility to win the race.
    Though this rationale has some validity, it also is true that the anchor runner actually covers the least distance of the four members of the team. Because of this fact, it may be more important to find an anchor runner who can accelerate on the turn but yet

**Figure 5.5.** When using the alternate hand exchange the second and fourth runners assume a starting position on the outside of the lane. The left leg is back to facilitate a view of the incoming teammate.

cannot maintain speed quite so long as a stronger teammate. The anchor runner also must be a "fighter," a person who is courageous under pressure.

The placement of team members is not just a matter of whim, for a split second gained or lost during exchange may mean the difference between victory and defeat. The coach should consider all extenuating factors, and only after experimentation should a final decision be made regarding running order.

2. When using the blind pass it is recommended that no voice signal be given about putting the hand back. With the confusion that exists at most exchange areas verbal cues usually are of little help. A better method is to take full advantage of the international, or acceleration zone. When the incoming runner is about twenty feet away from the acceleration line the outgoing runner takes off at full speed. At the first exchange (it would alternate thereafter) the outgoing runner pumps the left arm four times and then extends the hand rearward, palm up. The strides taken during this time would place both runners about five yards inside the exchange zone. The baton is then passed between a point from five to ten yards inside the exchange area.

While some might argue that it would be well to vary the point of exchange to better utilize the speeds of the runners involved, it has been my experience that one will win more races by being conservative, than by changing the exchange point from meet to meet.

## Teaching Relay Racing Skills and Tactics

Teaching emphasis in the relay events is on handling the baton. Whether a large group or just two individuals are involved, the procedure is the same. The teacher explains the different types of baton exchanges, demonstrates them, and has the runners drill under supervision.

### Running in Place

One effective starting point is a drill in which two athletes assume the relative positions of the incoming and outgoing runners so they may practice the exchange while running in place. This drill is used for both the visual and nonvisual exchange, with learners working together until they can accurately coordinate their movements.

### Left-to-Right-Hand Exchange

When the stationary drill is perfected, attention is shifted to the moving exchange. It is my belief that there is no need to work at full speed so long as the relative speeds of the participating runners are the same. I would recommend that a majority of the learning and practice time be expended on the turn.

We use a three point stance where the outgoing runner is concerned. The outgoing runner assumes this stance just inside the shadow mark for the international acceleration zone. The feet are placed in the regular sprint start position, the arm not involved in receiving the baton is extended to the track and the athlete looks back under the free shoulder at the incoming teammate.

Using a go mark some twenty feet beyond the point of acceleration, the outgoing runner turns and sprints into the exchange zone as noted earlier. The coach carefully notes how and if the baton is exchanged and makes adjustments with the go mark accordingly. Considerable drill is essential to perfect this highly technical skill.

## Modifications for the Physical Education Class

There are many drills for perfecting the baton exchange. These drills also can be used as a means of improving running form and endurance. Following are two drills that the writer has used successfully.

### Multipassing Drill

This drill is most effective when there are twelve to sixteen runners participating. These students are given numbers and are distributed equally among the four exchange zones. When an arbitrary go line has been established at each zone, the person numbered one sprints toward person number two and passes the baton. Person number two receives the baton,

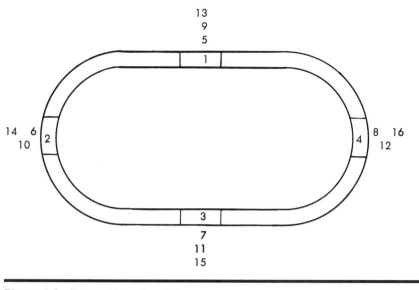

**Figure 5.6.** The multipassing drill.

runs to the next passing zone, and exchanges the baton with person number three. The drill continues around and around the track, with a new student receiving the baton at each station until all have completed a specific number of exchanges.

The teacher should be stationed at any one exchange area and observe all of the students during a period of several minutes. If there are several individuals running, the teacher has ample time to make appropriate comments to each during the interim between passes.

The multipassing drill also can be effectively adapted for team use. To do this, the teacher organizes two or more teams having five members, with the first and fifth runners on each team starting from the same exchange zone. The race is started, and the participants run and run and run, moving to a new zone each time they exchange the baton. When this drill is used, individuals are challenged to run faster and to give close attention to the proper mechanics of relay racing.

The author has used the foregoing team drill for many years and has found that it offers an extremely good incentive for pushing beyond the normal limits of fatigue. Athletes love to run this way, and they tend to forget the hard work that they are imposing upon themselves.

## Shuttle-Pursuit Drill

This drill incorporates the nonvisual exchange and the face-to-face exchange used in some shuttle relays and can be utilized out-of-doors or in the gymnasium (fig. 5.5). Here again five or more individuals can participate, twelve being a very workable number.

The drill is initiated by the first runner at station A, who sprints to station B and exchanges the baton with a nonvisual pass. The second person sprints to station C and exchanges the baton with the third person, also using a nonvisual pass. The third runner sprints to station D and exchanges the baton with a face-to-face (visual shuttle exchange) pass with the fourth runner who sprints back to Station C to repeat the procedure.

The shuttle-pursuit drill is best adapted to a running distance of 100 feet or more. This drill gives a large number of individuals baton-exchanging practice in a minimum amount of time.

**Coaching Considerations**

## Nonvisual Exchange

Careful scrutiny of international competition over the past several years has revealed a nearly universal shift from the underhand to the overhand exchange. Even the Russians, who tend to be ultratraditional, are now using the "slap down" as their method of exchange.

One step taken by coaches to achieve improved performance is the timing of the outgoing sprinter through the 30-meter zone (10 M + 20 M). A time of 3.5 seconds would indicate world class ability, with 4.0 seconds outstanding for a high school team. But more important, the use of the watch provides hard information as to the quality of the effort being put forth during practice. Since this is a sprint event, effort through the exchange zone must be maximal.

Another key to success is elevating the arm and hand to shoulder height at the instant of exchange. This action simplifies the reach and slap, with maximal free space being accrued. To achieve this optimum position, the outgoing sprinter must work repeatedly at pressing the hand upward to receive the baton.

Another effective coaching technique is to practice with relay members one and two, sprinting against three and four, or four and one sprinting against two and three. This should be done on the turn, with sufficient distance to permit full acceleration. There is no such thing as a half-speed start or baton exchange once the team members have warmed up.

## Visual Exchange

Every member of a track and field team should be skilled in the visual exchange. Here again, the trend nationally and internationally seems to be the inward turn to effect the handoff. This method places the outgoing runner in a position to see the inside lane marking, making it possible for the runner to maneuver without fear of fouling an adversary.

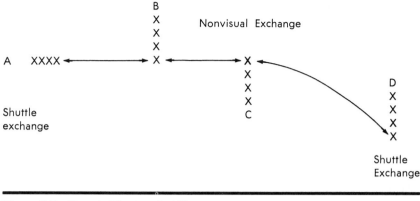

**Figure 5.7. The shuttle-pursuit drill.**

The continuous relay is an excellent method for teaching the visual exchange. It also constitutes one of the better means for building running endurance. Sometimes called either the Parlaf (two runners) or Zenderlaf (several runners), this drill is based on time, rather than on distance, with ten, fifteen, and twenty minutes of continuous running being the goal for different phases of the season. When this drill is used, no particular zones are employed, but all participating members are required to turn inward, reach back, and take the baton with their left hand from the extended right hand of a teammate. Free space is a goal here as well.

**Selecting Team Personnel**

Although there is a difference of opinion as to the wisdom of having sprinters run time trials, it is the writer's belief that such an event for selecting relay team personnel is a sound procedure. Thus, it is recommended that all 440 relay team candidates run a 110-yard time trial early in the season. While there is risk of injury, this seems to be the fairest method and surely is best for team morale.

Another possible method is to have five athletes run a continuous relay wherein each would effect several exchanges. In so doing the coach can observe passing and receiving, both into and out of the turns and evaluate team candidates accordingly.

# 6

# Hurdling

Someone has suggested that the hurdler must have the speed of a leopard, the spring of a deer, and the heart of a lion. Surely those who have observed the flawless form and the reckless courage of the expert hurdler will agree. No other track and field event demands such a carefree approach to a purposefully imposed barrier. Perhaps no other event offers the same challenge or so great a personal reward as running at and over ten hurdles in the course of an all-out sprint race.

Hurdle races for girls and women are run at distances ranging from 50 yards to 100 meters. A hurdle race of 400 meters is run in open competition at the national and international levels. Men run the 110 high hurdles and the 400 meter hurdles. High school boys often run a low hurdle race at 180 yards distance. (See appendixes for hurdle height and spacing.)

## The Start

The start for the hurdle race is exactly the same as the sprint start, though it may be necessary for the hurdler to reverse the feet in the starting blocks to arrive at the hurdle with the preferred foot forward. Most hurdlers take eight strides to the first hurdle, in which case the back foot in the starting blocks is the lead foot in clearing the hurdle. When seven strides are taken, the forward foot in the starting blocks would be the lead foot over the hurdle.

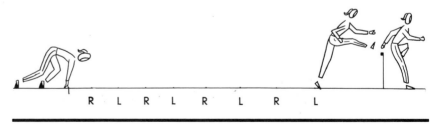

R   L   R   L   R   L   R   L

**Figure 6.1.** The start, stride pattern, and clearance of the first hurdle.

**Figure 6.2.** The athlete must arrive at the first hurdle under control. The point of takeoff for women is about 6 feet from the hurdle, for men the point of takeoff is about 7 feet.

Some hurdlers elevate their hips slightly higher than the recommended height for the set position, and they use their arms more vigorously so that they can attain their maximum speed more quickly than a sprinter. A hurdler must arrive at the first hurdle balanced and ready for the lift forward and upward over the barrier; these modifications help in this respect.

The takeoff point for women (distance between the takeoff foot and the hurdle) is about six feet, the takeoff point for men is closer to seven feet. Ordinarily a hurdler will take off closer to the first hurdle than to subsequent hurdles. This probably has something to do with stride adjustment and the psychology of shifting from a sprint to hurdle action.

When the point of takeoff is too close to the hurdle, the performer is forced to elevate the center of gravity too high for economical hurdle clearance. If the takeoff point is too far from the hurdle, precious time is lost over the barrier. There also is a tendency to come down too close on the opposite side, forcing the athlete to overstride, in an attempt to negotiate the next barrier. The touch down point beyond the hurdle should be between three and four feet.

## Lead-Leg Action

The first modification of sprinting form is the higher lift of the knee and thigh to permit hurdle clearance. This is accompanied by a slight bucking action of the trunk and a forceful drive against the track by the takeoff leg. All available forces are expended forward and slightly upward. The lead leg is kept in perfect alignment as the performer sprints over the hurdle (figs. 6.3-6.4).

**Figure 6.3.** There is a slight bucking action as the lead leg drives through.

**Figure 6.4.** All available force is expended forward and slightly upward in negotiating the hurdle.

### Trail-Leg Action

Action of the trail leg, described by the word *punch,* is a reflection of current thinking regarding this event. The action is unlike the "flattened split" required of the male high hurdler (or the short-legged female). Rather, the performer assumes a more upright position during hurdle clearance, with the thigh and knee extended slightly downward from the horizontal. Following a slight delay as the lead foot reaches for the track, the trailing knee punches upward, across the hurdle, toward the chest.

**Figure 6.5.** The effective hurdler sprints off the barrier, thus expending as little time as possible in the air.

The quick, high knee facilitates the sprint action so essential to this event. (Beginners have a tendency to rush the trail leg, bringing both legs over the hurdle almost simultaneously in a jumping-floating movement. This pattern seriously limits the length of the stride and forces the performer to lope between hurdles.)

## Hurdle Clearance

Since the hurdler can only gain speed while in contact with the track, one should constantly strive to shorten the time it takes to clear the hurdle. One way to realize this objective is to avoid too much float during the period of clearance. Perhaps this can best be accomplished by working endlessly on the action sequence over the hurdle. Certainly a mastery of the clearance components is imperative to championship performance (fig. 6.5). (The expert requires from 0.1 to 0.2 second longer to clear the hurdle than to take a normal sprinting stride.)

## Arm Action

Tall performers will find that with practice they can sprint over the hurdle with little modification in sprint form. Shorter athletes must lift their lead leg proportionally higher and buck sharply to clear the hurdle. Thus, while the tall, long-legged hurdler merely reaches toward the lead leg with the opposite arm to control balance, the shorter athletes finds it necessary to buck sharply and reach toward the lead leg with both arms. This double reach facilitates forward lean and lift of the lead leg. The arm on the same side as the lead leg should be carried as normally as possible, for the tendency to develop a side swing is common among be-

**Figure 6.6.** The lead foot lands beneath the body, arms and legs are in alignment, and the performer concentrates on the next hurdle.

ginners and heavy-legged hurdlers. An excessive side swing pulls the shoulders out of alignment and seriously affects the pattern of subsequent strides.

### The Stride Off the Hurdle

Getting over the first barrier is the most important problem facing the hurdler. A second hurdle is then placed at a point where it can be negotiated without straining. The introduction of a second hurdle both challenges the athlete to drive through the first barrier and catch a sense of rhythm so essential to this event. The sprint off technique involves placement of the lead foot beneath the center of gravity with the foot in alignment with the direction of the race (fig. 6.6).

**Teaching Beginners to Hurdle**

One of the most important lessons to be learned from experience is that skill habits are extremely difficult to change. For this reason one ought always consider a beginner to be a potential champion and insist that a skill be learned correctly. Perhaps no place is this principle more important than in the hurdle event where beginners invariably "sit on" the hurdle out of fear of hitting the barrier top. Once established, this habit is very resistant to change.

Skillful performers attack the hurdle "butts under" at the instant of takeoff. This action is an exaggerated sprint stride and captures the driving power so essential to the event. The steps to learning the hurdle sprint have appropriately been described by Wilt as the "sticks and

**Figure 6.7.** The trail leg drill also is utilized by the skilled performer as a means of quickening the knee punch across the barrier.

bricks" method of hurdling.[1] This is a method which progresses from a line on the track, to a brick, to bricks with cross sticks, and the like. The concept is simple; sprint the line, sprint the bricks, sprint the sticks, each with "butts under," and you are on your way to being a hurdler.

## Trail-Leg Action

With several hurdles properly spaced along the track, a number of students can practice trail-leg action together. With their trail legs to the inside, they walk in single file past the hurdles. Forward progress is controlled as each attempts to adjust the strides so that the outside or lead foot falls several inches ahead of each hurdle. If one is sufficiently close to the hurdles, this action forces the trail leg up and over to avoid banging the side of the barrier. The movement skill which the beginner is attempting to learn is a quick sequential act involving a step, a buck, and a punch. This drill can be speeded up the next time around so that the learner can develop a sense of timing, first walking, then jogging, and finally running as they are able to. Because the quick punch action of the trail leg is so important, this drill should be a part of the daily schedule of all hurdlers, beginners and experts alike. They should work toward the development of quick trail-leg action, taking five short, light, prancing steps between the hurdles and an exaggerated drive step just ahead of the hurdles, followed by the explosive punch through of the trail leg.

---

1. Fred Wilt, *Run-Run-Run* (Los Altos, Calif.: Track and Field News, Inc., 1964).

## Lead-Leg Action

Teaching lead-leg action poses a particular problem, for there really is no substitute for going over a hurdle. About the only thing that the teacher can do is to create a barrier that presents as little psychological disturbance as possible. This can be achieved by placing bamboo poles, lightweight tubes, or strings across the tops of two hurdles. The beginner thus hurdles a barrier that can be handled without injury.

There is no substitute for practice, and no amount of discussion will reveal to the beginner what it really is like to stride over a barrier. Perhaps it is best at the outset to let the beginner "jump" the hurdle any way they want to; then when they have convinced themselves that it can be done, they will be ready to consider proper form.

It has been noted by the writer that most beginners crowd the hurdle in the fear that they cannot clear it with a normal sprinting stride. It thus becomes necessary to establish a takeoff mark that permits straight alignment of the lead leg. To assist in the process a marker is placed on the track between six and seven feet from the barrier. The distance depends upon whether one is working with male or female athletes. As the learner works over one hurdle, the teacher comments on alignment, the bucking action, arm action, and the like.

## Drill over Two Hurdles

As soon as the learner has developed confidence over one hurdle, a second hurdle needs to be introduced into the learning situation. Initial drill over two hurdles might be done with five short steps between the barriers rather than three. This permits the athlete to concentrate on the hurdles rather than the strides between.

When the athlete can negotiate two hurdles with three strides between, it is time to introduce the start. Usually the learner starts from a stand with the feet in the normal sprint stride position. The back foot at the start is the lead foot over the hurdle. During the initial trials, the second hurdle should be moved to the side so the learner can sense its location without having to worry about negotiating two hurdles at one time. The performer is urged to sprint off the first barrier and on past the second. A mark is made where the takeoff foot lands on stride three and the second hurdle is placed six feet beyond this point for subsequent training.

Next the starting blocks are put in place and the procedure just described is repeated again. With patient encouragement and modification of the spacing needed, the learner soon will have mastered the toughest part of this event. From then on it is a matter of working at a variety of hurdle drills to improve hurdle technique. Rhythm drills over several hurdles, along with sprint training, bounding, depth jumping, and weight training rounds out the preparation of the hurdler.

## Five-by-Five Shuttles

This drill is often used early in the season for the purpose of developing strength and endurance. Ten hurdles are used, five facing one direction, and a second five, beside the first, facing the other direction. Using either five short steps or three regular strides, the performer runs several shuttle repeats (down and back). Each is taken from a flying start with emphasis on quickness over the hurdle.

## Continuous Knee Punches

With several hurdles spaced from four to six feet apart the performer drills alongside the barriers, stepping-punching, stepping-punching, stepping-punching to achieve improved flexibility and ballistic action with the punching knee. It is important that a hurdler use the hip flexor muscles to punch the trail leg through, rather than just pull the trail leg along with the momentum of the body.

## Rhythm Sprints

Better hurdlers manifest a sprint rhythm throughout the race. For this reason it is essential to train over the number of hurdles for which one is preparing. An effective means of achieving this goal is to place eight to ten hurdles on the track, eighteen to twenty-four inches less than regular spacing. The performer, using a flying start, attempts to sprint the entire flight without overstriding or floating. As the performer tires, the spacing should be readjusted so that the sprint rhythm can be maintained the entire distance. (During the fall and winter it is far more important to develop a rhythm than to worry about proper spacing.)

## The Accelerated Stride-Stretcher

It is difficult for beginners to believe that they can take off six feet or more from the hurdle and get all the way to the other side. To help them do so with courage and quickness, this drill requires a single stride between two hurdles that have been spaced from ten to twelve feet apart. The performer sprints at the hurdles, taking the first in stride and the second with the following stride. The foot pattern would be Left (take-off), Right (sprint down), Left (takeoff), and Right (sprint down). When a rhythm has been established, the hurdles are moved farther and farther apart until the desired stride lengths have been achieved.

## Stepping to the Wall

A good technique for teaching and perfecting the "butts under" sprint stride at the hurdle is to have the performer stand facing a wall from a distance of three to four feet. On command the performer lifts the thigh and steps forward, with the lead foot contacting the wall absolutely flat. When done properly the hips are under the trunk, which assumes a nearly erect, sprint posture. (Having the performer step above a line which has been drawn at hurdle height improves this drill.)

At best, drills are merely drills, and what a hurdler really needs is full speed—full flight training. While American athletes have tended to train over four or five hurdles, two or three days a week, European hurdlers train almost daily at race distances. Perhaps this accounts for the superior performances of European hurdlers.

## Training Schedules for the Beginning Hurdler

Speed and flexibility are the important physical attributes for hurdling success. The accompanying schedule for a beginning athlete seeks to maximize the development of sprint speed, flexibility in the hips, and quickness over the hurdle.

### Training Activities Appropriate for the Beginning Hurdler

| Code | J | Jog | ( ⅓ speed) | | AD | Acceleration-Deceleration |
|------|------|------|------|------|------|------|
| | ST | Stride | ( ⅔ speed) | | B | Block Work |
| | FS | Fast Stride | (Relaxed sprint) | | M | Minutes |
| | BU | Build Up | (Jog to fast stride) | | S | Seconds |

| Date | Warm Up | Distance | Time | Reps | Recovery | Other |
|------|---------|----------|------|------|----------|-------|
| 1 | 10 M J | 75 | FS | 5 | Walk back | |
| | Stretch | 4 hurdles | 15 M | | | Lead-leg and trail-leg drills |
| | | 440 | J | | | |
| 2 | 10 M J | 100 | BU | 3 | 440 walk | |
| | Stretch | 2 hurdles | 15 M | | | Accelerated stride-stretcher |
| | | 25 | B | 5–6 | | Wt. training |
| 3 | 10 M J | 75 | BU | 5 | Walk back | Sprint out of turns |
| | Stretch | 5 hurdles | 3 step | 5 | Walk back | 5 x 5 shuttle drill |

| Date | Warm Up | Distance | Time | Reps | Recovery | Other |
|------|---------|----------|------|------|----------|-------|
| 4 | | Fartlek | 25 M | | | Wt. training |
| 5 | 10 M J | 150 | FS | 2 | 440 walk | |
| | Stretch | 8 hurdles | 3 step | 3 | Walk until rested | Rhythm sprints |
| | | 25 | B | 5–6 | | |
| 6 | 10 M J | 210 | AD | 3 | 230 walk | 70 ST, 70 FS, 70 ST |
| | Stretch | 2 hurdles | 15 M | | | Accelerated stride-stretcher |
| | | 440 | J | | | |
| 7 | Stretch | Easy J | 20 M | | | |
| 8 | 10 M J | 4 hurdles | 3 step | 6 | Walk back | Rhythm sprints |
| | Stretch | 220 | FS | 1 | 880 walk | |
| | | 110 | FS | 1 | | |
| 9 | 10 M J | 100 | BU | 5 | Walk back | Sprint into turns |
| | Stretch | 5 hurdles | 5 step | 5 | Walk back | 5 x 5 shuttles |
| | | | | | | Wt. training |
| 10 | 10 M J | 3 hurdles | B | 6–8 | Walk back | |
| | Stretch | 330 | AD | 1 | | 110 ST, 110 FS, 110 ST |
| 11 | 10 M J | 50–100 | 20 M | | | Freewheeling |
| | Stretch | hills | | | | |
| | | 4 hurdles | 20 M | | | Lead-leg and trail-leg drills |
| 12 | 10 M J | 440 | ST | 1 | 880 J | |
| | Stretch | 5 hurdles | 3 step | | | Rhythm sprints |
| | | | | | | Wt. training |
| 13 | 10 M J | 75 | BU | 3 | Walk back | |
| | Stretch | 150 | AD | 3 | Walk back | 50 ST, 50 FS, 50 ST |
| | | | | | | Time middle 50 |
| 14 | | Fartlek | 25 M | | | Try to run where it is possible to jump various barriers |

## Training Schedules for the Mature Hurdler

## Fall Training Schedule

| Code | J | Jog | ( ⅓ speed ) | | AD | Acceleration-Deceleration |
|------|-----|-----|-------------|---|----|--------------------------|
| | ST | Stride | ( ⅔ speed ) | | B | Block Work |
| | FS | Fast Stride | ( Relaxed sprint ) | | M | Minutes |
| | BU | Build Up | ( Jog to fast stride ) | | S | Seconds |

| Date | Warm Up | Distance | Time | Reps | Recovery | Other |
|------|---------|----------|------|------|----------|-------|
| 9/1 | 15 M J<br>Stretch | Fartlek | 30 M | | | Wt. training<br>Depth jumping |
| 9/2 | 15 M J<br>Stretch | 75<br>5 hurdles | BU<br>3 step | 5<br>10 | Walk back<br>Walk back | 5 x 5 shuttle |
| 9/3 | 15 M J<br>Stretch | Work with sprinters | | | | |
| 9/4 | 15 M J<br>Stretch | 150<br>4 hurdles<br><br>440 | FS<br>10 M<br><br>AD | 2<br><br><br>1 | 290 walk | Accelerated stride-<br>stretcher<br>110 BU, 220 J,<br>110 BU |
| 9/5 | 15 M J<br>Stretch | 5 miles | J | | | Wt. training<br>Depth jumping |
| 9/6 | 15 M J<br>Stretch | 75<br>150<br>225 | FS<br>FS<br>AD | 1<br>1<br>1 | 150 J<br>440 J<br>10 M J | 75 FS, 75 J, 75 FS<br>Repeat 75,<br>150, 225 |
| 9/7 | | Active rest | | | | |
| 9/8 | 15 M J<br>Stretch | 6 hurdles<br>2 hurdles | 3 step<br>B | 4–5<br>5–7 | Walking<br>Walk back | Rhythm sprints |
| 9/9 | | Fartlek | 30 M | | | Wt. training |
| 9/10 | 15 M J<br>Stretch | Work with sprinters | | | | Depth jumping |
| 9/11 | 15 M J<br>Stretch | 8 hurdles<br><br>400 | Time<br>trial<br>AD | 2<br><br>1 | 10 M J | 200 J, 100 ST,<br>100 FS |
| 9/12 | | Hills | 25 M | | | Wt. training |
| 9/13 | 15 M J<br>Stretch | 180<br>3 hurdles | AD<br>15 M | 2–3 | 5 M<br>walking | 60 FS, 60 J, 60 FS<br>Lead-leg and trail-<br>leg drill |
| 9/14 | | Rest | | | | |

## Winter Training Schedule

| Code | J | Jog | ( ⅓ speed ) | | AD | Acceleration-Deceleration |
|------|-----|------------|---------------------|--|----|---------------------------|
| | ST | Stride | ( ⅔ speed ) | | B | Block Work |
| | FS | Fast Stride | ( Relaxed sprint ) | | M | Minutes |
| | BU | Build Up | ( Jog to fast stride ) | | S | Seconds |

| Date | Warm Up | Distance | Time | Reps | Recovery | Other |
|------|---------|----------|------|------|----------|-------|
| 1/1 | 15 M J | 220 | 32–34 | 4 | Walk back | |
| | Stretch | 5 hurdles | 3 step | 5 | Walk back | 5 x 5 shuttle |
| | | 2 hurdles | B | 5–8 | Walk back | Wt. training |
| 1/2 | 15 M J | 75 | FS | 5 | Walk back | |
| | Stretch | 3 hurdles | 3 step | 5–8 | Walk back | Rhythm sprints |
| | | 2 miles | J | | | |
| 1/3 | 15 M J | 550 | ST | 1 | 880 J | |
| | Stretch | 330 | AD | 1 | 880 J | 110 FS, 110 J, 110 FS |
| | | 220 | ST | 1 | 110 walk | |
| | | 75 | BU | 1 | 150 walk | |
| | | 50 | FS | 1 | | Sprint into turn |
| 1/4 | 15 M J | 8 hurdles | Time trial | 3 | Walk until recovered | |
| | Stretch | | | | | |
| 1/5 | 15 M J | Sprint drills | 30 M | | | Wt. training |
| | Stretch | | | | | |
| 1/6 | 15 M J | Work with sprinters | | | | |
| | Stretch | | | | | |
| 1/7 | | Active rest | | | | |
| 1/8 | 15 M J | 330 | ST | 1 | 880 J | |
| | Stretch | 20 | B | 5 | Walk back | Without hurdles |
| | | 20 | B | 5 | Walk back | With 2 hurdles |
| 1/9 | | Fartlek | 30 M | | | Wt. training |
| 1/10 | 15 M J | 150 | 19–21 | 3–5 | 290 walk | |
| | Stretch | 4 hurdles | 15 M | | | Lead-leg and trail-leg drill |
| 1/11 | 15 M J | 1 hurdle | B | 1 | Walk back | Time step off 1 |
| | Stretch | 2 hurdles | B | 1 | Walk back | Time step off 2 |
| | | 3 hurdles | B | 1 | Walk back 10 M J | Time step off 3 Repeat 1–2–3 drill |
| | | 880 | J | | | |
| 1/12 | | 4 miles | J | | | Wt. training Depth jumping |
| 1/13 | 15 M J | 10 hurdles | 3 step | 3–5 | Walk until recovered | Rhythm sprints |
| | Stretch | | | | | |
| 1/14 | | Rest | | | | |

## Spring Training Schedule

| Code | | | | | | |
|---|---|---|---|---|---|---|
| | **J** | Jog | ( ⅓ speed ) | **AD** | Acceleration-Deceleration | |
| | **ST** | Stride | ( ⅔ speed ) | **B** | Block Work | |
| | **FS** | Fast Stride | ( Relaxed sprint ) | **M** | Minutes | |
| | **BU** | Build Up | ( Jog to fast stride ) | **S** | Seconds | |

| Date | Warm Up | Distance | Time | Reps | Recovery | Other |
|---|---|---|---|---|---|---|
| 3/1 | 15 M J<br>Stretch | Work with sprinters | | | | |
| 3/2 | 15 M J<br>Stretch | 4 hurdles | B | 5 | Walk back<br>10 M J | Time between 3–4 |
| | | 180 | AD | 3 | 260 walk | 60 ST, 60 FS,<br>60 ST<br>Wt. training |
| 3/3 | 15 M J<br>Stretch | Sprint drills | 30 M | | | On the grass<br>Relay work<br>to finish |
| 3/4 | 15 M J<br>Stretch | 75<br>8 hurdles<br>220 | B<br>B<br>ST | 1<br>7–10<br>1 | 10 M J<br>Walk back | Time 75 |
| 3/6 | | Competition | | | | |
| 3/7 | Stretch | Rest | | | | |
| 3/8 | 15 M J | 50<br>75<br><br>150<br>4 hurdles | B<br>FS<br><br>17–19 | 3<br>3<br><br>1 | Walk back<br>Walk back<br>10 M J<br>10 M J | Flying start<br><br><br>Rhythm sprints |
| 3/9 | 15 M J | Work with sprinters | | | | Wt. training |
| 3/10 | 15 M J | 10 hurdles | 3 step | 2 | Walk until<br>rested | Timed using<br>flying start |
| 3/11 | 15 M J | 330<br><br>3 hurdles | AD<br><br>B | 2–3<br><br>5 | 10 M J<br><br>Walk back | 110 FS, 110 ST,<br>110 FS |
| 3/12 | 15 M J | 6 hurdles<br><br>1 hurdle | 3 step<br><br>B | 3–4<br><br>5–6 | Walk until<br>recovered<br>Walk back | Rhythm sprints |
| 3/13 | | Competition | | | | |
| 3/14 | Stretch | Rest | | | | |

Analysis of movies taken of Annelie Ehrhardt during her world-record performance gave dramatic evidence that the side view at the instant of takeoff should reveal a sprint attack, with the hips well under the performer. This view also should reveal a slight forward bend at the hips and a thigh lift that places the knee several inches above the level of the hip. The forward bend ensures a constant height where the center of gravity is concerned. The extreme thigh lift facilitates the all-important sprint off the hurdle.

Were one to view a male hurdler of comparable ability the differences in technique to be seen would be a more significant bucking action at takeoff and a so-called layout position on top of the barrier. The male hurdler's trail knee also tends to come through at a steeper angle seeming to lift almost to the armpit to facilitate the sprint off stride.

Check the points of takeoff and landing. Reasonable distances for women are approximately six feet and four feet respectively, with comparable marks for men being seven feet and four feet. These distances reveal that the hurdler has attained maximum height between eight inches and fifteen inches in front of the hurdle. This is important since the hurdler must sprint down off the barrier to achieve maximum speed. (When the center of gravity reaches its high point over, or beyond, the hurdle, the performer has expended too much force in a vertical direction. This happens when the takeoff is too close to the hurdle.)

Look for two parallels during hurdle clearance, the forearm and the thigh (fig. 6.8). This is what Walker calls the "doorknob" test, a reach forward with the leading arm as if to turn a knob and open a door.[2] Check the trailing knee. It should punch upward, close to the hurdle top and on through to a normal sprint stride.

Also from the side, study the stride cadence of your hurdler. What changes do you see? There really should be little difference between sprinting and hurdling, except the slight buck and exaggerated lift of the lead leg. Time your hurdler as well. An outstanding high school hurdler should be 2.5 seconds at contact over the first hurdle and 3.6 seconds over two. (This is equivalent to running the 100-meter race in 14.5 to 15.0 seconds.) A national level performer, on the other hand, will be 2.4 and 3.5 seconds over hurdles one and two (equivalent to 13.5 to 13.7 seconds for the 100-meter hurdle event). The major difference between good hurdlers and great hurdlers is sprint speed. While each can negotiate a hurdle in approximately 0.2 of a second, the sprinter covers the distance between hurdles considerably faster than a slower adversary.

---

2. Leroy Walker, Unpublished lecture notes, National Collegiate Athletic Association Track and Field Coaches Clinic, Sacramento State University, June 1971.

**Figure 6.8.** Look for two parallels as the performer negotiates the hurdle, the forearm, and the thigh.

**Stride Pattern for Successful Performance in the 100-Meter Hurdle Event**

| Strides | | Stride Length | Elapsed Time |
|---|---|---|---|
| R | | | |
| | L | | |
| _____ starting line | | | |
| R | | 20″ | |
| | L | 3′8″ | |
| R | | 4′2″ | |
| | L | 4′8″ | |
| R | | 5′2″ | |
| | L | 5′8″ | |
| R | | 6′ | |
| | L | 5′8″ | |
| _____ 1st hurdle | | 6′1″ .... 10′1″ | |
| R | | 4′0″ | 2.4-2.6 |
| | L | 5′6″ | |
| R | | 6′1″ | |
| | L | 5′11″ | |
| _____ 2nd hurdle | | 6′4″ .... 10′1″ | |
| R | | 3′9″ | 3.5-3.7 |
| | L | 5′7″ | |
| R | | 6′0″ | |

| Strides | Stride Length | Elapsed Time |
|---|---|---|
| _____ 3rd hurdle | 6'4" . . . . 10'1" | |
| | 3'9" | 4.3–4.7 |
| 4th hurdle | Little variation | 5.4–5.9 |
| 5th hurdle | hereafter | 6.5–7.1 |
| 6th hurdle | | 7.6–8.3 |
| 7th hurdle | | 8.7–9.5 |
| 8th hurdle | | 9.8–10.7 |
| 9th hurdle | | 11.0–12.0 |
| 10th hurdle | | 12.1–13.2 |
| Finish | | 13.7–15.0 |

Note that the takeoff stride is slightly shorter than the preceding stride to put the performer in an attack position.

## The Front View

Stand in the middle of the track and look for a square body position when the performer is on top the hurdle. The hurdler should be driving straight toward you. If the hips are open, or closed, the performer is torquing. Why? Does it stem from the lead arm reaching across the body or from the knee punch for which there is no counter force? (Remember action-reaction.)

Hurdling is a straight-line event. To maintain this alignment certain reactions must occur. One which the author recommends is to let the arm opposite the punching knee swing freely to the side. This action negates the tendency of the body to rotate toward the knee, which invariably results in a shortening of the following stride. A freely swinging arm is especially important in the 400-meter hurdle event because the performer tends to be more erect, and thus is more readily affected by counterforce.

Give the "sole test" from the front. The lead leg should come straight at you, thigh first, then the knee, then the sole of the shoe, spikes showing for an instant. Then look the performer in the forehead. The eyes should be fixed on the hurdle top just ahead.

**400-Meter Hurdle Event**

The 440-yard hurdle race is one of the most demanding events in track and field. Candidates for this event must have good quarter-mile speed, discipline, the ability to manifest a sort of relaxed concentration, and anaerobic strength similar to that possessed by the middle distance runner. The 440-yard race for men is called the intermediate hurdle race with the barriers set at thirty-six inches, where women are concerned the race is the low hurdle event with the hurdles set at thirty inches.

**Figure 6.9.** Utilizing a left lead leg helps to prevent the hurdler from flying off at a tangent to the turn.

**Hurdle Technique**

Because of the lower hurdle the participant in this event tends to assume a more vertical posture than is the case with the high hurdle race. For the tall athlete, hurdle clearance is little more than an exaggerated step. For most, the modification in technique having the greatest impact on performance would be the development of a left, lead-leg style. The latter is very important in that hurdling with the left leg leading around the turn tends to negate the tendency of the performer to fly off at a tangent while in the air over the barrier. A widely swinging arm on the lead-leg side also helps to keep the athlete in alignment (fig. 6.9).

**Stride Plan**

Because of the distance to and between the hurdles in this event, beginners have great difficulty in establishing a consistent stride pattern. Fatigue is also a factor to be reckoned with, making it necessary for most performers to modify their stride pattern at some point after the middle of the race. The following stride plan has been provided for the female performer. Note the shift from seventeen to nineteen strides between the sixth and seventh hurdles. (For men the stride plan likely would shift from 13 to 15, with the number of strides to the first hurdle being more in the range of 21 to 22.)

This is a relative point, depending on such factors as the wind, one's level of condition, the condition of one's adversaries, and the like. While some hurdlers will try to maintain the same stride plan during the entire race, most will add two strides somewhere between the fifth and eighth hurdles.

## Stride Pattern for Successful Performance in the 400-Meter Hurdle Event

| Strides | Stride Length | Number of Strides | Elapsed Time |
|---|---|---|---|
| R | | | |
| L | | | |
| ———— starting line | | | |
| R | | | |
| L | | | |
| R | | | |
| L | | 22–26 to 1st LH | |
| L | 6'–6'6" | | |
| ———— 1st hurdle | | | 6-9–7.2 |
| R | 3'–3'9" | 17 | |
| L | | | |
| L | 6'–6'6" | | |
| ———— 2nd hurdle | | | 11.6–12.0 |
| R | 3'–3'9" | 17 | |
| ———— 3rd hurdle | 3'–3'9" | | 16.3–16.9 |
| | | 17 | |
| ———— 4th hurdle | 3'–3'9" | | 21.1–21.9 |
| | | 17 | |
| ———— 5th hurdle | 3'–3'9" | | 25.9–26.9 |
| | | 17 | |
| ———— 6th hurdle | 3'–3'9" | | 30.8–32.0 |
| | 5'10"–6'2" | 19 | |
| ———— 7th hurdle | 3'–3'6" | | 35.8–37.2 |
| | | 19 | |
| ———— 8th hurdle | 3'–3'6" | | 41.0–42.6 |
| | | 19 | |
| ———— 9th hurdle | 3'–3'6" | | 46.3–48.1 |
| | | 19 | |
| ————10th hurdle | 3'–3'6" | | 51.7–53.7 |
| | | 20–25 | |
| ———— Finish line | | | 58.6–61.5 |

Careful study of the time plan will reveal that the 400-meter hurdle event, like the open 440 (or 400 meters) is a maximum acceleration—minimum deceleration race.

The development of the 400-meter hurdler is similar to the development of performers in the 440 and the 880. Primary emphasis should be on the speed-endurance factor; thus a holistic schedule must include cross-country running to build a foundation for subsequent interval training. (See training schedules for middle distance performers.) Considerable attention must also be given to stride plan work and the overall rhythm of this event.

**Training Schedules for the Beginning 400-Meter Hurdler**

## Training Activities Appropriate for
## the Beginning 400-Meter Hurdler

| Code | J | Jog | ( ⅓ speed ) | | AD | Acceleration-Deceleration |
|------|------|------------|------------------------|--|----|---------------------------|
| | ST | Stride | ( ⅔ speed ) | | B | Block Work |
| | FS | Fast Stride | (Relaxed sprint) | | M | Minutes |
| | BU | Build Up | (Jog to fast stride) | | S | Seconds |

| Date | Warm Up | Distance | Time | Reps | Recovery | Other |
|------|---------|----------|------|------|----------|-------|
| 1 | | Work with quarter-milers | | | | Wt. training |
| 2 | 15 M J Stretch | 1 hurdle | B | 6–7 | Walk back | Work for consistent stride |
| | | 2 hurdles | ST | 4–5 | Walk back | Work over hurdles 6–7 off the turn |
| | | 550 | ST | 1 | | |
| 3 | | Work with middle distance runners | | | | Wt. training |
| 4 | 15 M J Stretch | 2 hurdles | FS | 5 | Walk back | Flying start over 1–2 |
| | | 3 hurdles | 20 M | | Walk back | Work over 3–4–5 on back stretch |
| | | 150 | FS | 1 | | |
| 5 | 15 M J Stretch | 75–150 | 30 M | | | Hill sprints |
| 6 | 15 M J Stretch | 1 hurdle | B | 1 | Walk back | |
| | | 2 hurdles | B | 1 | Walk back | |
| | | 3 hurdles | B | 1 | 880 J | |
| | | 660 | ST | 1 | | |
| 7 | | Active rest | | | | |
| 8 | | Work with middle distance runners | | | | Wt. training |
| 9 | 15 M J Stretch | 220 + 2 hurdles | ST | 2–3 | 5 M J | Run a 220, continuing on over LH 1–2 |
| | | 1 hurdle | 15 M | | Walk back | Form work over 1 hurdle on the turn |
| 10 | | Work with quarter-milers | | | | |
| 11 | 15 M J Stretch | 4 hurdles | B | 2 | Walk until recovered | Time step down off no. 4 |
| | | 400 | ST | 1 | | |
| 12 | 15 M J | Work with sprinters | | | | Wt. training |
| 13 | 15 M J Stretch | 440 + 2 hurdles | ST | 1 | 20 M J | Run a 440, continuing on over LH 1–2 |
| 14 | | Active rest | | | | |

| Code | | | | | AD | Acceleration-Deceleration |
|------|------|-------------|---------------------|--|----|---------------------------|
| | J | Jog | ( ⅓ speed ) | | B | Block Work |
| | ST | Stride | ( ⅔ speed ) | | M | Minutes |
| | FS | Fast Stride | ( Relaxed sprint ) | | S | Seconds |
| | BU | Build Up | ( Jog to fast stride ) | | | |

| Date | Warm Up | Distance | Time | Reps | Recovery | Other |
|------|---------|----------|------|------|----------|-------|
| 9/1 | | Work with cross-country team | | | | |
| 9/2 | 15 M J Stretch | 440 | 70–73 | 5–6 | 440 J 10 M J | |
| | | 1 hurdle | 15 M | | Walk back | Flying start over no. 1 |
| 9/3 | | Work with quarter-milers | | | | |
| 9/4 | 15 M J Stretch | 3 hurdles | 20 M | | Walk back | Form strides over 1–2–3 |
| | | | | | 10 M J | |
| | | 330 | 55 | 1 | 110 J | |
| | | 330 | 53 | 1 | 110 walk | |
| | | 330 | 51 | 1 | J down | |
| 9/5 | 15 M J Stretch | 150 | 20–22 | 6–8 | 290 J back 10 M J | |
| | | 1 hurdle | 10 M | | Walk back | Form work on the turn |
| 9/6 | | Fartlek | 30 M | | | |
| 9/7 | | Active rest | | | | |
| 9/8 | 15 M J Stretch | 100–200 hills | ST | 8–12 | Walk until recovered | |
| 9/9 | | Work with cross-country team | | | | |
| 9/10 | 15 M J Stretch | 1 hurdle | FS | 1 | Walk back | Flying start |
| | | 2 hurdles | FS | 1 | Walk back | |
| | | 3 hurdles | FS | 1 | 10 M J | Repeat 1–2–3 drill 3 times |
| 9/11 | | Work with middle distance runners | | | | |
| 9/12 | 15 M J Stretch | 3 hurdles | 30 M | | Walk back | Work over LH 6–7–8 for stride form |
| 9/13 | 15 M J Stretch | 4 hurdles | B | 2 | Walk until recovered | Time step down off no. 4 |
| 9/14 | | Rest | | | | |

## Winter Training Schedule

| Code | | | | | | | |
|------|------|-----------|-------------------|------|------|---------------------------|
| | **J** | Jog | ( ⅓ speed ) | | **AD** | Acceleration-Deceleration |
| | **ST** | Stride | ( ⅔ speed ) | | **B** | Block Work |
| | **FS** | Fast Stride | ( Relaxed sprint ) | | **M** | Minutes |
| | **BU** | Build Up | ( Jog to fast stride ) | | **S** | Seconds |

| Date | Warm Up | Distance | Time | Reps | Recovery | Other |
|------|---------|----------|------|------|----------|-------|
| 1/1 | 15 M J Stretch | 880 | AD | 1 | 880 J | 660 ST, 110 J, 110 FS |
| | | 660 | AD | 1 | 880 J | 440 ST, 110 J, 110 FS |
| | | 550 | AD | 1 | 880 J | 330 ST, 110 J, 110 FS |
| | | 1 hurdle | 10 M | | Walk back | Form work |
| 1/2 | 15 M J Stretch | 3 hurdles | B | 6 | Walk back 10 M J | Wt. training Depth jumping |
| | | 550 | ST | 1 | | |
| 1/3 | 15 M J Stretch | Fartlek | 30 M | | | |
| 1/4 | 15 M J Stretch | 330 + 2 hurdles | ST | 2–3 | 10 M J | Run a 330, continuing over LH |
| | | 75 | BU | 5–6 | Walk back | 1–2–3 |
| 1/5 | 15 M J Stretch | 100–150 hills | 30 M | | | Wt. training |
| 1/6 | | 5–6 miles | J | | | |
| 1/7 | | Active rest | | | | |
| 1/8 | 15 M J Stretch | 440 | ST | 1 | 290 J | |
| | | 150 | FS | 1 | 10 M J | Repeat 3 sets |
| | | 1 hurdle | 15 M | | Walk back | Form work out of turn |
| 1/9 | 15 M J Stretch | Work with quarter-milers | | | | Wt. training |
| 1/10 | 15 M J Stretch | 6 hurdles | ST | 2 | 10 M J | Work over hurdles 1–2–3–4–9–10 |
| 1/11 | 15 M J Stretch | 75–150 grass | ST | 10–15 | Walk back | |
| 1/12 | 15 M J Stretch | 5 hurdles | B | 2 | 10 M J | Time step down off no. 5 |
| 1/13 | | Fartlek | 30 M | | | |
| 1/14 | | Rest | | | | |

## Spring Training Schedule

| Code | | | | | | |
|------|------|------|------|------|------|------|
| | **J** | Jog | ( ⅓ speed ) | | **AD** | Acceleration-Deceleration |
| | **ST** | Stride | ( ⅔ speed ) | | **B** | Block Work |
| | **FS** | Fast Stride | ( Relaxed sprint ) | | **M** | Minutes |
| | **BU** | Build Up | ( Jog to fast stride ) | | **S** | Seconds |

| Date | Warm Up | Distance | Time | Reps | Recovery | Other |
|------|---------|----------|------|------|----------|-------|
| 3/1 | 15 M J | 3 hurdles | B | 3–5 | Walk back | Stride work |
| | Stretch | 3 hurdles | ST | 3–5 | Walk back | Flying start over hurdles 5–6–7 |
| | | | | | 10 M J | |
| | | 550 | 1:20–1:25 | 1 | | |
| 3/2 | 15 M J | Work with quarter-milers | | | | Relay work |
| | Stretch | | | | | Wt. training |
| 3/3 | 15 M J | 6 hurdles | B | 2–3 | 10 M J | Time step down off no. 6 |
| | Stretch | | | | | |
| | | 75 | BU | 4–5 | Walk back | |
| 3/4 | 15 M J | 2 hurdles | 30 M | | Walk back | Work over 2–3, 5–6 and 8–9 for form |
| | Stretch | | | | | |
| | | 660 | 1:40–1:45 | 1 | | Wt. training |
| 3/5 | 15 M J | 330 | AD | 2 | 10 M J | 110 FS, 110J, |
| | Stretch | 75 | BU | 3–5 | Walk back | 110 FS |
| 3/6 | | Competition | | | | |
| 3/7 | | Rest | | | | |
| 3/8 | 15 M J | 600 | ST | 1 | 440 J | |
| | Stretch | 400 | ST | 1 | 440 J | |
| | | 300 | ST | 1 | 440 J | |
| | | 150 | 17–18 | 1 | 290 J back | |
| | | 150 | 17–18 | 1 | 10 M J | Wt. training |
| 3/9 | 15 M J | 440 + 2 hurdles | ST | 2 | 10 M J | Run a 440, continuing on over LH 1–2 |
| | Stretch | | | | | |
| | | 1 hurdle | B | 5–6 | Walk back | |
| 3/10 | 15 M J | 220 + 2 hurdles | B | 2 | 880 J | Run 220 at race pace, continuing on over LH 6–7 |
| | Stretch | | | | | |
| | | | | | 10 M J | |
| | | 550 | 1:20–1:25 | 1 | | |

## Spring Training Schedule—Continued

| Date | Warm Up | Distance | Time | Reps | Recovery | Other |
|------|---------|----------|------|------|----------|-------|
| 3/11 | 15 M J Stretch | 180 | AD | 4–6 | 440 J | 60 FS, 60 ST, 60 FS Relay work and wt. training |
| 3/12 | 15 M J Stretch | 3 hurdles 1 mile | B J | 4–5 | Walk back | |
| 3/13 | | Competition | | | | |
| 3/14 | | Rest | | | | |

It should be noted in the preceding training schedules that emphasis is placed on drills involving various combinations of hurdles. Considerable attention is given to hurdles one through three and seven through ten. Power drills for this event might include several repeats of hurdles one and two, or nine and ten. For strength endurance the hurdler could be timed over hurdles one through five, or six through ten, with complete rest between trials. (Ten to fifteen minutes of walking.)

Psychological preparation of the more advanced 440 hurdler would include drills such as running 500 yards, taking hurdles one and two on the way out and on the way in. This is a very demanding training session. It helps the athlete put a finish on the race as well as giving one confidence.

**Analysis of Performance**

In general the technique of running the 440 hurdles is very similar to that used in the high hurdle event. There are some minor variations. If possible, develop a left lead-leg performer. If not, get the hurdler off the hurdle as quickly as possible to shorten the time during which the center of gravity can be pulled at a tangent to the turn.

There is much less bucking action at takeoff or layout on top the hurdle barrier. The posture is more erect and, for some, the hurdle action is similar to an exaggerated step.

Arm action on the trail leg side may be more pronounced, swinging to the side to compensate for the torque produced when the trail leg is punched through.

Watch carefully to see where the athlete adjusts the stride pattern between the hurdles so as to be in step over the hurdle. All such adjustment should be made soon after coming off the hurdle so that the runners momentum can be carried through the race. A loss of momentum is often a disaster to the intermediate hurdler. This is especially true when it occurs after the seventh hurdle.

# 7 Middle Distance Running

This analysis of the middle distance events includes races between 880 yards and two miles,—exclusive of the steeplechase. As noted earlier an assumption underlying this analysis is that running events are classified according to tradition, performer speed, and the duration of the event. As will be seen throughout this chapter, each of these factors have some influence on both the development of the middle distance runner and on performance technique.

Until recently it was assumed that the middle distance events were the 800 to 1500 meter races (or yard equivalency). Records seem to indicate that both men and women have been racing at these distances since the early 1900s. Official records, however, date back to about 1912 for championship performances by men and the early 1930s for women.

A comparison of world records for men and women seems to indicate that during the past two or three decades women have been improving at a faster rate than men. Since 1934 the women's record for 800 meters has been improved by more than seventeen percent, while the men's record for that distance has been improved by just over six percent. At 1500 meters the women's record has been improved by nearly ten percent since 1954, with the record for men showing a gain of 7.33 percent.

An even more revealing statistic is the fact that the differences between world records for men and women have been narrowed by more than ten percentage points in just over two decades. The current difference is less than nine percent for both the 800 and 1500 meter events, with a projected difference of less than three percent by 1990.

In the 3000 meter race, which women have been running for less than ten years, the difference between the world record for men and women is about eleven percent. There are those who believe that this difference will be narrowed to two percent by 1990.

**Brief History of the Middle Distance Events**

**Factors to Be Considered in the Selection of Middle Distance Runners**

In addition to the performance factors noted in chapter 3 it is my belief that a majority of middle distance runners manifest a common core of personality characteristics. Several are delineated below.

## Highly Disciplined

These athletes are willing to pay a price in time and energy to achieve a high and worthy goal. All across the world one sees a similar sight where the middle distance runner is concerned. From early morning until late at night they take to the roads, the parks, and the trails to "get in the miles" essential to the achievement of their goals. Successful performers are indeed disciplined.

## Manifest a Sense of Vision

The middle distance runner looks to the future as well as to the present. Most recognize that improvement comes slowly, daily gains are measurable only over time, thus they are able and willing to bridge the gap between where they are and where they plan to be.

## Take Great Joy in Running

Shortly after his startling sub four minute mile, Roger Bannister noted that his greatest joy was "running off into the sunset" to be caught up there in the rhythm of the universe. Not all running training can be joyous, but enough is, and must be, if the athlete is going to do both the quantity and quality of work essential to achieve maximum performance.

## Tough Minded

There is pain in serious training and the successful performer must be tough enough to deal with that pain. There also must be a toughness of mind in the face of frustration, or defeat and of missing out on some of the creature comforts that may deter the athlete in his or her quest for "greatness." Most manifest a tough and fighting spirit.

## Listen to and Are in Tune with Their Bodies

At least one survey out of Montreal indicated that the primary reason for the Olympic athletes' involvement in sport was the intrinsic sense of being in tune with one's body. There seemed to be a special aesthetic quality to feeling the body at work, of sensing its response to the direction of one's will.

**Figure 7.1.** Biomechanically the running gait of the female is different than that of the male. Thus, at every rate of speed the female has to work harder than the male to cover the same amount of distance.

It should be recognized that there are significant differences between male and female middle distance runners. These are noted in body size (anthropometric) and in oxygen uptake (cardiopulmonary) measures. A third significant difference between men and women is the difference in the running gait of male and female performers. Indeed, biomechanical analysis has revealed that the female runner has a shorter contact time per stride and thus a longer swing time than does her male counterpart. What this means in terms of performance efficiency is that at every speed the female runner must work harder than the male.

There are at least two implications of the above statement that ought to be noted at this time. One is that a female middle distance runner should not train exclusively with male runners as this may adversely affect her natural running stride. The other is that because of the greater work that the female runner must do/stride, her overall work load at a given distance could be dramatically greater than that performed by a male runner. Thus, a ten mile run at a six minute per mile pace very likely has different implications for the female than for male. Or, stated differently, there is no reason to assume that women and men should have comparable work loads even if their performance records are identical.

Once the candidates for the middle distance events have been identified the genius of coaching, where these athletes are concerned, is understanding the energy demands imposed by a specific race and training the

**Other Considerations in the Selection of Middle Distance Runners**

**Training Concepts**

athlete in such a manner as to maximize the mechanism of specific adaptation. Where the middle distance runner is concerned, the energy systems involved are about fifty percent aerobic and fifty percent anaerobic.

Since there are differences of opinion as to how one achieves specific adaptation, I will simply say that it is possible to achieve the same end by different means. The key, I believe, is to recognize that there are anaerobically oriented (440 type) athletes who have moved up and aerobically oriented (three mile types) who have moved down. Thus, you have middle distance runners who are successful on forty to sixty miles of training a week and those who run 100 or more miles each week. This leads to the current world wide trend to emphasize "strong side" training where middle distance runners are concerned.

Following are selected principles of training regardless of the means that one might choose to effectively train athletes for these events:

1. Whatever method of training one adheres to, it is essential for success in the middle distance events to train both the aerobic and the anaerobic systems.
2. Training for the middle distance events must be viewed as a long term process if both the training effects and the trainee's potential are to be maximized.
3. There is an extremely narrow line between training too much and not training enough, and that line is different for everyone. Which is to say that all middle distance runners must be approached as individuals.
4. Because of the differences between male and female performers, it must be recognized that the female is not just a scaled down version of the male, she is a unique and highly specialized individual.
5. There are limits to one's capacity for responding positively to training. Since this is a fact, it should be recognized that training loads and maintenance loads differ significantly. For the most part it takes a training load of about eighty percent of one's current capacity to effect further positive change, whereas a work load of approximately sixty percent will maintain gains already accrued. The simplest way of monitoring the magnitude of the stress load is by checking heart rates. Heart rates between 120 and 160 to 165 beats per minute reflect stress that falls between the low aerobic and high aerobic threshold (60 to 80 percent). Work that increases the heart rate beyond 160 to 165 beats per minute tends to be anaerobic (80 percent and above). Another rule is that when one can no longer run and talk, the lactic-alactic threshold is near.

6. It should always be remembered that there is a difference between training to train and training to race. Our primary responsibility as coaches is to train our athletes to race.

7. One achieves the best results by training the strong side; which is to say that the aerobically gifted athlete should be trained aerobically, whereas the anaerobically gifted athlete should be trained to utilize his or her speed-endurance.

8. When speed and endurance are in competition for time and attention it ought to be recognized that one can more readily adapt to work stress than one can improve one's speed, i.e., it is more efficient to adapt to a slightly faster pace throughout a race than it is to try to win with the big kick at the end of the race.

9. Too much anaerobic training too fast tends to be destructive. One cannot reach down to the bottom of the barrel either in training or competition too often and expect to maintain any kind of peak.

10. If there is any question, it is better to be undertrained than to be overtrained. This is true for a meet, a season, or a life time.

11. It is to be remembered that there is a difference between optimum training and maximum training and that best results stem from optimum not maximum training.

## The Holistic Approach

The holistic program covers twelve months. (When working with high school athletes, it is recommended that a general format be developed for a period of three years.) The table on page 94 suggests how one could emphasize the development of the fuel systems during a one, two, and three year training cycle.

It should be noted in the following format that there is a progressive shift over the year from aerobic to anaerobic training. Note as well a similar general shift from an aerobic to an anaerobic commitment over the three years depicted above. The exact nature of this shift would be determined by the potential that each runner brings to the training situation. In the event one is working with an exceptional, aerobically endowed athlete, the training schedule would reflect this both by the magnitude of the aerobic activity and its continuation throughout the year. The same would be true of an exceptional anaerobic performer. (This is referred to as a strong side commitment and seems to be the direction that coaches are taking all over the world.)

Long Term Development of the Energy Systems Essential for
Competitive Racing at 800-1500 and 3000 Meters

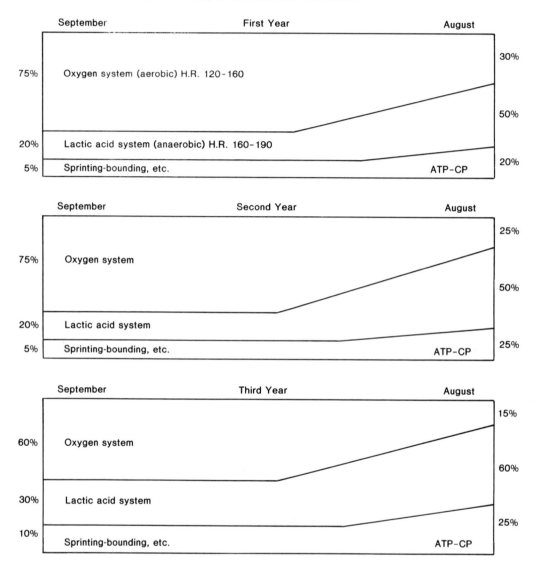

The next table represents a more detailed yearly format. This table includes the elements that one might incorporate in the training of the middle distance runner, as well as the relative time commitment to each element throughout the year.

Perhaps some explanation is in order relative to the generalizations made in the Comprehensive Training Program. The first is that I would recommend training in fourteen day cycles. Each cycle aims at achieving positive change by means of alternating hard days with easy days, with

# A Comprehensive Training Program for Middle Distance Runners

| Month | Sept. | Jan. | May | Aug. |
|---|---|---|---|---|
| **Total Miles** | 300 | 280 | 280 | 200 |

*Elements*

| | Sept. | Jan. | May | Aug. |
|---|---|---|---|---|
| Strength training | | | | |
|   weight work | 3 time/wk. . . . . . . . . . . . . 2 time/ wk. | | | |
|   bounding | 1 time/wk. . . . . . . 2 time/mo. | | | |
|   depth jumping | | 1 time/wk. | | |
| Flexibility work | Daily . . . . . . . . . . . . . . . . . . | | | |
| Long distance-slow (Oxygen system) | 4 time/wk. . 3 time/wk. . 2 time/wk. . 1 time/wk. | | | |
| Long distance-fast (Oxygen-lactic acid) | 1 time every other wk. . . . . . . . . . . . | | | |
| Fartlek (Oxygen-lactic acid) | 1 time/wk. . 2 time/Mo. . . . . . . | | | |
| Power runs (Lactic acid) | | 1 time/mo. . 3 time/mo. | | |
| Interval running (Oxygen-lactic acid) | | 1 time/wk. | | |
| Interval training (Lactic acid) | | | 2 time/wk. . 1 time/wk. | |
| Hill work (Oxygen-lactic acid) | 1 time/wk. . 2 time/mo. . Occasional use for peaking | | | |
| Sprint work (Lactic acid) | | | 1 time/wk. . 2 time/wk. | |
| Pace work (Steady state) | | 2 time/mo. . 1 time/wk. | | |

one day off each week. It is my belief that the training week ought to include ten to fourteen training sessions. A session would by definition, be a morning run, a weight training session, a session of bounding, a long, slow run, etc. Although we cannot accurately weigh each of the sessions that one might engage in, we should recognize that such weighting is the course of the future. Indeed, the day is not far off when we can say with a high degree of validity that the training load equivalency is between an hour of stretching and weight training, and a 12 mile run.

A second principle implicit in the comprehensive program, which needs some explanation, is the practice of "lifting" the training pace from September to August. This utilization of the overload principle varies from coach to coach but nevertheless is utilized by most.

My personal commitment is toward a progressive "lift" which drops from 1.0 to 1.5 seconds from the training pace each month from September to June. The range of such a "lift" in the training pace would be from ten to fifteen seconds per season. In arriving at the initial training pace for September one merely adds from ten to fifteen seconds to the anticipated one-half race time for the month of June. (Example: anticipated 800 M time for June 1:50. The one-half race time would be fifty-five seconds, thus the training time for September would be from sixty-five to seventy depending upon the maturity and strength of the runner involved.)

Another factor to be considered is that of work load or intensity. Most writers on this subject argue, and I agree, that both volume and intensity can be, and often are, overdone. In a positive sense I would recommend aerobic training runs of eight to twelve miles in length at heart rates between 120 to 150 beats per minute. (These would follow the frequency suggested in the comprehensive program.) Guidelines for the anaerobic training sessions would be interval repeats covering a distance approximating 2.5 to 3.5 times race distance at heart rates between 180 to 190 beats per minute.

It is my strong belief that most middle distance performers ought not dip too deeply, too often during the anaerobic training sessions. This is especially so when working with young or immature athletes. Indeed, if I had my way the high school athlete would seldom engage in intense, anaerobic training. (According to our research it takes from three to six days to recover from an intense work load.)

In recent years I have come to believe that hill work is a positive adjunct to the training of the middle distance performer. This is true both in terms of long-term preparation and as a means of peaking. Properly used, hill work represents a positive mechanism for developing strength in the antigravity muscles and a means whereby one can effect change in both the aerobic and anaerobic pathways.

Working with a computerized treadmill in our laboratory we have discovered that training runs at fifty to sixty percent of maximum velocity, at a ten to fifteen percent grade will produce heart rates of 180 to 190 in most performers. A recommended coupling of uphill running of this magnitude in an aerobic-anaerobic program would be as follows:

Subsequent to a warmup the trainee runs on the level approximately 440 yards aerobically (H.R. 120 to 150), to be followed immediately by an uphill run at a ten to fifteen percent grade, at a velocity that represents fifty to sixty percent of maximum. The length of the uphill run is determined by time with forty to sixty seconds suggested as a target (H.R. 180 to 190). This segment of the training run is completed with a level run out of approximately 440 yards which permits the heart rate to return to the aerobic range of 120 to 150 beats per minute.

                                                         440 yds. aerobic
                                              _____/
            40-60 seconds anaerobic
            10-15% grade
440 yds. aerobic
              _____/

Two further comments about this type of training: (1) Like any kind of interval work it can be overdone. (2) This is especially beneficial for the female athlete, who in our society needs significantly more strength work than the typical male performer.

Perhaps at this point it would be appropriate to be more specific in terms of suggested daily training sessions. It is to be recognized that these are indicative of what a middle distance runner might do during a specific season. In each instance the training activities relate back to the recommendations made in the comprehensive training schedule. The first schedule does not follow the usual format. The reason for this is to make the point that every aspect of the training program needs some form of quantification. This has relevance to all events, but particularly to the middle distance and distance events where performers have a tendency to train more than one time each day. The suggestion here is that one needs to consider the number of training sessions each week as relevant. It also is to be noted that rest is considered to be part of the overall preparation of the middle distance and distance runner.

## Typical Training Format

**Fall-September**

| | | |
|---|---|---|
| Monday | Anaerobic run (8-12 miles) | 1st session |
| | Weight training . . . upper body | 2nd session |
| Tuesday | Morning run-low aerobic (5-6 miles) | 3rd session |
| | Fartlek (45 minutes with some short, high intensity bursts) | 4th session |
| Wednesday | Hill work . . . continuous, aerobic-anaerobic | 5th session |
| | Weight training | 6th session |
| Thursday | Morning run-low aerobic (5-6 miles) | 7th session |
| | Afternoon aerobic-anaerobic-aerobic | |
| | 4 easy miles . . . 1 hard mile . . . 4 easy miles | 8th session |
| Friday | Active rest . . . i.e., hiking, swimming, cycling, etc. | 9th session |
| Saturday | Aerobic run (10-14 miles) morning | 10th session |
| | Weight training afternoon | 11th session |
| Sunday | High aerobic run (8-10 miles) | 12th session |
| Monday | Morning run-low aerobic (5-6 miles) | 13th session |
| | Fartlek (30 min. with some high intensity running) | 14th session |
| | Finish workout with several 220's at adjusted pace | |
| Tuesday | Morning run-low aerobic (6-7 miles) | 15th session |
| | Weight training, preceded by several form strides | 16th session |
| | on the football field | |

## Typical Training Format—Continued
**Fall-September**

| | | |
|---|---|---|
| Wednesday | Active rest, i.e., hiking, swimming, cycling, etc. | 17th session |
| Thursday | Hill work . . . repeats, aerobic-anaerobic-aerobic (400 m flat, 300 m 10-15% grade, 400 m flat run out) | 18th session |
| Friday | Morning run-low aerobic (3-4 miles) | 19th session |
| | Afternoon run-low aerobic (3-4 miles) | 20th session |
| Saturday | Competition in cross country | 21st session |
| | Followed by weight training-light | 22nd session |
| Sunday | Recovery run (8-12 miles) | 23rd session |
| Monday | Rest | 24th session |

Total miles approximately 150. Training sessions 11.5 per week. Two days of active rest. A mix of both aerobic and anaerobic training, though the major commitment is to aerobic or base running. During the second fourteen day training cycle the number of training sessions per week would increase to 12.5. It is assumed that each session will be preceded by fifteen minutes of stretching.

The beginning, or immature middle distance runner very likely would do the same kinds of things as those noted above. The difference between the immature and mature runners would be in the magnitude of the stress loads, with the beginner maximizing aerobic as against anaerobic training.

## Special Training Activities

*Segment running* is a drill adaptable to any large open area. The triangle drill is a typical example, with the participating runners divided between three stations. On signal the runners at station 1 run to station 2 and then jog back. Arrival of the first group of runners at station 2 is the signal for that group to run to station 3. The trick is for the first group to recover back to station 1 before the arrival of group 3.

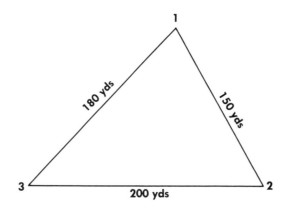

To fully utilize this drill the participants are instructed to run at four different speeds at each station; that is, they run the first leg at one-fourth speed, the second at one-half speed, the third at three-fourths speed, and the final leg at full speed. After each set of four repetitions, the groups move up to the next station and the running continues. One full cycle constitutes twelve segments.

The *Red Flag Special* is a continuous feedback drill having as its purpose training at a steady state. When using this drill, the quarter-mile track is divided into eight fifty-five-yard sections. (We use red flags to mark the segments, thus the name Red Flag Special.)

Participants in this drill are grouped according to ability. Following the initial signal to start running, a whistle is sounded at intervals commensurate with the steady state pace being sought. The participants attempt to pace themselves so that they are opposite a red flag each time the whistle is sounded. When a runner no longer can keep up, falling two or more strides off pace, he or she drops out and recovers by jogging.

Although the steady state drill is adaptable to the training of sprinters as well as of distance runners, a split-time schedule for milers is provided for the reader's consideration.

| Target Time | 1 | 2 | 3 | 4 | 5 | 6 | 7 | 8 | |
|---|---|---|---|---|---|---|---|---|---|
| 5:00–5:05 | 9.5 | 19 | 28.5 | 38 | 47.5 | 57 | 66.5 | 76 | **Steady State Running Split-Time Schedule** |
| 5:06–5:10 | 9.7 | 19.4 | 29.1 | 38.8 | 48.5 | 58 | 67.9 | 77.6 | |
| 5:11–5:15 | 9.9 | 19.8 | 27.7 | 39.6 | 49.5 | 59.4 | 69.3 | 79.2 | |
| 5:16–5:20 | 10.1 | 20.2 | 30.3 | 40.4 | 50.5 | 60.6 | 70.7 | 80.8 | |

The *55 alternate drill* (AD) drill utilizes the same section markers as the steady state drill. In this drill, however, runners alternate their pace each 55 yards. Pace times are determined for each group of runners by apportioning the 110-yard steady state time into fast stride and recovery segments. Using the 5:00-minute target time as an example, one might choose to divide the steady state time of 19 seconds into AD segments at 7.5 and 11.5 seconds respectively (19 seconds being the 110-yard steady state time for a 5:00 minute miler).

Here again the runners start on a specified signal, attempting to pass each flag as successive signals are given. (In this instance the signals are given at intervals of 7.5 and 11.5 seconds.) Experience has shown that the well-conditioned athlete can repeat many 440-yard runs in this manner. Experience has also shown this to be an excellent technique for teaching runners to relax while changing their pace.

*Power runs* offer a variety of training options. Short-distance power runs involve running all out for a specific time and then measuring the exact distance run—that is, yards, feet, and inches. This is both an excellent training technique and a diagnostic tool for selecting candidates for the 440, 400-meter hurdles, and the 880. Since it is an intense anerobic activity, however, it should be used infrequently, and then only with well-conditioned performers.

Another version of the power run involves distances of 660 yards or longer. A typical training session employing the power run concept might include runs of 1,320, 880, and 660 yards, respectively. Each 220 yards, at each distance, would be run at a progressively faster pace, with the final 220 yards being the fastest. A good variation when using this drill is to run all but the final segment on the grass, inside the curb, with the final 220 yards on the track simulating a finishing kick.

All of the drills and training activities heretofore discussed are now put into Winter and Spring Training Schedules for the readers consideration.

The reader is reminded that coaching is both a science and an art. Almost everyone knows the science of coaching, the x's and o's, the miles, reps, recoveries, and the like. The art of coaching is more tenuous. It is the art of coaching wherein we "listen to the athlete," sense how he or she is responding to the work loads prescribed. A part of the art also is recognizing that there are many ways to reach a particular goal and of then convincing your athletes that your way is best.

As the training of the middle distance runner must be perceived holistically, the athlete also must be perceived holistically. He or she needs to improve aerobically, anaerobically, in terms of strength, flexibility, and endurance, as well as in technique and in the subtlety of being ready mentally. How one accomplishes all of this cannot be clearly delineated in the mere printing of a schedule. Thus, I would repeat that it is the art of applying what we know that is the genius of coaching. One of the things that we know is that the stress loads necessary to "get there" must be eighty percent or more of the athlete's current level of development in a specific bio-physical factor, though a sixty percent stress load is sufficient to maintain that which has been accrued.

**Training Schedules for the Mature Middle Distance Runner**

## Winter Training Schedule

| Code | | | | | |
|------|------|-------------|-------------------|----|---------|
| | **J** | Jog | ( ⅓ speed) | **YD** | Yards |
| | **ST** | Stride | ( ⅔ speed) | **MI** | Miles |
| | **FS** | Fast Stride | (Relaxed sprint) | **M** | Minutes |
| | **BU** | Build Up | (Jog to fast stride) | **S** | Seconds |

| Date | Warm Up | Distance | Time | Reps | Recovery | Other |
|---|---|---|---|---|---|---|
| 1/1 | 2 MI J<br>Stretch | 1320<br>880<br>550<br><br>110 | ST<br>ST<br>ST<br><br>BU | 1<br>1<br>1<br><br>4–6 | 880 J<br>880 J<br>880 J<br>10 M J<br>Walk back | Kick the last 110<br>Kick the last 110<br>Kick the last 220<br><br>Run through turn |
| 1/2 | 2 MI J<br>Stretch | Fartlek | 45 M | | | Wt. training |
| 1/3 | 2 MI J<br>Stretch | 440 | Pace | 8 | 440 J | J 1 MI mile loop<br>between 4–5<br>J down |
| 1/4 | 2 MI J<br>Stretch | 150<br>grass<br>150 | FS<br><br>FS | 3–5<br><br>3–5 | Walk back<br>10 M J<br>Walk back | <br><br>15 M J to finish |
| 1/5 | 2 MI J<br>Stretch | 110<br>220<br>330<br>440<br>660 | FS<br>FS<br>Pace<br>Pace<br>ST | 1<br>1<br>1<br>1<br>1 | 220 J<br>330 J<br>440 J<br>440 J<br>10 M J | <br><br><br><br>Repeat the cycle<br>J down |
| 1/6 | | 7–8 MI | J | | | |
| 1/7 | | Active rest | | | | |
| 1/8 | 2 MI J<br>Stretch | 300<br>Long hill | ST | 5–7 | 5 M J | 15 M J to finish |
| 1/9 | 2 MI J<br>Stretch | 220 | 33–35 | 12 | J back | Run in sets of 4<br>440 J between sets |
| 1/10 | 2 MI J<br>Stretch | 660<br>80<br>150<br>150<br>150 | Pace<br>FS<br>22–23<br>21–22<br>20–21 | 1<br>1<br>1<br>1<br>1 | 200 J<br>880 J<br>J back<br>J back<br>J down | <br>Repeat 3 sets |
| 1/11 | | 3 MI<br><br>4th MI<br><br>3 MI | 7–8<br>MI/HR<br>5:45<br><br>7–8<br>MI/HR | | | Steady state<br>running<br>Continuous<br>running<br>7 MI total |
| 1/12 | 2 MI J | 660 or<br>1320<br>75 | Time<br>trial<br>BU | 1<br><br>10 | 15 M J<br><br>J back | <br><br>Run as finish kicks<br>out of the turn |
| 1/13 | | Rest | | | | |
| 1/14 | 2 MI J | 110<br>110<br>220<br>220<br>220 | FS<br>FS<br>33<br>31<br>29 | 1<br>1<br>1<br>1<br>1 | 110 J<br>880 J<br>J back<br>J back<br>J down | <br>Repeat 3 sets |

## Spring Training Schedule

| Code | | | | | | | |
|------|---|---|---|---|---|---|---|
| | J | Jog | ( ⅓ speed ) | | | YD | Yards |
| | ST | Stride | ( ⅔ speed ) | | | MI | Miles |
| | FS | Fast Stride | ( Relaxed sprint ) | | | M | Minutes |
| | BU | Build Up | ( Jog to fast stride ) | | | S | Seconds |

| Date | Warm Up | Distance | Time | Reps | Recovery | Other |
|------|---------|----------|------|------|----------|-------|
| 3/1 | 1 MI J | 1100 | Power run | 1 | 10 M J | Begin power runs with a J; |
| | Stretch | 770 | Power run | 1 | 10 M J | increase the speed each 220 |
| | | 110 | FS | 4–6 | Walk back | Kick off the turn |
| 3/2 | 1 MI J | 550 | Pace | 1 | 220 J | |
| | Stretch | 110 | FS | 1 | 5 M J | Repeat |
| | | 330 | Pace | 1 | 110 J | |
| | | 330 | 2 S faster | 1 | 10 M J | |
| | | 150 | 19–20 | 2–4 | 290 J | Finish kick drill |
| 3/3 | 1 MI J | 220 | 30–32 | 16 | J back | Run in sets of 4 |
| | Stretch | | | | | 440 J between sets |
| 3/4 | | 6–8 MI | J | | | Wt. training |
| 3/5 | 1 MI J | 220 | Pace | 1 | 440 ST | |
| | Stretch | 220 | Pace | 1 | 10 M J | |
| | | 150 | BU | 3–5 | Walk back | Run off the turn |
| 3/6 | | Competition | | | | |
| 3/7 | | Rest | | | | |
| 3/8 | 1 MI J | 800 | ST | 1 | 440 J | |
| | Stretch | 600 | ST | 1 | 440 J | |
| | | 400 | Pace | 1 | 440 J | |
| | | 60 | ST | 1 | | |
| | | 60 | FS | 1 | 60 ST | |
| | | 150 | 19–20 | 2 | J back | Finish kick drill Go right from 60 ST to 150 kick |
| 3/9 | | 6–8 MI | | | | Steady state running |
| 3/10 | 1 MI J | 440 | 11–7 | 6–8 | 5 M J | 55 AD drill; continuous change of pace at 55 YD markers |
| | Stretch | | | | | |
| 3/11 | 1 MI J | 1320 | ST | 1 | 880 J | |
| | Stretch | 220 | ST | 1 | | |
| | | 220 | Pace | 1 | | |
| | | 110 | FS | 1 | 440 J | Repeat 3–5 sets J down |

| Date | Warm Up | Distance | Time | Reps | Recovery | Other |
|------|---------|----------|------|------|----------|-------|
| 3/12 | 1 MI J | 220 | Pace | 1 | 220 J | Pace for 1st 220 |
|      | Stretch | 220 | Pace | 1 | 220 J | Pace for 2nd 220 |
|      |         | 220 | Pace | 1 | 220 J | Pace for 3rd 220 |
|      |         | 150 | 19–20 | 3 | 290 J | Finish kick drill |
| 3/13 | 1 MI J | Competition | | | | |
|      | Stretch | | | | | |
| 3/14 |         | Rest | | | | |

The wise coach works to achieve a desired level of development in a given area, shifts to maintenance loads where that area is concerned, and bears down in another area. And as the process of physical development continues, the mental side is fortified and strengthened as well.

Of all the topics concerned with the development of an athlete perhaps none is so important, or so difficult to deal with as the mental, or psychological side. The writer is under no illusion that he has the answer to this important dimension of coaching, but believes that there are certain psychological principles, which if applied with care and wisdom, can positively affect performance.

**Peaking, Tapering, and Mental Preparation**

Historically it has been assumed that peaking is something that one does once or twice a year. The typical approach to peaking has included a reduction in the volume of work, a lowering of the magnitude of the stress loads, an increase in tempo training (moving from quantity to quality), and an effort to get set mentally. The emphasis has been on "the doing of something near the end of the season" as against the idea of getting ready all year long.

While it may be unrealistic to assume that one can retain a competitive edge year-round, it may be equally unrealistic to assume that an athlete can only respond to the "big challenge" once or twice a year. Surely the professional golfer has taught us something about the mental side of performance in that many of them "stay up" for months while eating or starving on the basis of their competitive edge.

During my early coaching experience I followed the textbook in almost everything I did. The middle distance runner ran cross-country in the fall and road races during the winter for the purpose of building a base. In the spring we forgot the overdistance, shifted to the track and worked to build the competitive edge. Invariably some of my athletes had better times following cross-country season than they did in the spring. One such athlete was a shy soul who will hereafter be referred to as Doris. An athlete with profound commitment to excellence, an amazing ability to tolerate stress, a great cross-country runner, yet having only limited success on the track.

One day in the past we were invited to run in what was advertised to be the premier mile race of the century. A set up, actually, so that the Canadian record holder would have a chance to break the existing world indoor record in the mile. About that time I heard a Navy psychiatrist speak about the psyche of the athlete. He noted that many participants in individual events were there for their own inner needs. Among these was the need to affirm one's self, to build a sense of personal autonomy. "Many need to learn to win," he said, "to recognize that they can be better than the rest." Armed with this insight an effort was made to change Doris' perception of herself. At all times she was referred to as madame champion. We set training goals that were difficult, yet reasonable and achievable. During every workout an effort was made to surround Doris with positive images, she was affirmed with positive feedback, encouraged to risk herself for greatness, to dare to dream of being the best.

On race day the strategy, which we had developed, was to lead from behind, to push without passing, to let the adversary know that she was running against a viable competitor. From the start the Canadian runner took over the lead, setting the kind of pace that would be needed if the record were to be broken. At the 880 mark she had shaken all of the competitors except Doris. Soon she began looking back to see who this dogged pursuer was. At the three-quarter mark Doris made her move and the two athletes ran stride for stride for the next 220 yards. Thereafter Doris put on a torrid kick, went on to win the race and break the world record by five seconds.

In her athletic postmortem the Canadian noted that her first inkling of disaster was "the sounds of those feet . . . those awful footsteps which she could hear behind her." She had not been prepared to deal with such a sound, the longer it lasted, the louder it became, and the more certainly it eroded her confidence in herself. Doris, on the other hand, said "I could hear her breathing more heavily, I began to believe I could win and I did."

Bill Morgan and Peter Hansen of the University of Wisconsin are studying the competitive edge from another point of vantage. It is their assumption that "staleness" may be the factor that diminishes human performance. Maybe one is engineered to be successful most of the time, not just once or twice a year and it is this "psychic burn out" that is the problem with which we need most to deal.*

To test this hypothesis Morgan has utilized the "Profile of Mood States" to evaluate the athletes psyche during the school year. Thus far the data have shown that the athlete who is going stale, or succumbing to the stress of fatigue, emotional deprivation, boredom and doubt mani-

---

*Bill Morgan and Peter Hanson, report to the American College of Sports Medicine, Las Vegas, May 29, 1980.

**Figure 7.2.** In a tactical race the kicker has the advantage if the opening pace is too slow.

fests more anger, greater depression, and less vigor as the year moves along. If left unchecked these mood changes become irreversible, and the athlete who is "over the hill" in January likely will not make it back by spring.

The upshot, I believe, is that peaking and mental preparation are one and the same thing. This is not something that we do at a point in time, but something that we do all of the time. Recently the writer attended a banquet at which there were a number of world record holders. One of these was a middle distance runner who was there with his mother and his father/coach. It was an interesting and revealing experience: the quiet, yet positive attitude of the athlete; the near arrogant, though positive attitude of the father/coach; and the supportive strength of the mother. All of these attitudes are reflected in a champion's performance on the track.

From the tactical standpoint the coupling of the "sense of certainty" with one's physical endowments should result in maximum achievement most of the time. Though I personally deplore the slow, plodding opening pace with everyone rushing for position at the end of the race, this may be the best strategy for the great kicker.

A better strategy yet may be to attempt to control the race early on, setting a faster pace if you are aerobically endowed than would be the case if you are a kicker. The kicker, on the other hand, refuses to get pulled in over his/her head at the outset, but getting into position to kick before the final turn.

From the standpoint of physiology an even pace is still the most economical and thus the best pace for positive racing results. At 800 meters this would mean a differential of 1.0 to 2.5 seconds between the first and second quarters. A faster first quarter seems to be best. In the mile or 1500 meter event the differential between the first and second half of the race would be 2.5 to 3.5 seconds. Again the first half is usually faster than the second.

If there is a trend in the world today it seems to be toward the anaerobically endowed runner moving up in both the 800 and 1500 meter events. With the exception of the Olympic Games where tactics were fundamentally important to getting through the heats and perhaps winning the Olympic Gold, the great middle distance races of the 1980s tended to be maximum acceleration-minimum deceleration events. Indeed, a top American miler was quoted recently as decrying the fact that too many middle distance runners were just along for the ride, while those few who wanted to win and expected to win, continually went out after the victory from the very start.

Kazankina's incredible world record at Zurich in August 1980, surely reflected the new trend among female middle distance runners, as well as the tactic of maximum acceleration-minimum deceleration racing. Kazankina was 2:04.5 at 800 meters (0.4 seconds ahead of the pace for the men's Olympic 1500 meter final at Moscow) going on to win in 3:52.47.

And so we have come full circle. Throughout all of history men and women have improved in whatever it has been that they have elected to do. To continue this trend we must apply what we know as carefully and yet with as much daring as we can muster. In my mind the task is strong side training of the physical being and holistic, year around strengthening of the will and lifting of the human spirit. It is a total being who comes to our tracks, a bio-psycho-socio-spiritual being capable of incredible heights of achievement. We must meet each being where he or she is and help them to see and become that which they have been created to be.

# 8 Distance Running

These events include the three mile (5000 m), six miles (10,000 m) and marathon. Both men and women participate in all three events at the national and international levels. It is generally concluded that due to her higher percentage of body fat, a primary source of aerobic fuel, the female may be more nearly competitive with the male as the distance of the race increases.

Indeed, the reader is reminded that as one moves from the sprints to the marathon, the energy systems change form anaerobic to aerobic. Estimates of the energy source for selected races is to be found below. These estimates provide a significant clue as to the development of training schedules for the various running events.

## Estimated Energy Source for Selected Track Events

| Event | ATP/CP-Lactic Acid Systems (anaerobic) | Oxygen System (aerobic) |
|---|---|---|
| Marathon | 2% | 98% |
| 10,000 m | 10% | 90% |
| 5,000 m | 20% | 80% |
| 1,500 m | 50% | 50% |
| 800 m | 65% | 35% |
| 400 m | 85% | 15% |
| 200 m | 95% | 5% |

**Characteristics of the Successful Distance Runner**

Both from the standpoint of selection and performance, distance runners reflect those characteristics previously delineated for the middle distance athletes. They are, however, leaner, lighter, and smaller in body structure. They are genetically superior in aerobic capacity. They tend to take shorter strides and run with a more nearly vertical posture. Arm action is less vigorous and the height of both the knee and the foot during the swing phase of the stride is less pronounced than any other track performer.

It is generally concluded, the successful distance runner internalizes thought and emotion during both hard training and competition. It has been argued that most marathon runners will let their minds drift or float during the early portion of this event, but that ultimate success is dependent on "listening carefully to one's body."

**Characteristics of the Successful Training Program**

The most obvious characteristic is the comprehensive nature of the successful program. Such a program contains activities that are generally classified as continuous and interrupted. Continuous running includes marathon training and long distance slow or long distance fast. Interrupted training activities for the distance runner are Fartlek, Tempo running, and interval training.

Marathon running is part of the comprehensive program advocated by Arthur Lydiard. The germ idea of the Lydiard System is that one should adapt one's training to the geographic area in which one lives. While the overall system seeks a balance between speed and endurance, the marathon concept advocates the running of one hundred or more miles a week, with the athlete covering from ten to twenty miles a day. With mileage the backbone of the system, runners work on the track to develop rhythm and sprint hills to build strength.

LSD, which has reference to "long slow distance," is a term first used by Joe Henderson. Like marathon running, this system advocates mileage, but at a slow and easy pace. For young and immature runners LSD would mean a jog, covering from four to five miles an hour. For the mature runner the pace would be increased to six to seven miles an hour.

Fartlek is a program developed by Gosta Holmer, formerly the chief Olympic coach of Sweden. This program grew out of the need to train runners in a geographic area where the summers were short and the winters long and severe. The word Fartlek thus describes a kind of "speed play" in which individuals run through the woods, along a sandy beach, or in the open fields, moving with a zest that reflects the freedom of the spirit and the beauty of nature. Running of this kind is not without direction, however, as individuals are urged to change their pace—sprinting, striding, walking-working, recovering, working-recovering, ever striving toward greater speed and endurance.

Tempo running involves training at specified distances without concern for time. The purpose of this training is to make the transition from cross-country running to running on the track. Rhythm over prescribed distances is emphasized, though the keeping of time is not.

Interval training, on the other hand, involves the keeping of accurate records where time is concerned. This system was developed by Dr. Woldemar Grechler and his colleague, the eminent cardiologist Dr. Herbert Reindel. Perhaps the most widely used of all systems, interval training involves repeated runs at fixed distances with the aim of achieving certain target rates as far as the heartbeat is concerned. When originally described Grechler and Reindel suggested that the intervals for this kind of training would range in length from 100 to 400 meters. It is now recognized that intervals of from one hundred yards to three miles can be effectively used for training purposes.

The key to training for the distance events is aerobic activity. During the fall this would include a variety of aerobic games, some tempo running and cross-country. A large volume (40 to 50 miles) of aerobic running would be carried through the winter and into the spring. This is especially important for young athletes about whom most authorities would argue that "it is not the distance that kills, but the speed."

In other respects training for distance races is essentially the same as training for middle distance events. The major difference is that, as the distance for which one is preparing increases, the need for speed work (anaerobic training) decreases. During the fall both middle distance and distance runners engage in cross-country. (Half milers tend to run cross-country more for the work than for the competition.)

In the winter and spring when the training emphasis shifts to interval work, the distance runner would likely run repeat 880s, 1,320s and miles, rather than the 220s, 440s, and 660s covered by the middle distance performer. The longer intervals reflect the factor of specificity—a factor of prime importance where running rhythm is concerned.

For races longer than 10 thousand meters, participants frequently engage in staggering work loads. In addition to training runs of fifteen miles or more, it would not be uncommon for a marathoner to repeat as many as twenty to twenty-five 880s during a single workout session.

Suggested training loads for distance runners are shown below. These have not been put into the formal Training Format that has been used throughout the book, but the principles are the same. That is, the training cycle would be fourteen days. The practice of alternating hard and easy days would be adhered to. Each fourteen day cycle would have one day of active rest and one of complete rest. And, the number of training sessions per week would range between twelve to fourteen.

**Training Schedules for Distance Runners**

## Suggested Single Week Work Load for Mature Distance Runners—Preseason

| | |
|---|---|
| 4 morning runs—continuous | 7-8 minute mile pace |
| 2 afternoon runs—continuous | 6-7 minute mile pace |
| 2 afternoons Fartlek | 7-8 miles |
| 1 afternoon hills | 220-440 segments |
| 1 afternoon tempo running | adjusted race pace for date |
| 3 sessions of weight training | |

Total miles 80-100; energy distribution: 85 percent aerobic; 15 percent anaerobic

Suggested Single Week Work Load
for Mature Distance Runners—Competitive Season

| | |
|---|---|
| 4 morning runs—continuous | 7 minute mile pace |
| 2 afternoon runs—continuous | 5:30-6:30 minute mile pace |
| 1 afternoon tempo running | adjusted race pace for date |
| 1 afternoon Fartlek | integrate flat sections at race pace |
| 1 afternoon interval running | slightly faster than adjusted race pace |
| 2 sessions of weight training | |
| Competition | |

Total miles 75-90; energy distribution: 70 percent aerobic; 30 percent anaerobic

**Cross-country Training**

Since most distance runners engage in cross-country as a competitive sport, special emphasis will be given to this activity, both as a training tool and as a competitive event.

**Physical Characteristics of the Cross-country Runner**

Since distance runners usually double as cross-country performers, the physical characteristics manifested by these athletes have been discussed in the chapter on distance running. One additional characteristic, however, should be considered, that is, the characteristic of physical toughness. Because of the variation in terrain, the rough running surface, and the steepness of the hills, cross-country performers must be strong. Much of the time and energy utilized in their training should be aimed at the development of general toughness and physical strength.

**Psychological Characteristics of the Cross-country Runner**

Again it is safe to say that those characteristics which tend to describe the distance runner also tend to describe the cross-country performer. It is true, however, that not all successful distance performers enjoy cross-country running, nor do all successful cross-country runners like to compete on the oval track.

In a very real sense, the cross-country runner is a unique individual. Most thoroughly enjoy just running and likely would do this even if it were not possible to compete. These athletes particularly enjoy open places, with the challenge of an occasional hill, and a fence or stream to jump. These are the athletes who become bored by the monotony of interval training and who often ask if they can get away from the track to run alone through the woods or beside the crashing sea.

**Mechanics of Cross-country Running**

The mechanics of cross-country running vary with the terrain. On flat, open areas the performer utilizes a relaxed, economical style. The body is essentially erect, with the eyes focused from fifteen to twenty yards ahead. The arms are carried loosely, with the elbows fixed at near ninety

**Figure 8.1.** In flat, open areas the cross country runner utilizes a relaxed, economical style. The body is erect, the arms are carried loosely, the height of the feet and knees is minimal to conserve energy.

degrees. The partially flexed hands swing from the side rearward to the midchest forward. The running stride is relatively short. There is little knee lift. Foot action involves a ball-heel-ball sequence.

Running up hills demands a marked modification of style. The performer assumes a decided forward lean in order to utilize the powerful gluteal muscles in hip extension. Arm action is vigorous to accommodate the driving legs. Eye focus is approximately five yards in front of the runner. The energy expenditure in running up hills demands weeks of specific preparation for effective execution.

Downhill running also requires special modification. Indeed, running downhill can be the most fatiguing and mechanically ineffective segment of a race, if the performer has not learned the proper technique for this activity. Since balance often is a key factor in downhill running, the novice tends to markedly shorten the running stride to control forward progress. This tendency, of course, is inappropriate. The stride actually should be lengthened in downhill running, with the arms carried away from the body for purposes of balance. Successful performers learn to "roll" their hips when running downhill, thus lengthening their strides in a somewhat free-wheeling action. To perfect the mechanics of downhill running, as well as those essential to running uphill, the cross-country performer must practice many hours on hilly terrain.

## Training Techniques for Cross-country Runners

Marathon training is the foundation for success in all long-distance running. The cross-country runner should participate in this type of training at least two, perhaps three, times each week. It is not too much to expect that both the female and male athlete can run from eight to twelve miles during a workout of this type. For most effective results a fixed course should be followed. Times should be recorded to provide an incentive for working up to capacity. Recorded times are indicative of improvement, though for psychological reasons time should not become the preoccupation of the performer.

*Fartlek,* or fun running, should also be a part of the weekly schedule. The wise coach looks for different and exciting places for runners to train. Sometimes this demands bussing the team to an entirely new area; yet the rewards of such activity far outweigh any inconvenience incurred. Boredom is a constant threat to the all-important mental attitude of the runner and must be avoided at all costs.

*Hill work* has already been emphasized. It is important, however, to recognize that hill work involves more than just running up and down an inclined plane. Hills are the places where cross-country races are won. Hills must therefore become a special kind of challenge to the serious performer. All must believe that it is possible to catch and pass any adversary on a hill. A good drill for developing mental toughness on hills is to start individual athletes fifteen to twenty yards behind the pack and chase the other runners to the top of a hill. This kind of drill might well be used at least once a week during cross-country season.

Hillwork should also involve some type of strengthening activity such as running stairs or upward through loose sand. This is painful and the uncommitted hate it, but the serious performer looks forward to a weekly challenge of this kind.

### Novelty Reemphasized

Surely one of the keys to the successful preparation of cross-country runners is the integration of novelty into the training program. While each kind of training activity already described is essential, novelty must be a primary concern of the serious coach. Several examples of the types of variation that might be utilized follow. The readers are encouraged to explore these and to develop novel ideas of their own.

Since cross-country is a team event, runners are encouraged to train as often as possible in a group. Two training sessions each day are advocated, with the morning session mostly fun. Follow-the-leader is an example of fun running, with individuals leading the group in their particular "thing." Running in Indian file with the last person taking the lead at some designated signal is an effective way to initiate this activity.

Cross-country golf, or segment running, is a good means of attaining motivation through variation. When this scheme is used, a long course (perhaps even an actual golf course) is divided into several segments of varying length. Through experimentation, times are affixed to each segment which, if equaled in practice, constitute par for that leg of the run. Differentials of five-second increments are also established so that each runner can score oneself on par, one stroke, two strokes, three strokes over par, or under par, as the situation might be. If score is kept, each time the cross-country golf course is run, improvement is readily noted.

Obstacle courses have a special appeal to most cross-country runners. These might involve different running surfaces such as sand, short grass, dirt roads, or leafy trails. Fences, walls, a stream to jump, or sharp turns also are effective. Some coaches even prepare a different obstacle course for each training session. Small cards with directions are affixed to trees or posts. The performers run a given segment, read the new directions, and run on to the next station. This is similar to an activity done by foresters who are learning to use a map and compass. It is particularly effective because it keeps runners alert, giving them little time to worry about fatigue.

Team relays constitute another excellent means of motivating individuals to work to their capacity. These can be conducted in various ways, though one which some coaches have found to be particularly appealing is the *zenderlaf*, or continuous run for time. The course for such a training session is established by placing flags at varying intervals throughout a park. The number of flags is determined by the number of runners. At the outset, one runner from each team is stationed at each flag. At an appropriate signal, the leadoff performers run to the next flag, passing a baton to their respective teammates. The pace for each runner is determined largely by the distance between flags and the overall time for the continuous run. The winning team covers the greatest distance in a predetermined period of time. For best results the course should be open so that team positions are never in doubt.

**Strategy in Cross-country Running**

Because of the nature of this activity, strategy is in some ways less specific than for running a fixed distance on the track. On the other hand, strategy is an integral part of every race and often is the difference between victory and defeat.

Perhaps the most obvious strategy in cross-country is the need for keeping the team together as a group. This means that each runner must maintain contact with the closest teammate. When this contact is broken, one does not panic but works on the opponent who separated the group, with every intention of moving up one position at a time. This approach of setting immediate, realizable goals is particularly important for the young runner. It keeps one alert and builds the team spirit so essential to success.

Because there is a high degree of specificity in every activity, it is always wise to explore the cross-country course before an important competitive event. Such an exploration should provide information concerning potential bottlenecks where precious time might be lost if caught there with the pack. Hazardous turns or obstacles should be noted, with time expended in determining how best to negotiate these during the competitive race. Hills should also be carefully explored for the purpose of fixing an appropriate racing pace.

The importance of pace was discussed in the chapter on distance running. It is mentioned here to give emphasis to the fact that the even distribution of energy becomes increasingly essential with the length of the race. The wise runner starts fast to get out of the pack, then settles into a rhythm at a tolerable pace. One does not necessarily want to be the "rabbit," or leader, but assumes this role if one must. There is no need to panic in cross-country.

Because distance running is largely an act of the will, attitudes are particularly important in this event. Successful runners, therefore, seldom give the impression of being fatigued. By acting fresh they weaken the confidence of their less-experienced adversaries. Winners are often heard to say, "I made my move when the runners in front of me seemed to tire."

## Cross-country Training Schedules

It is strongly recommended that all runners participate to some extent in cross-country training. It is also strongly recommended that all athletes preparing for races 880 yards or longer, as well as 400-meter hurdle candidates, participate in the competitive cross-country program. Thus in preparing cross-country training schedules all runners should be considered.

Adhering to the holistic principle, better coaches predicate current practices on future expectations. Every day of training has a purpose as far as each individual athlete is concerned. To effect such a comprehensive program one must expend a large block of time organizing and planning (see chapter 1). The development of monthly, as well as of daily, training schedules is an effective means of putting one's ideas into perspective.

An example of the month-long training schedule is given here. Like all of the other schedules to be found in this book, this one was taken from the authors' working files. Note that it encompasses most of the elements to be found in the more popular systems of training which were discussed earlier. Study the schedule from the first day to the last and you also will see a progression in terms of overload demands.

Cross-country and road racing are both an end and a means. Some runners peak for the cross-country season, while others participate in cross-country as a means of getting ready for competition on the track. Whatever one's purpose for participating in cross-country running, continued improvement is dependent upon frequent timed activity.

# Comprehensive Cross-country Training Schedule—September

| | | | |
|---|---|---|---|
| **M** | 8–10 miles of continuous running, Seward Park | "Neckers Knob" loop; run from school, even pace | Lincoln Park 2 loops<br><br>13.6 MI | Golden Gardens loop; run from school, even pace |
| **T** | Track<br>8 × 440 (75–80)<br>440 J back<br>75 BU, walk back<br>J down<br>Weights | Track<br>5–6 × 880-AD<br>440 J back<br>3–5 × 150–23–25<br>Walk back<br>J down | Track<br><br>Red Flag<br>  Special—run<br>  your pace for<br>  this date | Track<br>1320 power<br>440 J<br>1100 power<br>440 J<br>880 power<br>4 M hill loop |
| **W** | Green Lake hill<br>  repeats<br><br>5 × 330<br>J back<br>Run lake to<br>  finish | Mt. Baker<br>3 MI step down<br>7M–6:30M–6M<br>Jog 10 M<br>4 MI steady<br>2 MI step down | Green Lake<br>  hill repeats<br><br>6 × 330<br>J back recovery<br>Run back to<br>  college | Woodland Park<br>  hills, 30 M<br><br>Run first M loop<br>  of college course<br>  for time |
| **Th** | Arboretum<br>3 MI Fartlek<br>Stretch<br>3 MI-7M/MI<br>  pace last<br>  440 hard | Wallace Field<br>30 M grass<br>Striding<br>150–200 repeats | Arboretum<br>Pick a partner<br>  and share the<br>  beauty together<br>45 M continuous | Fort Lawton<br>20 M segments<br><br>Finish with 30 M<br>Fartlek |
| **F** | Fort Lawton,<br>  segments as<br>  directed<br><br>Hills to<br>  finish | Discovery Park,<br>  hill trails<br>30 minutes<br><br>3 MI J down | Wallace Field,<br>10 × 100 FS<br>Walk back<br>10 × 150 FS<br>Walk back<br>5 × 200 form<br>3 MI J down | Jackson golf<br>  course, 6–8 MI |
| **S** | Time trial<br>3 MI<br>All compete | NW AAU Green<br>  Lake 3 MI<br><br>All compete | Fort Casey<br>  Invitational<br>**5 MI**<br>All compete | Seward step<br>  down<br>6:45–6:15–5:30<br>J 3 MI loop<br>  Through park<br>Step down 2 MI<br>5:30–All out |
| **SU** | 8–10 mile<br>Recovery run<br>  on your own | Complete rest | Fun run on the<br>  beach 30–40M | Complete rest |

It is well known that individuals adapt to imposed demands. Thus one could become a very efficient performer at ten-minutes-per-mile pace, without further improvement if no greater demands were imposed. Strangely enough, however, many coaches still instruct their athletes to "just go out and run" with the hope that improvement will occur.

The step-down drill referred to in the comprehensive schedules has proved to be one of the best activities yet found to produce progressive improvement. Participants in this drill begin running without prior warm-up, quickening their cadence each successive mile. The drill is used twice a month, with the first step down in September making very modest demands on the participants (8 to 6:30 and 6 minutes per mile).

By the end of November the step-down pace has been quickened to 6:15 to 5:45 and 5:15 per mile. Not infrequently, members of our Club have run this drill on target for the first two miles, covering the final mile under five minutes. They have then jogged a three-mile loop to recover, finishing the workout with a two-mile step down at 5:45 and less than 5 minutes for the final mile of the day.

## Training for the Marathon

With more and more athletes running the marathon it seems as if some attention should be given to preparation for this very special event. The marathon is a race just over twenty-six miles in length. Since marathons are run over varying terrain, world records for this event have only relative meaning. Better times for male performers, however, are somewhere between two hours and ten to twenty minutes. Whereas comparable times for women would fall in a range between two hours and thirty to forty minutes.

From the standpoint of metabolic factors the marathon is primarily an aerobic activity. This fact alone, however, does not tell the full story where training is concerned. Current research seems to indicate that the secret to training for the marathon lies in the same direction as that noted for other track and field events. It is the factor of quality that matters most.

Before specifically delineating work loads, I want to express the opinion that immature persons should not engage in marathon competition. If this were to be translated into chonological time I would put the age at seventeen to eighteen when an individual should begin competing in this event.

The first step in preparation for the marathon must be the development of a sound aerobic base. This can be done by following the guidelines already delineated for middle distance and distance runners. Where maximum oxygen uptake measures are concerned the marathon runner must have a value of 65 ml/kg/min, or higher. The emphasis thereafter is on pushing up the effective working threshold. It is at this point that many "would be" marathoners make their most serious training mistake.

Typically a marathon runner covers 100 miles or more each week. While the pace of this running varies, it usually is well below the aerobic-anaerobic threshold. The nature of the running likely would be at a long, slow pace, with selected sessions of cross-country training, and tempo work on the track.

The key to success, however, lies beyond this. It is in practicing the principle of continuous overloading. If all one does is run miles at sub-maximum work loads, then one soon adapts to that level of stress. The marathoner must progressively increase the stress loads like any other developing athlete. My recommendation at this point is to monitor stress loads by checking the heart rate.

For well conditioned teenage and college age performers a working heart rate of 120 to 145 beats per minute would be considered low aerobic. Heart rates of 150 to 170 would be considered high aerobic and heart rates in excess of 170 likely would be anaerobic. Translating this into a reasonable and effective training program involves the setting of specific work loads at each of the stress levels noted above.

## Suggested Work Loads for the Marathon

### The Fall Season

Beginning in September the athlete should increase the volume of running to 100 miles per week. This would involve running over varying terrain with heart rates primarily in the low aerobic zone. When the desired volume of work has been achieved, one high aerobic training session of from eight to twelve miles should be integrated into the weekly schedule. Later a second high aerobic session can be added. All of this is done in preparation for the more strenuous training, which usually begins in January.

### Pre-season Training

Monday:      A long (12 to 15 miles) low aerobic run. Heart rates between 120 to 145.

Tuesday:     Competitive pace, or tempo running at heart rates in the high aerobic zone. (8 to 10 miles)

Wednesday: Repetition running on the track or well-calibrated trails. Aerobic-anaerobic with heart rates ranging between 120 to 180+. Examples would be 2 x 1.5 miles with recoveries as needed to get heart rates back to 120. This to be followed by 4 x 800 meters with 400 meter jogs between each.

Thursday:    A long (12 to 15 miles) low aerobic run.

| Friday: | Tempo running over 3 to 4 mile segments. Heart rates in high aerobic zone. |
|---|---|
| Saturday: | Rest or easy recovery run of 5 to 6 miles. Low aerobic. |
| Sunday: | Steady run over 18 to 20 miles at low aerobic rate. |

### Training During the Competitive Season (Typical minicycle)

Day 1: Run a 10 K "time trial" at race pace.
Day 2: A long (10 to 12 miles) low aerobic run.
Day 3: Repetition running at race pace. 5 x 1 mile, with jogging recovery back to minimum of 120 beats per minute.
Day 4: A long (10 to 12 miles) low aerobic run.
Day 5: A Fartlek-like run with heart rates ranging between low aerobic and anaerobic. Continuous over 12 to 15 miles.
Day 6: Low aerobic run (5 to 6 miles).
Day 7: Low aerobic run (5 to 6 miles).
Day 8: Rest.
Day 9: Rest.
Day 10: Competition warm-up over segments of the race course. (Cover several miles at race pace).
Day 11: Competition.
Day 12: Recovery run—long (10 to 12 miles) low aerobic.

There are several factors to be noted here. The first is that the heart rate is a self-adjusting mechanism. Work loads that produced a given heart rate in the fall will not be sufficient to produce the same heart rate in the spring. One, therefore, is working progressively harder and harder as the season moves along. A second factor is that the actual distribution of stress loads varies from about eighty percent low aerobic to twenty percent high aerobic in the fall, to forty percent low aerobic to sixty percent high aerobic during the competitive season. A third factor, which may not be so obvious, is that the work load prior to competition is markedly reduced.

It has been my experience that many marathon runners make three serious mistakes. First, they tend to do too much running too soon and are plagued by soft tissue injuries. Second, they spend too much time working at submaximal stress loads and thus do not improve. And, thirdly they work too hard during the week preceding competition. While all are serious mistakes, the latter is particularly destructive as it takes several days to recover from a hard training session. And, to enter a marathon when one is not fully recovered is the worst kind of self-inflicted torture.

By all rights the steeplechase is a unique event and warrants more extensive coverage than it will receive here. Perhaps when this race becomes part of the regular, high school, and college schedule it will receive the emphasis that it ought.

The steeplechase is run over a distance of 3000 meters. During the course of the race, the performer must hurdle twenty-eight 36-inch barriers and negotiate seven water jumps. The race was first contested internationally during the Olympic games of 1920. Only two Americans (Horace Ashenfelter, gold 1952 and George Young, bronze 1968) have ever placed in the steeplechase in Olympic competition.

Because this event is not contested in high school competition and only part of the time at the college level, steeplechase specialists are virtually unknown. The practice heretofore has been to convince a mediocre miler, or 5000-meter runner to shift to the steeplechase for the purpose of gaining points for the team. More appropriately the steeplechase performer ought to be selected because he is a good middle distance/distance type, who is well-coordinated, relatively tall, and rugged.

Running training would be essentially the same as that employed by the two-mile competitor. The extra work would be on the development of hurdle technique. Indeed, it has been estimated that the "typical" steeplechase runner in the United States could reduce his/her time in this event by as much as twenty seconds, simply by improving hurdle technique.

**Figure 8.2.** A key factor in improved performance in the steeplechase is the development of an effective hurdle technique.

**The Development of Hurdle Technique**

Unlike the hurdles used in the shorter events, the steeplechase barrier is heavy and rugged and will inflict injury to the performer when contact is made. Initial learning of the hurdle technique therefore, ought to begin by using the step by step procedure described in chapter 6. When adequate hurdle proficiency has been accrued the steeplechase candidate begins to work over the barriers several times each week. Such training should be preceded by extensive stretching and trail leg drills. It should always be done at the beginning of a training session, rather than at the end, when one is fatigued.

Considerable training also must be done at the water jump. Unlike the hurdle technique just described, the water jump is a specialized "stride" from a barrier, across a water filled obstacle twelve feet wide. The secret to taking this jump is to accelerate several strides from the obstacle to produce sufficient momentum to carry one onto the barrier. The runner meets the barrier with the hollow of the front foot, maintains a crouch position over a bent leg, and springs forward as the center of gravity is moving past the base of support. The action is smoothly coordinated, with the extension of the supporting leg driving the performer to a landing about two feet from the waters edge. During the spring off the barrier, the arms are held wide for purposes of balance.

Once the hurdle barriers and the water jump obstacles have been negotiated the runner resumes his normal running style as quickly as possible.

**Racing Strategy**

Del Hessel, Steeplechase coordinator for the USOC TAC Development Committee, says that "mastering the barriers means mastering the race."[*] Perhaps no event is more fatiguing than the steeplechase. Thus the best strategy, other than the development of good technique, is even pace running. Recent United States champions in this event have tended to lay back during the early laps to conserve strength, and then come on to attack the race during the final 220 to 440 yards. Whatever is done, it is imperative that one maintain his momentum throughout the race. To balk at a barrier or the water jump is to court disaster. Not only is balking, or shying away from the barriers a primary cause of injury, but to the fatigued runner it is certain defeat for it becomes virtually impossible to accelerate once one's momentum has been lost.

---

[*]Del Hessel. Presentation of the TAC/USOC Development Committee, The University of Florida, Gainsville, January 8, 1981.

# part 3 Jumping Events
## High Jump–Long Jump–Triple Jump–Pole Vault

There are four jumping events in track and field. These are the high jump, the long jump, triple jump, and pole vault. While each is a very specific (and in the case of the pole vault a complicated and technical event) all are subject to certain common principles of performance.

All jumping events demand the greatest possible, controlled speed. All are explosive in nature. In every instance, the approach determines the quality of performance. For this reason it can be said that all jumpers are "take off conscious."

A basic principle to remember in the jumping events is that vertical speed and linear speed are enemies of each other. Thus as one seeks greater height at takeoff (except in the pole vault) it is necessary to compromise speed. Too great a compromise will negate the effectiveness of the approach. The key, therefore, when participating in the long jump, triple jump, and high jump is to develop sufficient strength and quickness (power) to transfer linear speed to essential lift in an instant of time.

To effectively monitor the jumpers speed, check marks are used. There are check marks for the athlete as well as for the coach. The former provides instant feedback to the athlete, making it possible for the jumper to effect ground release with abandon. Check marks for the coach are usually set three to four strides out from the point of takeoff and provide a specific location for timing the approach as well as evaluating stride consistency.

In each of the chapters on jumping the individual event is described in terms of technique. Step by step procedures are given for teaching the events. Training principles and schedules are provided, as are cues for the analysis of performance.

# 9 High Jumping

## Straddle Roll

There are many variations to the straddle form of high jumping. These include the dive straddle, the straight-leg kick-up, and the bent-leg kick-up, with modifications. All straddle jumpers take off from the inside foot, with the free leg being used somewhat as a pendulum to impart lifting force to the body mass. The most common characteristics of the straddle form is the layout over the crossbar. In this instance, the performer faces the bar during clearance, as opposed to the back layout used by the flopper.

## Back Flop

One of the words which best describe life is *change*. Certainly one of the more fascinating dimensions of the life and history of track and field is the change that has occurred in performance technique during the past half century. The most recent of these changes in technique is the evolution of the "Fosbury Flop."

Careful analysis of this new style of jumping reveals a remarkably economical performance skill. Perhaps more so than any other style, this back-clearance technique permits the performer to expend a greater percentage of force in a purely vertical direction. This is possible since little eccentric thrust is needed to produce an adequate turning effect. Moreover, action of arms and legs seems to ensure a maximum utilization of all lifting forces because the performer may be able to "hang" large portions of the body below the crossbar during the time of clearance.

## Approach

Good jumpers have approached the bar from all angles, though the recommended angle for the straddle jump is thirty to forty degrees. The length of the approach is forty or fifty feet, with the jumper taking seven or nine full strides. The approach is relaxed; the final two strides are longer and faster than those that precede. Most jumpers use a single check mark to fix the starting point. The strides beyond this mark are taken with a detached confidence as the jumper mobilizes all of the available energies for the plant and explosive spring.

## Takeoff

Ideally the last stride is longer than the others, with the foot planted along the line of approach. During this stride the center of gravity shifts downward in perparation for the explosive lift. The takeoff foot strikes heel first as the leg appears to run out from beneath the body. It is imperative that the jumper's center of gravity be over the lifting leg the instant the lifting force is applied. The final application of force is off the jumper's toes.

Better jumpers take off from a point approximately twenty-four inches from the crossbar (measured at a right angle to the crossbar). This takeoff point is usually opposite the near jumping standard so that the flight carries the jumper over the center of the crossbar. The landing point for better jumpers is approximately thirty-six inches beyond the crossbar and from two to three feet from the far jumping standard. The linear distance covered from point of takeoff to point of landing is from eight to ten feet.

## Leg Swing

Ideally the kick-up leg should be straight, but since few jumpers have been able to master this technique, they should strive for a kick that carries the leg's center of gravity to the highest possible point in the shortest possible time. In other words, the kick-up is a ballistic act that helps to lift the jumper from the ground. During the last two strides the body moves away from the arms (reaching back forces the shoulders back). From the penultimate stride to the plant, the center of gravity is moving upward. The jumper seeks to maximize this lifting action by accelerating the hips and shoulders forward and then upward. This is done by explosively extending an extremely strong takeoff leg.

## Arm Action

The arms, which have fallen back during the final two strides, are permitted to drift slightly sideward. This action helps to counterbalance the exaggerated extension of the forward leg and places the arms in a position from which they can be driven explosively upward at takeoff. Initially both arms follow the line of flight of the body mass. As maximum height is attained, the inside arm is placed against the abdomen, while the outside arm reaches over the bar, then downward to assist in the roll.

Once the turning pattern has been established, the outside arm is driven ballistically upward again. This action, or force, produces a counteraction, or force, which facilitates trail-leg lift (see action-reaction, chapter 2).

## Bar Clearance

High jumping is a skill having two distinct parts, the lift and the cross-bar clearance. Since the lift is the key to successful jumping, the beginner ought to be encouraged to jump as if there were no bar. The total commitment is to getting up, not worrying about getting over, or around something.

The layout and turn come after height has been attained. With the chest, shoulders, and arms above the bar, the jumper simply drops the right side toward the landing surface. The body is extended in a face-down position. Rotation occurs by turning the kicking foot sharply inward and looking back under the crossbar.

## Landing

It is imperative that the straddle jumper rotate far enough to land on the kick-up foot and the outstretched hands. If the bar is pulled off with the second leg over, it usually stems from inflexibility, or not rotating far enough prior to landing.

## Approach

Often taken for granted, the approach determines the success or failure of the jump. The approach generally is ten or eleven strides. A shorter approach tends to crowd the jumper at the bar, a longer approach imposes too many variables. The speed of the approach ought to be the maximal speed that the jumper can control.

Most back flop jumpers use a J approach with an arc radius of sixteen to twenty feet. The range depends on both the strength and height of the performer. Usually there are from three to five strides within the arc, leaving four to eight strides for the initial run up.

The first step of the approach tends to be underrated. There should be a check mark for this step as it sets the tempo for the whole approach. When this step varies it is an indication that the jumper is using either more or less force than usual in the push off. The next several strides are on a straight line. Each stride is faster than the preceding one. The body is directly over the foot when it contacts the ground to insure that the jumper is in balance at all times.

**Comments on the Back Flop**

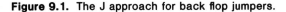

```
 ┌ ─ ─ ─ ─ ─ ─ ─ 0 ─────── 0
 │ 16-20'      ↓ 20-24"
 │            R  L  R
 │         R
 │       L
 │     R
 │   L
 │  R          11 strides
 │
 │  L
 │  R
 │  L
 │  R
LR
```

**Figure 9.1.** The J approach for back flop jumpers.

During training sessions a "turn mark" should be placed on the approach surface. This enables the jumper to develop a sense of position and permits the all important concentration of getting ready for the jump.

Some coaches and athletes make the mistake of minimizing the importance of the final three strides in the flop. If one argues that the approach is seventy-five percent of the jump, one might also argue that the final three strides represent ninety percent of the approach. Not only are these strides faster but they have a rhythm that sounds something like daa da dpp. During this phase the center of gravity is lowered between daa da and raised between da dpp. The stride before takeoff permits the center of gravity to settle so that it is moving upward at the instant of impact by the jumping foot.

One of the most common errors in the flop is to permit the center of gravity to fall toward the crossbar during the final approach. When this happens the jumper produces excessive linear force and tends to jump through, rather than over the bar. During the final approach (the last four or five strides) the jumper leans into the circle to create centrifugal force. This is often referred to as staying tight to the circle . . . or keeping the inside shoulder down. By leaning inward at ground impact vertical release is more likely to occur. Subsequently the body is subject to centrifugal force which flings the center of mass across the bar at a tangent to the turn.

I think it is an error to push the jumper into a stride pattern that demands either a shortening or a lengthening of the last stride before takeoff. There are good arguments for both of these mechanical adaptations. The overwhelming argument, however, is that vertical lift is a function of ground impact, meaning that the jumper must accelerate onto the takeoff foot to maximize jumping potential. Or, put more directly, the speed of the last stride is more important than its length, if one is only talking about two to three inches.

**Figure 9.2.** During the final three strides, the jumper aggressively attacks the cross bar, leaning into the circle to create centrifugal force.

Coaches and athletes frequently fail to establish the appropriate take-off point for the back flop. One often sees jumpers leaving the ground in the middle of the crossbar and landing on the outer edge of the landing surface. Because of the approach speed associated with the flop, some tend to take off too close to the crossbar. In this instance maximum efficiency is not achieved.

To effectively utilize one's speed and optimum trajectory, the point of takeoff should be opposite the near standard and at least the length of the arm (24 to 30 inches) from the crossbar. By taking off opposite the standard, the jumper passes over the middle of the crossbar which is the lower point along it's length.

There is another more subtle problem regarding crossbar clearance that often is overlooked. This is the problem of "riding the bar" or "sliding along" the crossbar between the points of takeoff and landing. When the latter occurs the jumper usually has difficulty timing the arch and pike, tending to catch the bar with the backs of the legs when descending into the pit.

If one remembers the earlier reference to centrifugal force, the cause of the problem is easy to discern. When the flopper releases from the ground the body flies off at a tangent to the curve of the approach. Thus, if the curve is tight the tangent to the crossbar will be closer to a right angle than it would be if the jumper were more nearly parallel to the crossbar at takeoff. There usually are two causes for the parallel position at takeoff and thus the tangent which causes the jumper to ride along the crossbar. These are a very wide approach or a jab step toward the bar on the penultimate stride. The latter problem has multiple consequences. The first is that it dissipates centrifugal force causing the jumper to lean toward the crossbar to effect clearance. The jab step also tends to slow the jumper down at a point when he/she should be accelerating and it flattens the arc causing one to "ride the bar" as noted earlier.

## Takeoff

For purposes of discussion the takeoff will include preparatory actions taken during the final two or three strides, the punching action of the arms and free leg, and the body position at ground release.

With good arguments for both the single and double arm punch and the elevated inside arm at takeoff, I will argue that the most common error relative to takeoff is the random, rather than specific use of the arms. Indeed, ask most high jumpers why they do what they do and they are hard pressed to give an answer.

My personal preference is the double arm punch to shoulder height, with the arms being extended back to the sides during bar clearance. To effect this skill the jumper drives into the turn using the arms and legs much like a sprinter. An instant before the penultimate stride, the outside (right arm in our diagram) hangs back while the left bent arm, first leading, circles quickly rearward so that both arms can be driven upward to achieve a transference of momentum. This is a difficult skill for some, making it necessary to teach them the simpler, single arm punch. Whichever is used the important point is to maximize the ground impulse by punching as the forward speed is checked when the takeoff foot impacts the ground. In so doing the third law of motion is utilized with the action-reaction resulting in optimum vertical lift.

A serious error during this final phase of the approach and takeoff is the insistence that the back is turned toward the crossbar by a vigorous knee punch toward the opposite shoulder. While this may help and at times is necessary, the more subtle, though fundamental truth about the turn toward the bar is that this should be happening through the hips during the last two strides (see figure 9.4). Indeed, a proper approach causes the hips to be turning as the takeoff foot lands so that the knee punch is a natural follow-through contributing its force to vertical lift, with little, or none being expended in the turning action.

The importance of the approach needs to be reiterated. The jumper first settles the jump in his or her heart, steps on the takeoff mark and accelerates along the line of the J approach, the focus of attention somewhere near the left standard. The turn-in is initiated by an application of pressure with the outside foot. The jumper leans into the turn, dramatically quickens the final three strides, checks the forward speed with

**Figure 9.3.** An instant before the penultimate stride the arms are permitted to drift back.

**Figure 9.4.** The double arm punch maximizes ground impact at takeoff. Note that the hips are turning inward at the instant of plant. This action results in the turn of the back toward the cross bar and permits the performer to expend maximum kicking force upward, rather than in an attempt to turn the body.

the takeoff foot and sort of sprints upward over the bar. The inward lean insures vertical release from the ground, a rigid body captures all lifting forces, the centrifugal force flings the body across the crossbar and the second phase of the jump begins.

## Crossbar Clearance

One of the more common problems at this point is the tendency to dive backward into the bar. Another is the anticipatory lean into the crossbar. Breaking these habits is difficult. Thus, any tendency toward either of these problems must be dealt with immediately and with positive measures.

My initial approach would be to convince the jumper that the crossbar must be ignored. The concentration in high jumping is as the name implies, it is *high jumping!* One's attention, therefore, must be on explosive ground release in a vertical direction, crossing the bar just happens.

Another problem in bar clearance is the extreme arch which typifies the style manifest by many flexible high school athletes. The arch may permit the performer to clear heights higher than the center of gravity, but it also tends to create a leg clearance dilemma. One must have a good sense of body position and excellent reflexes to lift the legs away from the crossbar when the body is in an exaggerated arch.

The optimum position, I believe, is with the back essentially flat on top the crossbar. The arms are extended along the sides. When the center of mass has cleared the bar the knees are lifted so that the heels drop beneath the buttock. In an instant the legs are strengthened and the performer rotates over to a landing on the upper part of the back. At the highest heights there is a tendency for the jumper to continue to rotate after the landing so that the feet touch the landing surface beyond the head in a sort of back somersault. Unless something like this occurs, the less flexible jumper tends to pull the crossbar off with the heels.

Perhaps the most common problem, when passing over the bar, is letting the buttock hang down so that it catches the bar, knocking it off. To determine if this is happening the coach ought to stand back thirty to forty feet on a line parallel with the standards. It becomes readily apparents where the low point is.

The coaching cue here is "press the navel up." The timing sequence from the plant and takeoff is vertical lift, arch back, press the navel up, head up-knees up (action-reaction) straighten legs, continue to rotate to a landing on the upper back, with the legs falling over the head as would happen in a back roll.

**Figure 9.5.** The back is essentially flat during crossbar clearance. The performer does, however, press the navel up to help lift the hips away from the bar.

A correct landing would be on the upper back, the legs completely extended to pike the body and the chin forward on the chest. The pike lengthens the turning radius to slow it down and effect control. (Beginners tend to tuck, shortening the radius and speeding up the turn.)

1. The jumper should approach the bar in a relaxed and confident manner, not rushing but using as much speed as can be effectively transferred into lift. (Remember the law of inertia.)
2. The high jump has two distinct parts. These are the lift and crossbar clearance. The jumper should give primary attention to getting lift; then should shift attention to the turn. This is a wise principle to follow with individual jumps as well as with the expenditure of time in learning how to jump. (Even though the jump is a two-part movement from a mechanical standpoint, it must be performed as a coordinated whole.)
3. The body tends to follow the head. In the straddle roll the turn is initiated by eccentric thrust at takeoff and is facilitated by looking back under the crossbar when the jumper is in the layout position. In the back flop the head is flexed forward to the chest when the jumper assumes a layout over the crossbar. This action, coupled with flexion of the legs on the hips, negates further turning and ensures a safe landing.

**Things to Remember When Teaching the High Jump**

4. Girls have a particularly difficult time retaining their straddle or legs-apart position while jumping. The straddle therefore should be emphasized during every practice session so that the trail leg is carried away from the bar during the landing.

5. The lifting force for high jumpers is determined by the factors of strength, distance, and time. The best jumpers will likely be those who can most effectively control these factors. They will be strong and will apply their force through a long power stroke as explosively as possible.

6. The jumper should kick vigorously to a point above the bar. A vigorous kick-up or leg swing will in effect lighten the body mass, and if coordinated with the drive of the takeoff leg, will produce the greatest possible body lift.

**Teaching Beginners to High Jump**

Determining the Takeoff Foot

The scissors style of jumping is very natural and an excellent means of determining the takeoff foot. Beginning jumpers approach a low bar (eighteen to twenty-four inches) from an angle of approximately forty-five degrees, swing the inside leg over the bar, and continue running after landing on the opposite side. If the action "feels good," they likely have taken off from the correct foot. If it does not, they should explore the takeoff from the opposite side. (Since 80 percent, or more, of a group of beginners will take off from the left foot, all should begin on the right side—facing the crossbar.)

When using the scissors style of jump, the performer takes off from the outside foot, swinging the inside foot over the crossbar. Most students can learn to scissor in one class session and are then ready to explore other jumping techniques. However else they may choose to jump, the takeoff foot will remain the same.

Mechanically the back flop is closely related to the scissors technique. Indeed, it now seems strange that in the evolution of jumping, the back-clearance style did not become fully developed before the advent of the eastern, western, or the straddle rolls. The flop, in essence, is a scissors jump with a quarter-turn outward, coupled with other modifications which control the body in flight. (Undoubtedly, the landing area has had much to do with the development of jumping techniques. The evolution here has been from sand to wood shavings to foam rubber to large, air-filled bags.)

The first thing the flopper must do is learn to turn the back toward the crossbar. Although this is unnatural to most individuals and thus is cause for some initial fear, the turning action is easy to effect. One need merely step forward on the left foot, turn the hips, stand up tall, and punch the right knee vigorously toward the left shoulder. This action should next be repeated from a five-stride approach, the learner attempting to spring upward as well as to turn.

When the jump and turn have been mastered, the learner is encouraged to drive upward from a short approach, impacting a resilient substance which has been placed against the wall. (A portable landing pit supported in a vertical position makes an excellent surface for this drill.) Practice should continue until the takeoff and turn, followed by a flat back impact of the resilient surface, have been achieved. (A performer who rebounds off the resilient surface has committed too much force in a horizontal direction and should strive for more vertical lift.)

When a beginner can takeoff vertically and turn the back toward the bar it is time to start jumping. The bar should be moved up in increments of one inch until the point where the jumper's form tends to "decay" is found. The bar is then lowered an inch or two and work continues at that point.

High jumpers tend to jump for height only once a week. There may be two additional jump sessions when the performer works from a short-approach. A recommended procedures for maximum height jumping is to begin at a point several inches below the performer's best height. Each time the bar is cleared it is moved up two inches. When the jumper misses, the bar is lowered one inch. Practice continues until the jumper has three consecutive misses.

**Training Schedules for High Jumpers**

A suggested single week work load for off-season training would include the following:

3 days of "sprint" work      75s—150s—220s—300s
1 day of Fartlek      2 to 3 miles
2 days of plyometric drills and bounding
3 days of weight training (usually following the sprint drills)

The following activities would be included in the single week work load during the competitive season:

2 days of curve sprinting (always in the direction of the approach)
2 days of short-approach jumping (specific technique work)
1 day of maximum height jumping
2 days of weight training
1 day of plyometrics
Competition and *rest*

More specific training schedules for both the beginner and the mature jumper are delineated on a day to day basis. The reader is again reminded that these are suggestive of what one ought to do and should not be followed without consideration of individual needs.

## Training Activities Appropriate for the Beginning High Jumper

| Code | J | Jog | (⅓ speed) | | SA | Short Approach |
|---|---|---|---|---|---|---|
| | ST | Stride | (⅔ speed) | | FA | Full Approach |
| | FS | Fast Stride | (Relaxed sprint) | | M | Minutes |
| | BU | Build Up | (Jog to fast stride) | | S | Seconds |

| Date | Warm Up | Running | Jumping | Recovery | Other |
|---|---|---|---|---|---|
| 1 | 440 J Stretch | 5 × 50 BU | | Walk back | Run sprints on turn to simulate HJ approach |
| | | 440 ST | | 440 J | Wt. training |
| 2 | 440 J Stretch | 3 × 75 BU | Jump Circuit 20 M | Walk back | |
| 3 | 440 J Stretch | Work with sprinters | | | |
| 4 | 440 J Stretch | 5 × 50 BU | 10–12 SA | | Turn sprints Concentrate on take off Wt. training |
| 5 | **440 J** Stretch | Work with hurdlers | | | |
| 6 | 440 J Stretch | 3 × 75 BU | FA drill | Walk back | |
| 7 | | Active rest | | | |
| 8 | 440 J Stretch | 2 × 100 BU | Jump Circuit 20 M | Walk back | Wt. training |
| 9 | 440 J Stretch | Work with sprinters | | | |
| 10 | 440 J Stretch | | FA drill | | Wt. training |
| 11 | 440 J Stretch | Work with hurdlers | | | |
| 12 | 440 J Stretch | 5 × 75 BU | 200 stair hops—sets of 20 | | Turn sprints |
| 13 | 440 J Stretch | | 10–12 SA | | Concentrate on vertical lift |
| 14 | | Active rest | | | |

# Fall Training Schedule for the Mature High Jumper

| Code | | | | | | |
|------|------|-------------|------------------------|------|------|--------------------|
| | J | Jog | ( ⅓ speed ) | | SA | Short Approach |
| | ST | Stride | ( ⅔ speed ) | | FA | Full Approach |
| | FS | Fast Stride | ( Relaxed sprint ) | | M | Minutes |
| | BU | Build Up | ( Jog to fast stride ) | | S | Seconds |

| Date | Warm Up | Running | Jumping | Recovery | Other |
|------|---------|---------|---------|----------|-------|
| 9/1 | 440 J<br>Stretch | 5 × 75 BU<br>440 J<br>3 × 50 FS | | Walk back<br>440 walk<br>Walk back | Turn sprints<br><br>Wt. training |
| 9/2 | 440 J<br>Stretch | 3 × 50 FS<br><br>2 × 150 FS | 10–12 SA | Walk back<br><br>290 J | Work on check<br>marks for SA |
| 9/3 | 440 J<br>Stretch | Work on second event | | | |
| 9/4 | 440 J<br>Stretch | 3 × 50 BU<br>3 × 75 FS<br>2 × 150 ST | | Walk back<br>Walk back<br>290 J | Wt. training |
| 9/5 | 440 J<br>Stretch | | Jump<br>Circuit 30 M | | |
| 9/6 | 440 J<br>Stretch | Work on second event | | | Wt. training |
| 9/7 | Stretch | Active rest | | | |
| 9/8 | 440 J<br>Stretch | Hill work with cross-country team | | | |
| 9/9 | 440 J<br>Stretch | 3 × 220 ST<br>5 × 50 BU | | 400 walk | Wt. training<br>Turn sprints |
| 9/10 | 440 J<br>Stretch | 3 × 50 FS | 10–12 SA | Walk back | Concentrate on<br>vertical lift |
| 9/11 | 440 J<br>Stretch | Work on second event | | | 200 stair hops—<br>sets of 20 |
| 9/12 | 440 J<br>Stretch | 330 ST<br>220 ST<br>150 FS<br>75 FS<br>75 FS | | 440 walk<br>220 J<br>220 walk<br>Walk back<br>J down | Wt. training |
| 9/13 | 440 J<br>Stretch | | Jump<br>Circuit 30 M | | |
| 9/14 | Stretch | Active rest | | | |

## Winter Training Schedule for the Mature High Jumper

| Code | J | Jog | ( ⅓ speed ) | | SA | Short Approach |
|------|------|------|------|------|------|------|
| | ST | Stride | ( ⅔ speed ) | | FA | Full Approach |
| | FS | Fast Stride | ( Relaxed sprint ) | | M | Minutes |
| | BU | Build Up | ( Jog to fast stride ) | | S | Seconds |

| Date | Warm Up | Running | Jumping | Recovery | Other |
|------|---------|---------|---------|----------|-------|
| 1/1 | 440 J<br>Stretch | 3 × 220 ST<br>5 × 75 FS | | Walk back<br>Walk back | Wt. training |
| 1/2 | 440 J<br>Stretch | 3 × 50 FS<br><br>3 × 75 BU | 12–15 SA | Walk back<br><br>Walk back | Accelerate<br>through the<br>heel plant |
| 1/3 | 440 J<br>Stretch | Work on second event | | | Wt. training |
| 1/4 | 440 J<br>Stretch | 3 × 50 FS | FA drill | Walk back | 10 M J down |
| 1/5 | 440 J<br>Stretch | Work on second event | | | Wt. training |
| 1/6 | 440 J<br>Stretch | | Jump<br>Circuit 30 M | | |
| 1/7 | Stretch | Active rest | | | |
| 1/8 | 440 J<br>Stretch | 330 ST<br>3 × 150 BU | | 400 walk<br>290 walk | 200 stair hops—<br>sets of 20 |
| 1/9 | 440 J<br>Stretch | Work on second event | | | Wt. training |
| 1/10 | 440 J<br>Stretch | 3 × 50 FS | FA drill | Walk back | 10 M J down |
| 1/11 | 440 J<br>Stretch | Work on second event | | | Wt. training |
| 1/12 | 440 J<br>Stretch | 5 × 75 BU | 10–12 SA | Walk back | Work on flat back<br>over the bar |
| 1/13 | Stretch | Rest | | | |
| 1/14 | 440 J<br>Stretch | | Jump<br>Circuit 30 M | | |

## Spring Training Schedule for the Mature High Jumper

| Code | J | Jog | ( ⅓ speed ) | | SA | Short Approach |
|------|-----|-----|-------------|---|------|----------------|
| | ST | Stride | ( ⅔ speed ) | | FA | Full Approach |
| | FS | Fast Stride | ( Relaxed sprint ) | | M | Minutes |
| | BU | Build Up | ( Jog to fast stride ) | | S | Seconds |

| Date | Warm Up | Running | Jumping | Recovery | Other |
|------|---------|---------|---------|----------|-------|
| 3/1 | 880 J<br>Stretch | 4 × 150 FS | | 440 walk | 30 M on second<br>event |
| 3/2 | 880 J<br>Stretch | 5 × 75 BU | FA drill | Walk back | Sprint turns<br>Wt. training |
| 3/3 | 880 J<br>Stretch | Work on second event | | | 100 stair hops,<br>sets of 25 |
| 3/4 | 880 J<br>Stretch | 5 × 75 BU | 10–12 SA | Walk back | Sprint turns<br>Form work as<br>needed;<br>J down |
| 3/5 | 880 J<br>Stretch | 330 ST<br>220 ST<br>150 FS<br>75 FS<br>75 FS | | 440 walk<br>220 walk<br>Walk back<br>Walk back<br>Walk back | |
| 3/6 | | Competition | | | Wt. training |
| 3/7 | Stretch | Rest | | | |
| 3/8 | 880 J<br>Stretch | Work on second event | | | Wt. training |
| 3/9 | 880 J<br>Stretch | 5 × 75 BU | FA drill | Walk back | 10 M J down |
| 3/10 | 880 J<br>Stretch | 220 ST<br>110 FS | | 220 J<br>440 J | Repeat set<br>100 stair hops,<br>sets of 25 |
| 3/11 | 880 J<br>Stretch | 5 × 50 FS | 8–10 SA | Walk back | Wt. training<br>Form work as<br>needed |
| 3/12 | 880 J<br>Stretch | Work on second event | | | |
| 3/13 | | Competition | | | |
| 3/14 | Stretch | Rest | | | |

From the Side—for Back Floppers

Watch the final approach strides. Is the jumper leaning away from the bar? Does the heel of the takeoff foot drive against the takeoff surface? Are the arms back, ready for the ballistic upward thrust?

Watch the hips during the final stride. Are they turning away from the crossbar? They should be for this is the first action in getting the back turned toward the bar. Is the knee punch explosive? This is a short lever, explosive event.

Watch for the "toe balance" at the instant of takeoff. (The body literally rotates around the takeoff leg which is fully extended.) This picture, the fully extended body, performer seeming to be balanced on the tip of the toe, gives evidence that the jumper has expended the forces vertically as if through the top of the head. (Less efficient floppers will prematurely pike and dissipate force into, rather than through, their body.)

Now shift your attention to the crossbar. Does the performer seem to be pushing the navel upward, helping the hips to rise above the crossbar? Are the knees partially flexed, heels back beneath the buttock? An instant after the hips pass over the crossbar, one ought to see the body configuration change from an arch to a pike. This is accomplished by first lifting the knees and then the feet. The landing should be on the upper back.

Continue your observations from the left side, looking next at the full approach. Is it a driving approach? Is each stride taken with certainty? Do the legs appear to sprint out from beneath the trunk just prior to takeoff? Do you see a definite checking of forward motion, an explosive lifting of an extended body? If not, you must encourage your jumper to "abandon oneself to greatness," to drive against the heel until it hurts!

A View from Behind the Jumper During the Approach

When a curvilinear approach is being used, watch the transition from straight-line to curved running. The point of transition is the place where the lean away from the crossbar should be initiated. Watch for the relationship between the takeoff point and the near standard. The takeoff foot should be opposite the standard, the body slightly more than an arm's distance out from the crossbar. One should sense a flow of motion as the performer approaches the takeoff.

Most jumpers using a curvilinear approach take between ten and eleven strides, with the final three or four strides on the turn. A shortening of these final strides, or failure to lean away from the bar, usually

Figure 9.6

Figure 9.7

Figure 9.8

**Figure 9.6.** During the curved portion of the approach, the jumper leans into the circle to build centripetal force. The final three strides are powerful, driving strides.

**Figure 9.7.** The fully extended takeoff leg indicates that the jumper has expended maximum force against the jumping surface.

**Figure 9.8.** Crossbar clearance is facilitated by pressing the hips upward. When in the layout position the knees are flexed, heels are beneath the buttock.

means that the curve is too sharp. Check the horizontal distance covered during the turn. While approach distances vary dramatically among better jumpers, it is probable that a turning point closer than fifteen feet from a line perpendicular to the near standard constitutes a turn that is too sharp.

**Figure 9.9.** A view of the top of the head during crossbar clearance reveals that the jumper's back is flat and that she is in position to clear the bar with the trailing legs.

## A View from Beyond the Landing Pit

Watch the jumper's head during the final approach. If you can look into the eyes, the performer is prepared to sprint through, rather than jump over, the crossbar. From this perspective one should see a marked tilt of the shoulders, with the right higher than the left. Eye focus should be above the crossbar.

At takeoff the body seems to possess a midbody swivel as the upper body twists sharply toward the crossbar. When the jumper is on top of the bar, you should see only the top of the head. If you can see the face, the jumper likely will pull the crossbar off with the legs.

# 10 Long Jump–Triple Jump

Not everyone agrees as to the best style of long jumping, the most common points of disagreement being the hang versus the stride in the air, the pike and step-out landing versus the limp leg fall to the side, and the arms forward versus the arms rearward position during the landing.

Since there have been world-class performers whose form involved the use of each of the variables just identified, there obviously are good arguments for each point of view. The jumping style advocated by the writer is thus based more on personal preference than on any supportive facts.

## The Approach

Perhaps the major change in long jumping during recent years has been the lengthening of the approach for the purpose of attaining greater takeoff speed. Better jumpers now approach from 115 to 130 feet, attacking the takeoff board from the very first stride. Commenting on this phase of jumping during a discussion with the writer, Ralph Boston stated, "This thing is like pouring water out of a pitcher; it just has to flow." He further emphasized relaxed speed, with "high knees and loose hands" during the sprint-up.

While working with Olympic team candidates, Gayle Hopkins, another former great long jumper, gave primary attention to the approach. He insisted that both the short approach (for pop-up jumping) and the full approach be accurately measured. Moreover, he would not permit a performer to jump without approaching from one of these fixed points.

Most jumpers use one check mark, take a single stride forward onto that mark, and sprint for the takeoff board. During the final two or three strides there is a change in rhythm referred to as *the gather*. At this point the jumper gets mentally ready to sprint off the board. There is no letting up as once was taught, but rather a settling of the center of gravity, followed by an explosive lift. This can be both seen and heard as there is a definite pop-pop when the correct takeoff rhythm has occurred. A good teaching cue here is to encourage the jumper to lead with the heel during the penultimate stride. This insures attainment of the so-called gather without any loss of approach speed.

141

## Takeoff

The takeoff is also critical to effective jumping. The foot plant is a deliberate downward, rearward step with the heel striking first (in much the same manner as in high jumping). One wants the whole foot level on the board to achieve maximum sprint-off force. Since horizontal velocity is at least twice as important as vertical lift, the expenditure of force must be forward and then upward. The stride off the board drives the chest out and up along the line of sight established during the final phase of the approach.

**Figure 10.1.** The center of gravity is slightly lower on the penultimate stride, but is moving upward at the instant of foot plant. During the plant the heel strikes first so that the whole foot can be used as a thrusting lever at takeoff.

**Figure 10.2.** At takeoff the center of gravity is driven aggressively forward and upward.

The jumper who applies force too soon (before the center of gravity has moved over the takeoff leg) will tend to stop forward momentum and impose a backward rotation to the body. This results in a jump that is fairly high, but causes one to land on the seat. If, on the other hand, the center of gravity has moved ahead of the lifting leg, a forward rotary effect is imposed on the body, and the jumper will tend to fly low and land on the hands and knees. It is absolutely essential, therefore, that the timing of the jump be perfect and the force be expended forward and upward to as near a twenty-degree angle as possible. (In actual practice jumpers seldom achieve an angle greater than twenty degrees.)

Perhaps the major distinction between the beginner and the skillful athlete is the difference in the lift which each obtains off the board. The beginner tends to lunge forward in a desperate search for distance, whereas the expert gets up and rides greater speed and height to victory.

## Flight in Air

Though it is difficult for some jumpers to maintain their run in the air, this style of carry is advocated by the writer.

A description of the run in the air must begin at the takeoff. If the left foot is the takeoff foot, the right leg naturally follows through with a high knee lift which is very similar to the stride over the hurdle. The leg is then thrust out and back, the foot is carried up behind and forward again, just as if the jumper were running on the ground. The opposite, or

**Figure 10.3.** During the stride in the air, the leg goes back fully extended and it comes forward flexed.

lifting, leg follows through in the normal bilateral manner. The principle here is that when the leg goes back it is fully extended, when it comes forward it is flexed.

Arm action during the flight tends to be fairly normal, counteropposing the action of the legs. At the center of the parabola all extremities are extended to counteroppose rotation. During the forward descent the jumper extends the arms forward, to be followed by a sharp rearward thrust of the arms to achieve maximum extension for the landing.

### Landing

An effective landing demands powerful hip flexor and abdominal muscles. Whether striding in the air or using a hang to negate angular force, the jumper when preparing to land must flex the legs powerfully at the hips to move the body mass as close as possible to the line of descent of the center of gravity. During flexion the legs are lifted toward the trunk which remains essentially vertical. This piking action shortens the body radius, quickening rotation just enough to permit the heels to contact the landing surface. The body then settle into a squatting position from which the jumper can step forward and out of the pit. (Ineffective performers flex the trunk toward the legs during the landing, rotate prematurely into the pit, and lose distance unnecessarily.)

**Figure 10.4.** During the landing, the trunk is carrier erect and the legs are elevated as high as possible.

1. The approach must be long enough to permit the jumper to achieve the maximum controllable speed. Moreover, the approach must be relaxed, making it possible for the jumper to apply force explosively.
2. The takeoff is essentially a stride forward and upward off the takeoff board. The lifting force should be applied as the center of gravity passes over the takeoff leg.
3. The takeoff foot should be flat and the takeoff leg slightly flexed an instant before the body is propelled upward and forward.
4. The long jumper should concentrate all effort on combining optimum height with optimum speed.
5. The training schedule for the jumper should include activities aimed at the development of strength (particularly in the abdominal area), explosive power (especially in the takeoff leg), and sprinting speed.
6. The long jumper must recognize that the approach, takeoff, flight, and landing are parts of a complex skill. Part practice should therefore seek the development of habits that will stand up under the stress of speed and competition.

Almost everyone has a preferred foot for jumping. Once determined the learner should be encouraged to work from a five-step approach. Since rhythm is fundamentally important to maximum jumping, the initial and all training sessions thereafter should give primary emphasis to this factor. The five steps are thus introduced as a 1-2-3-pop-pop rhythm. Additional strides are added one at a time with the rhythm remaining the same. When the learner loses the rhythm no additional strides are added.

## Learning the Hitch Kick

The first step is learning to take off with and hold the sprint stride. When this has been accomplished the jumper is told to take a five-step approach, assume the stride position, and land in stride in the sand pit. The actual landing will be on the foot of the lead leg and the knee of the trailing leg in a sort of modified split position. There is little likelihood of injury if the distance covered is five to six feet and the sand has been well loosened.

The next step in learning the hitch kick is to reverse the lead and trail legs prior to landing. This action results in a one-half hitch kick and can be learned by most beginners in a single session of activity. The final piked landing, with the trailing leg pulled forward, is much more complicated and requires extensive practice. Use of a springboard to achieve greater height and thus more time to stride and prepare for the landing is an effective aid to learning. The landing, however, would be on the feet, either in a sand pit or on crash pads in the gym.

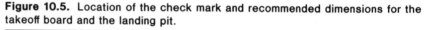

**Check Mark**

10' to 15'

Runway 120' or more in Length

Takeoff
Board

Landing Pit
9' wide-15' long

8" wide-4' long

**Figure 10.5.** Location of the check mark and recommended dimensions for the takeoff board and the landing pit.

Continued work on the hitch kick should be done from a specific checkpoint. Every jumper should have two such points, one for short-approach practice and the other for full-approach jumping. For beginners, the short-approach check mark should be from forty to fifty feet from the takeoff board, with the full-approach mark between ninety and one hundred feet from the board. These should be accurately determined and used with consistency during practice.

### Determining the Jumper's Check Marks

Check marks are determined on the track and away from the landing pit. A line is placed on the track and the learner is instructed to step onto the line with the takeoff foot, and sprint forward a distance of 150 feet or more. At a point 100 to 115 feet from the start the teacher or a manager marks the place where the toe of the takeoff foot strides the track during the sprint through. When a cluster of ten marks has been accrued, the distance is measured from the takeoff line to the center of the cluster and the marks are then moved to the long jump runway. Any adjustments that are needed are made on the runway.

### Learning to Lift

Some beginners have found that jumping over a height barrier helps them to obtain the desired lift at takeoff. One drill for teaching beginners to jump upward involves the placement of a bar or pole across the jumping pit. This bar should be several feet from the takeoff board and from two to three feet high. When placed too close, such an obstacle forces the performer to jump up rather than out, thereby minimizing, rather than maximizing, horizontal carry.

The true flight of the long jumper is a parabola similar to the flight of a projectile. If the jumper is forced to attain height too soon, this pattern is destroyed and one falls sharply back to the landing area. If, on the other hand, one achieves the proper angle at takeoff, height will be attained at the midpoint of the flatter trajectory and maximum distance will be accrued.

Learning to long jump correctly is a time-consuming and demanding activity. Because this is so, most practice jumps should be taken from a short approach. Following the initial exploratory jumps, work should be done off the board. When the board is used, the teacher or some other responsible person must become the "jumpers eyes," checking the exact position at takeoff. Every jumper, beginner or world-class performer, should lift the eyes toward the horizon four or five strides from the take-off board, to facilitate the pop-pop, jump with abandon.

Long jumpers, like high jumpers, vary in the amount of jumping that they can do. Perhaps it is partly a matter of conditioning, but many performers seem to lose their ballistic potential if they jump too often. For this reason long-jump candidates should engage in a second event. Sprinting, relay work, and hurdling are very compatible with long jumping and constitute excellent training activities for this event.

A suggested single week workload for off-season training would include the following:

**Training Schedules for Long Jumpers**

| | |
|---|---|
| 3 days of sprint training | 75s—150s—220s—300s |
| 1 day of Fartlek | 2 to 3 miles |
| 1 day of hill bounding | |
| 1 day of plyometrics | |
| 3 days of weight training (usually following the sprint work) | |

Since most long jumpers participate in a second event, the sprints, relays, the triple jump, it is difficult to state what they ought to do during the competitive season. The following schedules provide guidelines, however, for both the beginning long jump candidate and the mature performer.

## Training Activities Appropriate for the Beginning Long Jumper

| Code | | | | | | |
|------|---|---|---|---|---|---|
| **J** | Jog | ( ⅓ speed ) | | **SA** | Short Approach | |
| **ST** | Stride | ( ⅔ speed ) | | **FA** | Full Approach | |
| **FS** | Fast Stride | ( Relaxed sprint ) | | **M** | Minutes | |
| **BU** | Build Up | ( Jog to fast stride ) | | **S** | Seconds | |

| Date | Warm Up | Running | Jumping | Recovery | Other |
|------|---------|---------|---------|----------|-------|
| 1 | 440 J Stretch | 3 × 75 BU | | Walk back | 20 M work on full-approach marks<br>Wt. training |
| 2 | 440 J Stretch | 2 × 150 ST | 20 M work on on the runway FA | Walk back | |
| 3 | 440 J Stretch | Work on blind relay exchange | | | Wt. training |
| 4 | 440 J Stretch | 3 × 75 BU | Jump Circuit 10 M | Walk back | 20 M work on short-approach marks |
| 5 | 440 J Stretch | Work with hurdlers | | | |
| 6 | 440 J Stretch | 220 ST, 110 J, 75 FS 50 time trial | | 440 J J down | Wt. training |
| 7 | | Active rest | | | |
| 8 | 440 J Stretch | 150 FS | 8–10 SA | 440 walk | Work on stride off the board<br>Wt. training |
| 9 | 440 J Stretch | Work on blind relay exchange | | | 150 stair hops, sets of 25 |
| 10 | 440 J Stretch | | 6–8 SA<br>4–6 FA | | Look up; extend for distance<br>10 M J down |
| 11 | 440 J Stretch | Work with hurdlers | | | Wt. training |
| 12 | 440 J Stretch | 3 × 75 BU | 10–15 SA | | Landing drill |
| 13 | 440 J Stretch | 330 ST 150 FS, 220 J, 75 FS | | 440 walk<br>J down | |
| 14 | | Active rest | | | |

## Fall Training Schedule for the Mature Long Jumper

| Code | | | | SA | Short Approach |
|------|-----|-----------|----------------------|-----|----------------|
| | J | Jog | ( ⅓ speed ) | SA | Short Approach |
| | ST | Stride | ( ⅔ speed ) | FA | Full Approach |
| | FS | Fast Stride | ( Relaxed sprint ) | M | Minutes |
| | BU | Build Up | ( Jog to fast stride ) | S | Seconds |

| Date | Warm Up | Running | Jumping | Recovery | Other |
|------|---------|---------|---------|----------|-------|
| 9/1 | 880 J<br>Stretch | 3 × 220 ST | 8–10 SA | Walk back | Heads Up!<br>Wt. training |
| 9/2 | 880 J<br>Stretch | Work with sprinters | | | |
| 9/3 | 880 J<br>Stretch | | Jump<br>Circuit 30 M | J down | |
| 9/4 | 880 J<br>Stretch | Work with sprinters | | | Wt. training |
| 9/5 | 880 J<br>Stretch | 5 × 75 BU | 6–8 SA<br>3–6 FA | Walk back | Board work<br>Form jumps<br>10 M J down |
| 9/6 | 880 J<br>Stretch | Fartlek–<br>25 M | | | Wt. training |
| 9/7 | | Active rest | | | |
| 9/8 | 880 J<br>Stretch | Work with sprinters | | | Wt. training |
| 9/9 | 880 J<br>Stretch | 2 × 150 FS | Jump<br>Circuit 20 M | Walk back<br>J down | |
| 9/10 | 880 J<br>Stretch | Short hill<br>sprints<br>30 M | | | Wt. training |
| 9/11 | 880 J<br>Stretch | 5 × 75 FS | 6–8 SA<br>4–6 FA | Walk back | Landing drill<br>Form jumps,<br>1 for distance |
| 9/12 | 880 J<br>Stretch | 75–150 ST<br>Grass 30 M | | Walk back | 10 M J down |
| 9/13 | 880 J<br>Stretch | 75 Time trial | | 880 walk | 150 stair hops,<br>sets of 25 |
| 9/14 | | Active rest | | | |

# Winter Training Schedule for the Mature Long Jumper

| Code | J | Jog | ( ⅓ speed ) | SA | Short Approach |
|---|---|---|---|---|---|
| | ST | Stride | ( ⅔ speed ) | FA | Full Approach |
| | FS | Fast Stride | ( Relaxed sprint ) | M | Minutes |
| | BU | Build Up | ( Jog to fast stride ) | S | Seconds |

| Date | Warm Up | Running | Jumping | Recovery | Other |
|---|---|---|---|---|---|
| 1/1 | 880 J<br>Stretch | 3 × 110 FS | Depth<br>jumping 20 M | 330 walk | 10 M J down |
| 1/2 | 880 J<br>Stretch | Work with sprinters | | | Wt. training |
| 1/3 | 880 J<br>Stretch | 5 × 75 BU | 10–12 SA | Walk back | Let me be your<br>eyes; sprint<br>off, come<br>up tall |
| 1/4 | 880 J<br>Stretch | Relay work with sprinters | | | Wt. training |
| 1/5 | 880 J<br>Stretch | 220 FS<br>220 FS<br>3 × 75 BU | | 440 J<br>880 J<br>Walk back | 10 M J down |
| 1/6 | 880 J<br>Stretch | | 6–8 SA<br><br>6–8 FA | | Concentrate on<br>height<br>2 sets of 4, for<br>distance; 440<br>walk between<br>sets |
| 1/7 | | Active rest | | | |
| 1/8 | 880 J<br>Stretch | 10 × 50 BU | Depth<br>jumping 20 M | Walk back | 10 M J down |
| 1/9 | 880 J<br>Stretch | Work with sprinters | | | Wt. training |
| 1/10 | 880 J<br>Stretch | 5 × 50 BU | 12–15 SA | Walk back | Landing drill,<br>arms back,<br>hips forward |
| 1/11 | 880 J<br>Stretch | Work with sprinters | | | Wt. training |
| 1/12 | 880 J<br>Stretch | Fartlek—<br>25 M grass<br>and hills | | | |

| Date | Warm Up | Running | Jumping | Recovery | Other |
|------|---------|---------|---------|----------|-------|
| 1/13 | 880 J<br>Stretch | | Several SA<br>6 FA | | For warm-up<br>For distance;<br>time each<br>approach |
| 1/14 | | Rest | | | |

## Spring Training Schedule for the Mature Long Jumper

| Code | J | Jog | ( ⅓ speed ) | | SA | Short Approach |
|------|-----|------------|-------------------|--|------|------------------|
| | ST | Stride | ( ⅔ speed ) | | FA | Full Approach |
| | FS | Fast Stride | ( Relaxed sprint ) | | M | Minutes |
| | BU | Build Up | ( Jog to fast stride ) | | S | Seconds |

| Date | Warm Up | Running | Jumping | Recovery | Other |
|------|---------|---------|---------|----------|-------|
| 3/1 | 880 J<br>Stretch | Work with sprinters | | | Wt. training |
| 3/2 | 880 J<br>Stretch | 6 × 75 BU | 10–12 SA | Walk back | Concentrate on<br>pat-pop<br>rhythm<br>10 M J down |
| 3/3 | 880 J<br>Stretch | Work with sprint relay team | | | Wt. training |
| 3/4 | 880 J<br>Stretch | 220 ST, 220 J,<br>110 FS,<br>440 J | 4–6 FA | | Check marks<br>carefully; take<br>3 jumps for<br>form, 3 for<br>distance<br>10 M J down |
| 3/5 | 880 J<br>Stretch | Work with sprinters | | | |
| 3/6 | 880 J<br>Stretch | Competition | | | |
| 3/7 | | Rest | | | |
| 3/8 | 880 J<br>Stretch | 15 M ST on<br>grass | 8–10 SA | | Work on form<br>as needed<br>Wt. training |
| 3/9 | 880 J<br>Stretch | Work with sprint relay team | | | 100 stair hops,<br>sets of 25 |

## Spring Training Schedule for the Mature Long Jumper—Continued

| Date | Warm Up | Running | Jumping | Recovery | Other |
|---|---|---|---|---|---|
| 3/10 | 880 J Stretch | 5 × 50 FS | | Walk back | |
| | | | 4–6 SA | | Sit tall in landing, flex the legs to the trunk |
| | | | 6 FA | | For distance |
| 3/11 | 880 J Stretch | 330 ST, 440 J, 150 FS, 440 J Repeat | | 10 M J | Wt. training |
| 3/12 | 880 J Stretch | Block starts and grass striding | | | 10 M J down |
| 3/13 | | Competition | | | Several hill sprints following meet |
| 3/14 | | Rest | | | |

**Analysis of Performance**

Stand opposite the takeoff board, thrity to forty feet back. Watch the foot plant. Does the heel strike first? Is the full foot down on the takeoff board? If not, the performer is likely leaning too far forward and will sprint over, rather than off, the board. The result will be a flat and ineffective trajectory.

Listen for the pop-pop. If you hear it, you also will see a settling during the final two or three strides, the center of gravity moving down and then ballistically forward and up. When this change in rhythm cannot be achieved, it may indicate poor leg strength. Test your jumper with the standing long jump and the jump and reach. Eight and nine feet respectively for women and men in the long jump and twenty and thirty inches in the jump reach would seem to be minimum standards for an individual hoping to excel in the long jump.

Watch the jumpers chest and shoulders during the final four or five strides. Is the performer running tall, eyes focused "out beyond the horizon"? Remember, you must be the jumpers eyes.

Now move to the middle of the runway, still thirty or forty feet back. This time watch the entire run-through. The jumper should accelerate smoothly from the very first stride. This is an easing into the takeoff. Controlled speed is the stuff of which long jumps are made.

One way every coach can provide positive reinforecment for long jumpers is to determine their optimum approach times. This can be done by timing each jumper's approach from the first step to the stamp on the board and correlating these times with the distances achieved. Optimum times should then be compared with approach times during competition so that each jumper will better know the kinds of adjustments one needs to make.

**Figure 10.6.** As the jumper descends into the pit, the arms are extended forward and then rearward to maximize the extension of hips and legs.

Having given primary attention to the approach and takeoff, the coach should then move to a point opposite the landing site. Look first for a long body at the peak of the flight. Regardless of the style of flight, all jumpers must lengthen their bodies at the high point of the parabola to control rotary motion. Russian jumpers drill "on coming up tall" by touching their heads to an object suspended over the middle of the landing pit.

Watch the flight after the high point. Does the performer pike forward in anticipation of the landing? If so, there will be premature rotation into the landing pit. Since all parts of the body rotate in the same direction at the same rate of speed, the only way one can achieve greater distance by the position of the feet and legs during the landing, is to lift them above the body's center of gravity as it descends into the pit. Watch the arms carefully during the landing. They should first reach forward to aid in balance and then extend rearward to aid in extension of the hips and legs.

## The Triple Jump

In recent years the triple jump has become a regular part of the high school and college track and field schedule for the male performer. The standing triple jump also is frequently used as a training tool, as well as predictive measure for both male and female athletes and thus warrants some attention in a text of this kind.

Although the technique of this event differs from the high jump and long jump, the mechanical principles relating to all three are essentially the same. The distance gained in the triple jump is largely dependent on the speed of approach, and the ability of the performer to conserve and apportion this speed through the hop, the step, and the jump.

## The Approach

The approach in the triple jump would be similar to that already described for the long jump. Perhaps the key difference is that the triple jumper is almost totally committed to linear speed. To facilitate this commitment the triple jumper, like the high jumper, tends to sprint away from the arms during the last two strides. The arms are then used in a double arm punch to transfer momentum, from that part of the body, to the whole body in an aggressive reach for distance.

## The Hop

The first phase of this event is the hop. Unlike the long jumper who drives the lead knee to a position parallel with the ground, the triple jumper seeks to drive the knee forward, with a slight inclination upward. The takeoff leg is flexed with the heel carried into the buttock. Due to the comparatively low takeoff angle, the semiflexed lead foot is moved back in a quick, pawing action, the takeoff foot extending to make contact with the heel. The performer's body has again moved away from the arms, which will next transfer momentum to the step.

## The Step

To keep the momentum moving linearly the performer settles slightly into the supporting leg. The center of mass moves over the new base of support and the trailing leg and both arms punch forward again. Since this is a step, the landing will now be made on the opposite foot. To facilitate the stepping action, the performer assumes a wide "split stride" with both legs slightly flexed. In this position the knee of the stepping leg is parallel to the ground. The takeoff angle is again relatively low to conserve forward speed. The landing of the stepping foot is heel first and the arms drop behind for one final transfer of momentum.

## The Jump

Technique of the final phase is that of the long jumper. Due to the shorter time in the air, many triple jump performers use the hang style of jump. All are faced with a loss of momentum at takeoff and tend to rotate rearward onto the seat in landing. For this reason, the performer needs to remain over the takeoff foot slightly longer than would be wise or necessary in the open long jump.

**Things to Remember When Teaching the Triple Jump**

1. The distance gained in this event is largely dependent upon horizontal speed. Thus, the performer must produce the greatest possible controllable speed during the approach.
2. Due to the tendency to overextend the hop, jumpers are cautioned to develop a sense of rhythm in which all phases of the event have approximately the same duration. Such an even rhythm would sound and feel like pom, pom, pom. (In reality this ratio may vary, but the athlete will more effectively learn to conserve and utilize momentum if a sense of rhythm is achieved.)
3. Due to the tendency to rotate forward or rearward over the points of landing, the athlete is encouraged to keep the head up at all times.
4. A sound teaching cue for beginners, as well as advanced performers, is to encourage them to "wait for the ground" when landing. This tends to cushion the landing and contribute to a forward-upward impulse, rather than the jarring, breaking action that occurs when the landing leg comes down prematurely.
5. Because the triple jump is so physically demanding, candidates for this event must be well-conditioned before engaging in a training program.

**Teaching the Triple Jump**

The selection and early training of the triple jump candidate may well constitute one and the same process. This is because most triple jumpers expend a significant portion of their time working on bounding and jumping drills. It also is true that not all jumpers possess the coordination essential to this demanding event.

The initial bounding drills would involve single leg activity, namely r-r-r, l-l-l with a double arm punch. The arm action is tricky for beginners and involves a series of circular punches with the arms flexed at 90 degrees. Indeed, most beginners tend to punch with arms that are only slightly flexed and the longer lever will not permit the quick tempo essential to these drills.

A second series of drills would involve single foot combinations such as r-r-l, l-l-r, or r-r-l-l-r. When these have been mastered, the performer can go to the long jump runway and begin working on triple jump rhythm. To determine which ought to be the initial takeoff foot the athlete should explore both of the following combinations: l-l-r-jump and r-r-l jump. This is what Dean Hayes, successful triple jump coach from Middle Tennessee State University, calls teaching "thinking feet."

**Training Schedules for Triple Jumpers**

Due to the physical demands of this event, most triple jumpers work on strength, speed, and coordination away from the jumping pit. Perhaps one day a week of actual jumping, with two or three days of coordination drills would be sufficient jump training. A basic drill using eighteen inch boxes is depicted for the reader's consideration. (Space between the boxes 15 feet to 20 feet) R $^R$ L $^L$ R $^R$ L $^L$ R to landing in the sand pit. This can, of course, be done so that the final jump into the pit is from the left leg. A suggested single week work load is to be found below:

Off-season: work with long jumpers, plus running stadium stairs
Competitive Season:
2 days of sprint training, 75s-150s-220s
1 day of bounding and box jumping
1 day of short-approach jumping
1 day of rhythm drills on the grass or football infield
2 days of weight training (usually to follow sprint work)
Competition and rest

**Analysis of Performance**

From a position forty to fifty feet to the side of the runway look for a smooth transition from the approach, through the hop, step, and jump. Is the speed of the approach carried through from beginning to end? It should be. Is the performer in good balance? The head and torso erect? The athlete running tall? One should be.

Is the arm punch coordinated with the action of the legs? Remember, that with both the hop and the step, the athlete should let the ground come up to him (delay the landing) with initial contact being made with the heel of the supporting leg. In the step is the knee up? Better performers seem to ride the knee until extending the leg to the ground.

# 11      Pole Vault

One of the most exciting and surely the most difficult of all the track and field events is the pole vault. Dating back to the vaulting action needed to carry travelers across the small streams of the British countryside, the vault has undergone dramatic change over the years. Perhaps the most significant of these has been development of the fiberglass pole. Indeed, because of the flexible pole, vaulters are now attaining heights heretofore unheard of.

Effective performance in the pole vault demands exceptional speed, strength, and motor coordination. The vault itself is the result of coordinated effort between the athlete and the pole. Dyson has described this coordination as a double pendulum, the athlete being one pendulum and the pole the other pendulum.

To maximize the lifting force of this double pendular system the performer must impart maximum controlled speed to the pole at the point of plant, and transfer this to vertical lift.

## The Approach

While the length will vary with individuals, the range usually is from 100 to 150 feet. Better and stronger jumpers use the longer approach. An approach of 100 to 115 feet is adequate for most prep athletes. Regardless of the level of performance, vaulters usually use three check marks. The first is the takeoff point for the run-up, the second is a mark for the coach to use to evaluate the athlete's speed, and the third is the point of takeoff.

The approach must utilize maximum, controlled speed. During the run-up the position of the body is erect, both to counterbalance the pole and to put the performer in the attack position at pole plant. The term attack has been used advisedly here, as one key to success in vaulting is the attack of the box. This is facilitated by running tall during the final several strides.

## The Pole Carry

The hand grip on the pole places the preferred hand (right for most jumpers) on top, the left hand some eighteen to thirty inches below. The thumbs of both hands are up.

During the run-up, the pole is carried with the planting end at head height. Hand location with respect to the body places each approximately equal in distance from the center of the hips.

## Plant

The plant is the most important aspect of the vault. Although the vaulter once could get away with stepping as much as a foot on either side of the check mark, the newly designed, flexible pole demands a precise foot placement and plant.

The transition between the approach and plant is smooth and coordinated. When three or four strides out, the performer effects a curl press action slightly in front of the forehead. At the instant of planting the pole both arms are extended, with the right (top arm) being directly over the takeoff foot. Any deviation from this will result in a "snatching" of the performer off the ground, rather than the driving "step-off" which is imperative if adequate lifting force is to be achieved.

Since timing is a critical factor here, the attack should strive for what is best referred to as an "early plant." This results in an action that is aggressive, the athlete tending to drive the pole through the box, not just to the box.

During the plant, the shoulders are kept squared to the box. One must avoid the tendency to push the right side forward as the pole is extended. The latter motion tends to rotate the athlete toward the left at takeoff. The important concepts again are: extend the right arm, plant high, plant early, and plant aggressively.

## The Takeoff

Remembering the imperative of developing maximum lifting speed at takeoff, the vaulter is instructed to spring off the ground. The transition again is to curl-press the pole, sock it into the box, spring off the ground, and drive the lead knee (right in this instance) forward and upward. The left, or takeoff leg, remains extended. This keeps the center of gravity as low as possible and minimizes rotational inertia.

During takeoff, the pole is controlled by the firmly extended left arm. With the right arms pulling slightly to facilitate the bending of the pole, ground release is a natural and dynamic action.

## Swing and Roll Back

During the early part of the swing, there is a delay of further movement by the jumper. The idea here is to just hang and let the rotary forces imparted at takeoff give maximum lift to the pole. The arms are extended, the long body relaxed, only the right leg is elevated.

As the rise continues, the left leg catches up to the right leg. The athlete rocks back to maintain momentum, and the left arm holds the body away from the pole. The vaulter now enters the most critical part of the double pendular action. With the pole seeming to stall there is an urge to pull, to keep it moving. At this point, however, the pull is counterproductive, thus patience in the rock back is essential.

When the hips are elevated to a point where they are between the head and the pole, the vaulter works to keep the legs moving upward. The angular momentum, which was conserved in the hang, is now imparted to the pole. When the pole nears the perpendicular, the vaulter begins the pull and turn. The pull is powerful, vertical, and through the hips.

Figure 11.1                                   Figure 11.2

**Figure 11.1.** Subsequent to the plant and swing the vaulter rolls back to maintain momentum.

**Figure 11.2.** The vaulter must be patient, keeping the center of gravity close to the pole and the legs moving upward.

Figure 11.3                                    Figure 11.4

**Figure 11.3.** When the pole nears the perpendicular the vaulter begins the pull and turn.

**Figure 11.4.** The left leg passes behind the right to turn the vaulter into the cross bar.

The left leg shoots under the right to turn the athlete toward the crossbar. The action is upward, not outward, as all efforts are aimed at the achievement of maximum height. At the last possible instant the vaulter jackknives slightly at the hips. This action drops the legs and elevates the trunk so the performer can rotate around the crossbar (action-reaction).

Both arms push, first the left releasing, then the right. Both arms are lifted, thumbs rotating inward. With the body now beginning to fall the heels are lifted violently, the back is arched, and the trunk and arms swing clear of the crossbar (action-reaction). There then is a free-fall by the performer into the landing pit.

**Teaching the Pole Vault**

There seems to be a high correlation between gymnastic ability and the pole vault. Because this is so, talent evaluation frequently begins with a series of gymnastic activities. These include the rope climb, horizontal bar work, and somersaulting skills on the trampoline, etc. Selected gymnastic activities also represent a good place to begin when teaching the pole vault.

**Figure 11.5.** By dropping the feet and legs, the trunk and arms are elevated to clear the cross bar.

**Figure 11.6.** By lifting the heels vigorously (action), the performer is able to arch the back and pull the chest and arms away from the cross bar (reaction).

## The Front Pullover

When performing this skill the athlete takes a front grip on the horizontal bar and hangs with the arms fully extended. The initial action from the full hang is to flex the hips and lift the legs so that the fronts of the feet just touch the bar. (This requires good stomach muscles and puts the athlete in the "rock back position" from which the pull is initiated against the pole.)

The athlete next presses the fronts of the legs against the bar, pulls and shoots legs upward and rearward. When performed correctly, a rotary motion occurs and the athlete ends up in a front support position with the thorax above the bar.

## Front Pullover to Back Landing

If a high jump or pole vault landing pit is available, the latter should be placed against the high bar standards. The athlete performs the pullover as described above except that the rotary motion is continuous. Rather than terminate the skill in the front support position, the athlete pushes away from the bar and lands on the back as would be the case when actually vaulting.

## Swing and Vault—Using a Rope

The athlete takes a regular grip, thumbs up, right hand above the left. With the arms completely extended, the athlete takes a short run-up, flexes at the hips, and brings the feet and legs to the rope as is described in the front pullover. At the height of the forward swing the pull-shoot action occurs. In this instance, however, the left leg cuts behind the right turning the body so as to simulate the act of crossbar clearance.

When this drill has been mastered one can put up an actual crossbar and work indoors on vaulting fundamentals. Some coaches have expanded the drill by suspending a portion of a vaulting pole from a rope. In this instance the athlete actually runs to the point where the vault occurs and in so doing is able to attain considerable height. The drill builds strength as well as teaching motor coordination.

## The Grip and Plant—Using a Short, Rigid Pole

Using a pole from seven to nine feet in length the athlete takes a grip that places the hands about eighteen inches apart. The pole is carried with the right hand (top hand) below and behind the hips, the left hand in front of, and above the hips. The tip of the pole is carried at eye level.

With a run-up of five to seven steps the performer approaches, plants the pole and rides it into the landing pit. Concentration at the outset is on hanging onto the pole. As the drill continues the jumper grips the pole higher and higher, extending the approach as necessary to produce enough speed to accommodate the hand height.

When the learner can hang onto the pole with the top hand two to three feet above the head, the rock back, turn, and rotation to a landing should occur. Then all one does is to continue to raise the hands and lengthen the approach until the latter is from seventy to ninety feet. Thereafter a fixed approach should be worked out according to the guidelines delineated in the chapter on the long jump. At an appropriate point the athlete will shift to a stiff, though flexible pole. The hand grip will be elevated accordingly and the short-approach vaulting will continue.

## The Towel Drill

When the vaulter has selected a pole for preliminary practice, the towel drill becomes an effective means of producing confidence and accuracy in the pole plant. This works by placing a towel on the track to simulate the plant box. The athlete runs through as if actually vaulting, effects the curl-press action and drives the pole into the towel.

**Selection of the Pole**

All flexible poles are graded and marked according to flex. The lower the number the stiffer the pole, i.e. 5.0 is stiffer than 7.0. Initially the athlete should use a relatively stiff pole as the bending action introduces an element that is difficult to control. Once the flex is mastered, however, the performer should "get on" a pole appropriate for their body weight. Interestingly enough, as the athlete gains in strength, speed, and technique he/she again progresses to stiffer and stiffer poles.

One way to tell if the flex of the pole is appropriate for an individual is to watch the performer during the plant and swing. If little or no bend is put into the pole, it is obviously too stiff, or the athlete is too slow. A soft pole, on the other hand, would bend too much at takeoff causing the athlete to prematurely "mush" through the crossbar.

**Training Schedules for Pole-vaulters**

Because of the difficulty in learning this event, the beginner should vault as much as possible. The elements of strength, speed, and flexibility also need continuous improvement. A typical, off-season, single week work load for the vaulter might look as follows:

1 day of Fartlek like running (2 to 3 miles)
2 days of sprint work, 50s-75s-100s in and out
2 days of gymnastic activities (rope, rings, horizontal bars, parallel bars)
3 days of weights (to follow sprinting and Fartlek)
1 day working on the trampoline to develop a sense of "air mindedness"
2 days of plyometrics and bounding

In those areas where it is possible to vault during the winter months the athlete should begin working with the pole as early as December. The training schedule thereafter would be modified accordingly:

3 days of vaulting, i.e. either short- or long-approach
3 days of lifting (to follow vault training)
3 days of sprint work
1 day of gymnastics
1 day of trampoline
Competition and rest

The more formal training format for vaulters would be very similar to those prepared for long, triple, and high jumpers, except that the pole-vaulter tends to do more technical work. To make this possible, much of the vaulter's training is done from a short-approach, or with the short, stiff pole with elements of the total skill being the focus of attention.

**Analysis of Performance**

Little of any value can be seen from the rear of the runway, thus the coach assumes a position at the side and some thirty to forty feet out from the runway. At times the coach will want to stand parallel to the location of the plant foot and at other times will want to be parallel to the crossbar.

First watch the consistency of the run. There should be a gradual acceleration throughout, with the final steps taken at maximum, controllable speed. Watch the hands. Does the athlete move the bottom hand up? This is a very common error for beginners. The hands must remain fixed throughout the plant, swing, and rock back.

Remember that at takeoff the push-pull action of the arms is not perceptable. If you see the athlete pulling the pole back, caution him to stop, as it will destroy the natural pendular action. Also, at the plant notice the relationship of top hand to plant foot. Remember that this foot must be under the top hand. Next look at the body. There should be an initial hang with only the right leg flexed at the hip and knee. This long body is essential to keep the center of gravity low and minimize rotational inertia.

The rock back is a natural, though unnatural position. This is to say that one gets there naturally by flexing the hips and pulling the legs to the pole, but staying there with the back to the ground is not natural at all. This is, however, the most critical element of a good vault so the performer must be cautioned again and again and again to "stay back" and let the pole work before the pull occurs. And, it occurs when the pole is almost vertical.

It takes work to get away from the bar during crossbar clearance. Since the time is short one must explode off the pole, pike to rotate around the bar and arch to clear the torso and arms from the bar. Look to see if your jumper is working.

## A View from the Front

From this position the coach should look for any tendency to drift right or left during the final approach. Because of the weight of the pole, some jumpers tend to drift to the right. Others will plant across their body which dissipates energy in a rotary, rather than linear direction. Now listen for the pop of the pole in the plant box. Remember, one cannot be tentative in this event. The idea is to attack the box and drive into the pole.

# part 4

# The Throwing Events
## Shot–Discus–Javelin

Historically, American men have ranked among the best throwers in the world. This is particularly true where the shot and discus are concerned, and on occasion in the javelin as well. For many reasons, especially the social-cultural sanctions imposed on the American female, girls and women in this country have not done well internationally in the shot and discus. The United States has produced several women who have ranked among the world's best in the javelin.

These are among the most technically difficult events in track and field. They also tend to be the most demanding in terms of physical size, motor coordination, strength, agility, and power. Recognition of these demands, and the holistic effort necessary to develop each to the maximum, are essential to ultimate success. It takes time to be a thrower and is attested to by the fact that the average age of successful throwers is higher than any other group of track and field performers.

From the standpoint of mechanics the three throwing events are dependent upon an effective integration of both linear and rotary forces. (It is recognized that rotary force is used to produce the linear action essential to straight ahead running. In the throwing events rotary forces are used to produce torque.) Examples of this integration are the rotation of the discus thrower across the circle, the shift to the pretension position just prior to putting the shot, and the block, hip punch, turning-pulling action manifest by the javelin thrower.

The key term in the preceding paragraph was the word block. To fully understand the throwing events one must understand the significance of this term. The block, or checking action used by successful throwers is a manifestation of the hinged principle. A principle wherein one checks movement at one end of a lever to maximize the speed at the other. It would follow, that the greater the speed of the lever as a whole and the more sudden the block, the greater the speed to be transferred to the moving end of the lever. In one sense this is what throwing is all about. The shot putter, discus, and javelin throwers maximizing rotational and linear speeds in the preparatory phase of these events, blocking and transferring a summated speed to the implement to be thrown.

This also explains the need for physical size, great strength, and power where throwers are concerned. To produce essential speed, to check or block this speed in an instant of time, and then transfer the speed to a throwing implement requires a special blend of strength, agility, and physical size. A final note here about strength and size. It is the cautioning of teachers and coaches to recognize that most of the technical errors, which one sees among beginning throwers, stem from a lack of strength, rather than some inability to learn.

---

# 12

# Shot Put

The shot put is a power event. Where women are concerned the weight of the shot is eight pounds at the high school level and in collegiate and open competition the shot is 4K or 8 pounds, 13 ounces. The male competitor puts a twelve pound shot at the high school level and in open competition he puts a shot weighing sixteen pounds.

The initial stance is taken by the performer at the extreme rear of the circle, the right foot on a hypothetical center line, toe pointing out the back of the circle. The left foot, supporting little of the body weight, is also on the center line though comfortably forward of the right foot. The shot is held against the neck just above the shoulder. The left arm is down across the body, with the fingers pointing out beyond the right foot.

## The Shift

The shift is initiated by a simultaneous flexion of the right leg and hip, coupled with an extension of the left leg and foot toward the toe-board. As the powerful drive from the right leg moves the performer across the circle, the right foot is pulled back beneath the body to establish a new base of support.

## Drive and Thrust

Theoretically there is no distinction between one phase of the put and another. When properly performed, the shift, drive and thrust, and follow-through constitute a continuous, flowing movement which terminates in an explosive expenditure of all available force. For purposes of analysis, however, the drive-thrust period is the most critical period in this event.

The shift covers about half the length of the circle, depending upon the size and speed of the participant. Following the shift, the right foot is again planted on the hypothetical line dividing the circle. The left foot is planted immediately after the right, against the toeboard and

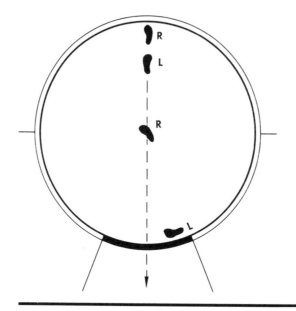

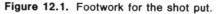

**Figure 12.1.** Footwork for the shot put.

several inches to the left of the center line. The right leg and hip are flexed well beyond forty-five degrees; the trunk, head, and free arm are extended toward the rear of the circle. The eyes continue to focus on the point ten feet outside the ring, an act which is essential if the body mass is to be properly retained over the source of driving power. When properly executed, the shift places the body in a controlled position, the powerful muscles of the legs and hips are on stretch, and the trunk is extended rearward. During the shift, the right foot is turned so as to land at 90 degrees to the force line through the center of the circle. The shoulders also remain at 90 degrees to the force line though the hips have begun to open. This action puts the performer in the so-called power position where pretension between the hips and shoulders produces a torque force.

When the performer lands in the power position the location of the shot must be such that if it were to fall it would land outside, or to the rear of the right foot. This is a key point since it insures a maximum range of motion during the lifting, thrusting action to follow.

The action sequence from the power position is a turn of the right knee forward to permit a lifting push from the toes of the right foot. A simultaneous action occurs with the left arm which is flung violently around and up to quicken the opening of the hips and apply speed to the shot. Next the chin and then the chest are turned forward and stopped as the blocking action from the entire left side provides a solid base for the thrusting, or "slapping" of the shot. As the transfer of power takes place, the shot is accelerated. The thrusting arm actually has trouble

**Figure 12.2.** Some shot putters begin from a down position. They initiate the shift by unseating, or dropping the body mass toward the toe board.

**Figure 12.3.** Simultaneous with the unseating of the hips, the athlete extends the free leg toward the toe board and drives to the power position. Although the hips are permitted to open slightly, the shoulders remain squared to the rear, putting the athlete in the position of pre-tension.

**Figure 12.4.** During the shift the shot is elevated slightly. When the athlete hits the power position the shot is outside the base of support, so that if it were to fall it would land beyond the right foot.

**Figure 12.5.** Action cues from the power position are elbow, chin, chest as the performer turns, lifts and slaps the shot with all available explosive force.

keeping up so that it can be said that the shot is "running free." The shot leaves the hand with the thumb in a down position. Wrist flexion and finger snap give the shot the final acceleration.

## Reverse

The reverse is actually a follow-through which comes somewhat naturally after the explosive expenditure of energy into the shot. Here too there are variations in technique. For some, the reverse involves a half-turn following the put, with the performer changing the position of the feet as a means of controlling momentum. For others, the reverse or exchange is not complete, as the athlete merely turns forward into the put and lowers the center of gravity by bending the hips and knees. Whichever follow-through is used must come after the expenditure of force, and it must permit the participant to dissipate all forces within the shot-put circle.

It should be remembered that the reverse really has nothing to do with the put, but rather is a means of controlling momentum following release of the shot.

a.                                                                 b.

**Figure 12.6.** The followthrough is a natural action implemented to dissipate the explosive expenditure of force. In reality it is a reaction to the action of the put and needs little, if any coaching attention.

**Things to Remember When Teaching the Shot Put**

1. The three key factors in shot-putting are (a) velocity of release, (b) angle of release, and (c) height of release. Thus the shot which is released at maximum velocity, at an angle of forty-five degrees, and at the greatest possible height will travel the longest possible distance. When a compromise in technique must be made to accommodate the human element, it is imperative that shot velocity be retained at the expense of either the height of release or the trajectory through which the shot travels. Release velocity is the most important factor in shot-putting.

2. In part, the speed which the putter imparts to the shot will be determined by the putter's own momentum. Since momentum is determined by the body mass times its velocity, an athlete with good speed can compete with one who possess greater body mass.

3. About 90 percent of the distance of the put is attained from the application of forces during the final thrust. This force comes primarily from muscular strength in the legs and hips and is most effective when applied through the maximum range of motion.

4. The performer should move in a straight line across the ring, increasing speed through the balanced putting position, driving solidly up, out, and over the extended left leg. Shot-putting should be seen as a smoothly coordinated sequence of action, not a loosely connected chain of events.

5. To negate any pause in the shift-lift sequence, the right foot plant at the center of the circle should constitute the trigger which initiates the explosive putting action.

6. Establish performance habits during practice. Don't foul, don't get sloppy, don't put halfheartedly. Develop confidence which is essenttial to a recklessly explosive effort.

7. Stay under and behind the shot. The equal and opposite reaction to expending all available force directly into the shot produces a reverse, or follow-through, without fouling.

8. Attention should be given to the act of snatching the right leg and foot beneath the body during the shift across the circle, and of turning it at right angles to the line of force prior to its contact with the throwing surface. While the landing should be on an essentially flat right foot, one should sense the weight of the body on the ball of the foot to facilitate the forward turn of the knee which follows.

**Steps in Teaching the Shot Put**

1. Holding the Shot

The shot is held so that its weight is centralized at the juncture of the hand and the fingers. The fingers should be spread, the three middle fingers behind the shot, the thumb and little finger adding support to the sides. As the competitor gains strength, the shot can be elevated until it ultimately is supported by the uppermost joint of the middle fingers.

**Figure 12.7.** The shot is held so that its weight is centralized at the juncture of the hand and fingers.

**Figure 12.8.** The shot is placed against the neck with the palm up. This provides support and permits the performer to apply maximum explosive force at the instant of release.

Placement of the shot against the neck is determined by the position of the hand when the shot is released. (The shot is released with the thumb down.) Thus the shot is placed against the neck with the palm up. This both helps to support the shot during all preliminary action and puts the wrist and hand in the best possible position for applying an explosive, slapping force.

## 2. Putting from a Stand

The putting motion should be learned from a stand. The athlete assumes the power position, with the shot held against the neck. To initiate the thrusting action, the center of gravity is shifted back over the flexed right leg. There is a momentary gather, then the right leg drives the body up and forward, and the shot is put with a quick, thrusting stroke. The performer is especially careful to keep the elbow behind the hand and the hand directly behind the shot.

The standing put is extremely important to successful performance. For most shot-putters, the standing put produces ninety percent of the distance attained. Only ten percent is produced by the shift. It is imperative, therefore, that the learner as well as the highly skilled athlete stand and put many, many times. It is this drill that

**Figure 12.9.** When putting from a stand the performer concentrates on utilizing the strength of the extensor muscles in the legs and hips. Note that the thumb is down, palm up and the elbow behind the shot to expend all forces through the shot.

teaches the performer to shift the weight over the power source and to explode into the shot. It is also this drill that produces much of the strength, balance, and control so essential to success.

## 3. Teaching the Shift

Since balance and control are important to shot-putting success, the serious competitor gives attention to the shift early in the training program. Being aware that putting from a stand is not identical to the coordinated driving-shifting motion; the learner incorporates both the shift and the thrust into a single practice situation.

There are two or three points of view about how to best reach the shift. The point of view that has proved to be most successful in the writers' experience is one which encourages a relaxed, natural approach. This point of view assumes that all individuals are different in their body structure and movement patterns; thus their adaptation to a skill must be individualistic. The learner is therefore shown the initial stance, the "teeterboard action" of dropping the shoulder and lifting the leg, and the powerful extension of the right leg and hip which shifts the body across the circle.

A good drill at this point is to stand facing out the back of the circle. Both feet are on the outer circumference of the circle, the arms are elevated to shoulder height and extended rearward. The performer flexes at the hips and knees, assuming a semisquat position and immediately shifts to the power position. By keeping the arms extended, with both continuing to point toward the back of the circle, the athlete has effectively created pretension between the hips and the shoulders and produced the torque so essential to this event.

Following exploration of this action, the so-called leg-drive drill is demonstrated to the learner. This is a drill that includes a series of drives from the right leg. The drill is continuous, the performer driving and snatching, driving and snatching, in a series of ten or more such maneuvers. The advantage of this drill is that when performed correctly it forces the athlete to stay low over the right leg. This, of course, is the power position from which the lifting-thrusting force is applied to the shot (see fig. 12.9).

The leg-drive drill is also an excellent means of developing explosive strength. While beginners have difficulty doing a series of three or four, skilled performers can leg drive twenty-five yards or more without difficulty.

**Modifications for the Gym Class**

Perhaps the most popular modification for the gym class is the medicine ball put. Medicine balls are larger, they come in various weights, and they are less likely to inflict injury to the participants. For activity class drill one need only have a line from which to put. If there is a large group of students, putting should be "on command."

**Training Schedules for the Shot-Putter**

Participants in the throwing events almost always are specialists. Because this is so, they are limited with respect to training activities. If one participates in both the shot and the discus, there is some latitude with respect to training, but even here there is sufficient conflict between straight-line performance and torque to make this a questionable combination.

It is the writer's opinion that techniques for putting the shot and flinging the discus should not be introduced simultaneously. If a coach deems it necessary to have a particular athlete "go both ways," it always is wise to insure the "mastery" of one set of skills before introducing the next. The common tendency of beginning shot-putters to throw, rather than put, the shot is magnified by the open hip position necessary for discus flinging. And, conversely, the straight-line emphasis in the shot negates the rotary commitment essential to the discus.

A suggested single week work load for off-season training would include the following:

4 days of lifting
2 days of short sprints        50s-75s
2 days of throwing various weighted objects (Light shots for speed, heavy shots for power)
1 day of shadow drills, leg drives, two hand-overhead throws
2 days of plyometrics and/or bounding (usually on sprint days)

A similar single week work load for the competitive season would shift in the direction of technique training, though there would be continued emphasis on the development of strength. Indeed, one cannot adequately discuss either the shot or discus without giving specific attention to strength training.

## Strength Training

Heretofore the writer has sought to avoid any authoritarian assertions regarding best teaching techniques or methods of training. For there are, as any experienced teacher or performer knows, different ways of achieving a particular goal. In general, this also may be true where the application of weight-training principles are concerned. But, where weight training and the improvement of physical strength as an adjunct to improved performance in the throwing events is concerned, there is no other position. If one wishes to rise above mediocrity in these events, one must seriously work at the development of strength.

In reality, American men are as strong, or stronger than other world class throwers. American women, however, are not. On two occasions I watched European women bench press well over 300 pounds and squat with nearly twice their body weight. When top American throwers have yet to bench press much more than their body weight, or do squats with more than one and one-fourth times their body weight, it is no wonder that top Europeans can stand and throw beyond our records for these events.

The specific program for throwers would include pressing, pulling, and squating activities. It is recommended that one train in six week cycles (see chapter 16) beginning the first cycle at sixty-five percent of one repetition maximum for each lift. The winter lifting program would involve fewer repetitions, at eighty percent of one's single repetition maximum. During the competitive season both repetitions and maximum poundage is reduced from five to ten percent.

## Representative Weight-training Schedule

| Time Period | Sets | Reps | Shot | Discus | Javelin |
|---|---|---|---|---|---|
| **1st Cycle** | | | Bench press | | |
| | | | Snap press | Flys | Pullover |
| 1st wk | 1 | 10 | Arm curl | | |
| 2nd wk | 2 | 8 | Leg press | | |
| 3rd wk | 3 | 10–8–5 | Upright pulls | | |
| 4th wk | 3 | 10–8–5 | Incline sit-up | | |
| 5th wk | 3 | 10–8–5 | Leg curls | | |
| 6th wk | 2 | 7–5–3 | Torque twists | | |
| | | | French curls | | |
| **3rd Cycle** | | | Alternate military press and bench press | | |
| | | | Snatch | | |
| | | | Reverse curls | | |
| 1st wk | 3 | 5–3–1 | Dead lift | | |
| 2nd wk | 3 | 5–3–1 | Front squat | | |
| 3rd wk | 3 | 5–3–1 | Hanging leg | | |
| 4th wk | 3 | 5–3–1 | lifts | | |
| 5th wk | 3 | 5–3–1 | Leg curls | | |
| 6th wk | 3 | 5–3–1 | Wt. throwing, two hands | Fling 5-lb. plate | Belly blast 4 K shot |
| | | | Back hyper | | |
| | | | Wrist roller | Torque twist | Javelin pull, heavy |
| **5th Cycle** | | | Alternate incline press and bench press | | |
| | | | Power cleans | | |
| | | | Bent-over | | |
| 1st wk | 3 | 7–5–3 | pulls | | Lat pulls |
| 2nd wk | 3 | 7–5–3 | Back squat | | |
| 3rd wk | 3 | 7–5–3 | Snatch | | |
| 4th wk | 3 | 7–5–3 | Snap press | Torque twist | Javelin pull, ballistic |
| 5th wk | 3 | 7–5–3 | | | |
| 6th wk | 3 | 7–5–3 | French curls | | |
| | | | Calf-raiser | Flys | |
| | | | | | Back hyper |

## Training Activities Appropriate for the Beginning Shot-putter

| Code | J | Jog | (⅓ speed) | SA | Short Approach (½ circle) |
|------|------|------|------|------|------|
| | ST | Stride | (⅔ speed) | FA | Full Approach |
| | FS | Fast Stride | (Relaxed sprint) | WT | Weight Training |
| | BU | Build Up | (Jog to fast stride) | | |

| Date | Warm Up | Running | Throwing | Recovery | Other |
|------|---------|---------|----------|----------|-------|
| 1 | 440 J<br>Stretch | 2 × 100 ST | 20 Min.<br>shadow puts | | 10–15 SA<br>to finish |
| 2 | 440 J<br>Stretch | 5 × 50 FS | | J easily | WT 1 set,<br>10 reps |
| 3 | 440 J<br>Stretch | 3 × 75 BU | 10 SA<br>15 FA | | Work on getting<br>the right leg<br>under the body |
| 4 | 440 J<br>Stretch | 5 × 25<br>stairs | | | WT 1 set,<br>10 reps |
| 5 | 440 J<br>Stretch | 4 × 100 ST | 15 Min.<br>shadow puts | | 10 × 10<br>leg drives<br>10–12 SA<br>to finish |
| 6 | 440 J<br>Stretch | Several FS<br>grass | | | WT 1 set,<br>10 reps<br>(upper body)<br>Depth jumping |
| 7 | | Active rest | | | |
| 8 | 440 J<br>Stretch | 2 × 150 ST | 12 SA<br>12 FA | Use two<br>shots | Alternate SA-FA<br>with emphasis<br>on "feeling"<br>the power<br>position |
| 9 | 440 J<br>Stretch | | | | WT determine,<br>3 rep maxi-<br>mum for legs<br>Upper body<br>as usual |
| 10 | 440 J<br>Stretch | 3 × 75 BU | 10–12 SA<br>10–12 FA | | Measure each<br>and note the<br>difference ½<br>circle and full<br>circle puts |
| 11 | 440 J<br>Stretch | 10 × 30 FS | | | WT 1 set,<br>10 reps |

| Date | Warm Up | Running | Throwing | Recovery | Other |
|------|---------|---------|----------|----------|-------|
| 12 | 440 J Stretch | 5 × 25 stairs | 12–15 SA 12–15 FA | | Alternate SA-FA while-exploring pretension |
| 13 | 440 J Stretch | | | | WT determine, 3 rep maximum for upper body Legs as usual |
| 14 | | Active rest | | | |

## Fall Training Schedule for the Mature Shot-putter*

| Code | J | Jog | ( ⅓ speed ) | SA | Short Approach ( ½ circle ) |
|------|-----|-----|-------------|-----|------------------------------|
| | ST | Stride | ( ⅔ speed ) | FA | Full Approach |
| | FS | Fast Stride | ( Relaxed sprint ) | WT | Weight Training |
| | BU | Build Up | ( Jog to fast stride ) | | |

| Date | Warm Up | Running | Throwing | Recovery | Other |
|------|---------|---------|----------|----------|-------|
| 9/1 | 440 J Stretch | 4–6 × 50 BU | 10–15 SA | J easily | WT 1 set, 10 reps |
| 9/2 | 440 J | 3 × 150 ST | 6–8 SA 15–20 FA | | Reach through the shot; lift and extend |
| 9/3 | 440 J Stretch | 10 × 25 stairs | | J easily | WT 1 set, 10 reps ( upper body only ) |
| 9/4 | 440 J Stretch | 4–6 × 50 BU | 10–15 SA 15–20 FA | | Work for pre-tension position "Slap" the shot |
| 9/5 | 440 J Stretch | 10 × 30 FS grass | | | WT 1 set, 10 reps "Burn out" on bench |
| 9/6 | | Rest | | | |
| 9/7 | 440 J Stretch | 3 × 150 ST | 15 Min. shadow puts | | Light weight work |
| 9/8 | 440 J Stretch | 5 × 75 BU | 10–15 SA | | WT 2 sets, 8 reps |
| 9/9 | 440 J Stretch | Several BU grass | 10–12 SA 20–25 FA | | Measure last 3 Measure and compare with SA |

*Note: Athletes preparing for the shot, discus, and javelin events follow the same weight training schedule, except in those instances where specific, event-related exercises are given.

## Fall Training Schedule for the Mature Shot-putter—Continued

| Date | Warm Up | Running | Throwing | Recovery | Other |
|------|---------|---------|----------|----------|-------|
| 9/10 | 440 J Stretch | 5 × 50 FS | | | Light weight work |
| 9/11 | 440 J Stretch | | | | WT determine, 5–3 rep maximums for upper body Lower body as usual |
| 9/14 | 440 J Stretch | | 8–10 SA 15–20 FA | | Warm up with heavier shot Put lighter shot for speed |
| | | Finish with 5 × 20 stairs | | | |

## Spring Training Schedule for the Mature Shot-putter

| Code | J | Jog | ( ⅓ speed ) | SA | Short Approach (½ circle) |
|------|-----|-----|-------------|-----|---------------------------|
| | ST | Stride | ( ⅔ speed ) | FA | Full Approach |
| | FS | Fast Stride | ( Relaxed sprint ) | WT | Weight Training |
| | BU | Build Up | ( Jog to fast stride ) | | |

| Date | Warm Up | Running | Throwing | Recovery | Other |
|------|---------|---------|----------|----------|-------|
| 3/1 | 440 J Stretch | 6–8 × 50 BU | 10–12 SA  25–30 FA | | Get under the shot Feel a solid push |
| 3/2 | 440 J Stretch | 5 × 50 FS | 5 × 15 leg drives with shot | | WT 3 sets, 5–3–1 reps |
| 3/3 | 440 J Stretch | 6–8 × 50 BU | 8–10 SA  24–30 FA | Use two shots | To loosen up. Put in sets of 6 Mark best put each set |
| 3/4 | 440 J Stretch | Several BU grass | 10–12 SA | | Extend yourself WT 2 sets, 7–5 reps |
| 3/5 | 440 J Stretch | 3–5 × 50 BU | 6–8 SA  18 FA | 440 J between sets | To loosen up. Put in sets of 6 |
| 3/6 | | Competition | | | |
| 3/7 | | Rest | | | |

| Date | Warm Up | Running | Throwing | Recovery | Other |
|------|---------|---------|----------|----------|-------|
| 3/8 | 440 J<br>Stretch | 10 × 30 FS | 10 SA<br>10 FA<br><br>10–15 FA | 440 J | With heavier shot<br>With heavier shot<br><br>With lighter shot<br>Think speed |
| 3/9 | 440 J<br>Stretch | | | | WT 3 sets,<br>5–3–1 reps |
| 3/10 | 440 J<br>Stretch | 3 × 75 BU | 10–12 SA<br>25–30 FA | Use two<br>shots | Concentrate on<br>pretension |
| 3/11 | 440 J<br>Stretch | 2 × 150 ST<br>grass | | | WT 2 sets,<br>7–5 reps |
| 3/12 | 440 J<br>Stretch | Repeat 3/5 | Same | Same | Same |
| 3/13 | | Competition | | | WT 2 sets, 5–3<br>reps following<br>competition |
| 3/14 | | Rest | | | |

## From Behind the Performer

Look at the right foot. The toe should be pointing directly toward you. Check the left arm. It should be flexed down across the body, with the hand extending beyond the right side. The initial movement sequence should be down and then across the ring. Give particular attention to the shoulders all the way to the power position. Watch for any tendency to anticipate the put, which is signaled by the left shoulder drifting upward. Effective putting demands a closed position until the final explosive instant, with the longest possible power stroke initiated in the shortest possible time.

Watch the whole action sequence again, this time focusing your attention exclusively on the head and shoulders. At the low point of the initial dip you should see only the back of the performer's head as the eyes are focused just outside the circle. Note where the shot is resting. It should be in the notch where neck and shoulder meet. The elbow of the putting arm should be viewed as an extension of the right shoulder. (The beginner tends to drop the elbow beneath the shot, which frequently results in a throwing, rather than a putting, action.) One way of negating the tendency to drop the elbow into a support position is to keep the thumb down and the palm up when placing the shot against the neck and shoulder.

## A View from the Left Side

Begin again with the feet. The performer should come off the toes of the right foot. There should then be an obvious snatching of the right foot beneath the body at the center of the ring. Check to see if the right foot turns so that the great toe is in position to apply lifting force. (A former world-record holder was observed failing to turn the foot at right angles to the line of movement and made dramatic improvement when this problem was corrected.) Also watch to see if the feet come down together. They should!

The observer should catch a sense of tension, a "mechanism" ready to explode out of the power position. This is what the experts refer to as the pretense position—the right foot turned at right angles to the line of force, the shoulders squared toward the back of the circle. Many athletes cannot assume this pretensed position because they are inflexible. Those who can have achieved the ultimate as far as range of motion is concerned (see chapter 2).

An important point here is the location of the shot relative to the right foot. Where would it fall if dropped in the power position? To maximize range of motion, it must be outside the foot.

The action out of the power position is almost too fast to see with the naked eye. What one should see, however, is the right knee turning in the direction of the put and the leg extending to send lifting force up

**Figure 12.10.** Action sequence in the upper body from the power position is elbow, chin, chest. The left elbow driving across the body to put the musculature of the chest on stretch. The chin and chest lifting up, out and into the put.

through the right hip, shoulder, and arm. On the left side, the shoulder and the arm, elbow leading, drive up, over, and down, stretching the putting muscles and priming them for an explosive "slap against the shot." Action sequence in the upper body is best depicted here with the cue terms, elbow, chin, chest.

Stand back about thirty feet and watch the whole action sequence. Movement out of the back of the circle is controlled, movement from the power position is "pure explosion." You should have a sense throughout that the hips are leading the shot to the point of delivery.

Now watch the actual pathway of the shot. There should be a slight rise of the shot between the low point at the beginning of the shift, to the power position. From the power position to the point of release the shot rises at an angle of forty to forty-five degrees. The point of release is at the maximum height attainable by the performer and slightly in front of the toe board.

A final thought, are the technical errors which you see due to learning, or a lack of strength. Remember, it is very easy for the implement simply to overpower the athlete. Size and strength are essential to this event.

# 13

# Discus

Careful study of track and field records covering the past fifty years reveals that the greatest improvement has been in the so-called throwing events. In the discus throw, improvement in the women's record has exceeded 75 percent, with the current men's record more than 125 percent better than it was fifty years ago. The two factors most responsible for these performance gains probably are the current emphasis on weight training and a better understanding of mechanical principles.

**Performance Technique**

The 1¾ Spin

The exact size of the discus ring is eight feet two and one-half inches in diameter. To produce the greatest possible turning force the participant begins the spin from the extreme back portion of this circle. The performer

**Figure 13.1.** The discus thrower assumes a preliminary position at the back of the circle with the feet slightly wider than shoulder width. The initial wind up involves a rotation of more than 180 degrees to the right.

faces the rear of the circle, feet approximately shoulder width, and the left foot is planted on an imaginary line bisecting the circle into a right half and a left half. The discus is held loosely in the hand, the body relaxed though poised for action. The spin is preceded by two or three preliminary swings of the discus forward and backward across the body.

**Figure 13.2.** Following the preliminary wind up, the performer shifts the body weight back to the left and initiates an unwinding action across the circle.

**Figure 13.3.** During the sprint step out of the back of the circle, the left arm is extended to maximize rotational inertia and produce separation between the trunk and the more rapidly turning lower body.

**Figure 13.4.** All of the weight has been shifted over the left leg and foot.

**Figure 13.5.** The discus is trailed well behind as the performer accelerates to the power position at the front of the circle.

A rhythm established, the discus back, and the weight over the right foot, the performer suddenly begins to unwind. The action is initiated by the legs and hips as the weight is shifted to the left. The upper body is completely relaxed, the right arm being pulled along behind with the discus at shoulder height. During this portion of the spin it is essential that the feet remain in contact with the ground as long as possible.

When the weight has shifted almost entirely to the left foot, the turning force actually lifts the right foot, which is then driven forward and inward to establish a new base of support. (There are differences of opinion as to how the right foot and leg ought to be used during the turnout of the back of the circle. Rather than confuse the reader by an explanation of each, the writer has chosen to describe the technique generally known as the "step out." This technique is assumed to be well suited to the tall, strong, and well-coordinated performer.)

The step out begins by shifting all of the weight over the left foot. A forward-facing position is assumed by spinning on the toes, after which the right leg, knee passing close to the left, steps quickly forward to establish a new base of support. The toe of the right foot contacts the throwing surface as nearly parallel to the center line as possible. The performer continues to turn on the right toe until the left foot contacts the throwing surface at the front of the circle. (The actual point of contact by the left foot is several inches to the left of the imaginary center line.)

**Figure 13.6.** Contact is made in the center of the circle on the right toe, the heel nearly facing in the intended direction of the fling.

**Figure 13.7.** The action sequence is continuous, the left foot extending to make contact to the left of the center of the circle in the shortest possible time.

The position at the front of the circle, known as the power position, makes it possible for the performer to apply an explosive lifting-turning force to the discus. This all happens in an instant, the left side lifting as the right side continues to unwind.

### The Fling

The fling of the discus begins before the performer "hits" the power position, the trigger being the contact of the right foot at the center of the circle following the step-out maneuver. The ballistic action sequence is as follows: right toe contact, left toe contact, and a torquing lift which literally flings the discus out of the performer's hand.

The actual point of release is at shoulder height, with the arm extended at right angles to the lifting left side. This right-angle position produces the longest possible lever and subsequent maximum release velocity. (The speed and angle of delivery determine the distance that a discus will fly. The optimum angle of delivery varies between twenty-five and thirty degrees, depending on the direction and velocity of the wind.)

**Figure 13.8.** The left side blocks, the right side continues to turn with the lifting, turning action producing maximum release velocity. The point of release is at shoulder height.

**Figure 13.9.** The follow through is a natural consequence of the explosive expenditure of energy essential to maximum performance in this event.

**Things to Remember When Teaching the Discus**

1. The learner should be made to recognize that the forces which impart distance to the throw are produced by the unwinding action of the body. The performer must first wind up to maximize torquing force, then conserve this during the driving turn across the circle and expend it explosively into the discus at the front of the ring.

2. Since torquing force is basic to the discus throw, the trend in this event is toward greater and greater range of turning motion. The transition thus has been from one and one-half turns to one and three-quarter turns and more. While as yet no one has been highly successful with two full turns, this undoubtedly will constitute the form of the future. The serious performer therefore must be committed to a throwing style that insures a long, fast, and explosive turn. Some tips to facilitate the attainment of such a goal are as follows:

   a. Rotate the whole body farther clockwise in the preliminary position, that is, place the left foot on the center line of the circle rather than the right foot as is typical of current technique.

   b. Following the preliminary swings with the discus, quickly shift all of the body weight over the left foot and sprint around this pivotal point, driving the right foot forward to a new and balanced base of support.

   c. Try to move the mass of the hips well ahead of the trunk and trailing discus. Do so by literally "picking up" the right heel from its preliminary position at the rear of the circle and placing it in an appropriate position at the center of the circle. Concentrate on a quickening action where foot placement is concerned.

   d. Keep the discus close to the body during the turn to minimize rotational inertia (the resistance to turning). Take a long preliminary swing to atttain the greatest possible range of motion, and then permit the discus to settle behind the body and downward over the left hip. Retain this position until the last possible instant when the discus is lifted upward to again utilize the long, fast-moving lever for maximum release velocity.

**Teaching the Discus Throw**

A logical series of steps to be followed when teaching beginners to throw the discus is listed.

1. Teach the grip.
2. Teach the swing and release.
3. Teach the step and fling.
4. Next, teach the step, pivot, and fling.
5. Early in the learning experience the learner should be introduced to the one and three-quarter spin. The spin should be explored with an attitude of relaxed abandon. The learner should be encouraged to let go, to spin with performance-level speed, to search until the balanced throwing position is found. (Speed will compound the errors

at first; though in the final analysis skillful performance will be more readily attained, for a skill learned at one rate of speed is a different skill than when learned at another rate of speed.)

## How to Hold the Discus

The most common handhold, or grip, is one in which the hand is placed on the discus with the fingers slightly separated, the first joint of each finger curled over the metal rim. The thumb is pointing away from the fingers and is lying against the discus surface. The wrist is cocked slightly toward the little finger, placing the forefinger in position to apply the final pulling force to the implement.

## Swing and Release

The beginner should concentrate on learning how to deliver the discus properly. This can be accomplished by assuming the throwing stance behind a line, the left side toward the direction of flight, right arm extended rearward, and weight over the back foot as described. The discus is swung back and forth across the body several times to establish a sense of timing. Its path is a line extended from a point well to the rear, and several inches below the height of the shoulder, to the forward delivery point which is about shoulder height. The discus is carried with the palm down, the force of the swing keeping it securely in the hand.

After several exploratory swings, attention is shifted to the delivery. In the discus event the point of delivery is sideward, with the index finger imparting the final force and clockwise spin to the implement. Mastery of these skills demands careful concentration and hours of practice. The learning throws should not exceed thirty feet, though the performer should try again and again to deliver the discus smoothly and with no sign of wobble.

For those individuals who cannot control the discus in the horizontal swing and release, an underhand bowling action might be explored. This drill involves a regular underarm swing with an attempt to release the discus over the forefinger so that it rolls away from the learner in a straight line. Whichever technique one uses to deliver the implement, it is essential that the wrist remain straight with respect to the arm and that thumb pressure be applied against the discus to negate its tendency to wobble.

## Step and Fling

When one can control the discus a good drill is the step and fling. This is performed by standing in the center of the circle, facing forward. The feet are shoulder width, the body is relaxed, the discus held loosely at the side. Following a preliminary leftward swing, the discus is carried back across the body, and the weight is shifted momentarily to the right side. Without hesitation the body follows the discus in its clockwise path, winding up for the powerful whipping action to follow. Immediately after the weight pivots back over the right toe, the left leg is extended forward to establish a wide, solid base. The weight is again shifted forward, and the discus is pulled to a release at shoulder height. (This motion actually is a right pivot on the right foot—a step forward onto the left foot and a transfer of the body mass from the right foot onto the left foot—with a long, coordinated pull.) The step and fling should receive extensive practice.

## Step, Pivot, and Fling

This drill is also initiated from the forward-facing position, except that the performer begins at the back, rather than at the center, of the circle. With the discus held between both hands at shoulder height in front of the body, the performer steps forward onto the right foot. As one steps, the discus is carried by the throwing arm to the right. This motion effects a pivot, shifts the weight to the right leg, and frees the left leg for the step forward. The new stance is a modified power position providing both linear and rotary force which can be imparted to the implement.

Most skillful performers in the discus event can achieve from 85 to 95 percent of their maximum throwing distance using the step, pivot, and fling. This is, therefore, an excellent drill for beginners as well as for accomplished throwers.

## 1¾ Turn

The preliminary position for learning this complicated skill is one in which the performer stands facing out the back of the circle. The feet are several inches more than shoulder width, the left foot on an imaginary line bisecting the circle into right and left halves. Following one or two preliminary swings, with the body rotated about ninety degrees to the right, the learner looks back to the left and begins to pivot.

The most important and difficult action sequence in the 1¾ turn follows. This involves a complete shifting of the weight down over the left foot while trailing the discus well behind the body. The tendency to fall toward the center of the circle and to rush off the left foot is almost overwhelming. Thus the teacher must patiently and firmly insist that the weight be shifted entirely to the left.

The action sequence is continuous. When the learner has turned so that the head and shoulders are facing forward, the right leg steps over the left in a move which is referred to as "crossing the X." The toes of

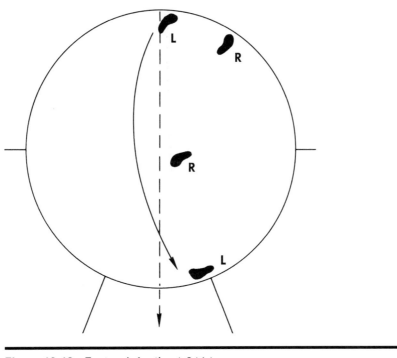

**Figure 13.10.** Footwork for the 1 3/4 turn.

the right foot contact the throwing surface, and the body continues to pivot until the left foot blocks further rotary motion. In that instant the performer explosively imparts all available force to effect the discus fling.

It takes thousands of turns to come out of the back of the circle in balance with just the right combination of linear and rotary forces. During the turning, turning, turning essential to develop this skill the coach continually reminds the athlete to keep the head up, to shift left, to step across onto the toes. The use of chalk marks is very effective during the weeks of learning. The marks show the performer where the feet are with respect to where they ought to be. A beginner who can "hit" the power position once in ten turns, is well on the way to learning this difficult skill. (For most beginners the one good throw in ten will require many weeks of serious practice.)

## Modifications in Discus Throwing for the Physical Education Class

Perhaps the best approach to mass instruction for the discus event is to begin with the basketball throw. This can be done in the gymnasium, using the regulation circle and spin. The throwing technique is similar to the turn and fling used when the discus is delivered. The ball is controlled by turning force as is the discus and is flung by a torque and lift at the front of the circle.

The sling ball, an implement imported from Sweden, also constitutes an excellent throwing device for the physical education class. (One can make a sling ball by taping a short rope handle to a basketball.) The inertia of this device helps the learner keep the right side back during the turn so that the delivery force stems from torque, rather than from flexion of the arm.

**Training Schedules for the Discus Thrower**

Due to the technical nature of this event a great deal of time must be spent in learning the fundamentals of performance. This creates somewhat of a dilemma for the coach for there also is need for great strength in discus throwing. Since both throwing and weight training are fatiguing activities, it is imperative that training schedules be developed to use time in the most effective manner.

### Hip Punch Drill

One way to effectively use time and teach fundamental skills is by utilizing good drills. A drill which we have found to be a valuable tool in teaching the hip punch is to work from the power position at the front

a.  b.  c.

**Figure 13.11.** (a) When practicing the hip punch drill, the athlete assumes a stance with the feet in the power position. (b) The weight is shifted over the right leg as the athlete rotates to the right. (c) The legs are flexed to put the performer in a position for applying lifting, turning force. The throwing (flinging) sequence is initiated by the left elbow flailing forward to put the throwing muscles on stretch. The left side blocks, and the right side lifts and turns to produce a flinging action where the right arm is concerned.

of the circle. The athlete assumes a relaxed stance, reaches well back with the implement to be thrown, and pops the hip through. Rotation occurs off the toes. When done ballistically the implement is flung into space without any conscious effort on the part of the arm flexor muscles. The arm acts like a flail, thus the term "fling" when referring to this event.

It is recommended that one practice the hip punch drill with objects other than the discus (though the discus will be used at times during the winter and spring). A sock filled with sand, or a metal rod are most effective since the athlete can actually hold onto these. Their inertia tends to hold the shoulder back during the initial part of the punch, so that primary acceleration comes from the hips, as is essential to good discus throwing.

## Balance Drill

Another excellent training tool is the balance drill. This is performed without a discus. One begins by standing at the back of the circle, the feet in the usual, preliminary position. A towel is carried in the right hand to help keep the right side back.

Start with one or two preliminary swings and execute a 360 degree turn back to the starting position. The knees should be slightly bent, the weight transferred over the left, pivot leg with turning force being imparted by the free right leg. This drill helps to negate the tendency that

**Figure 13.12.** The sprint out drill simulates the driving action from the back of the circle to the power position. The point of the drill is to capture the sense of torquing by creating a separation between the upper and lower portions of the body.

most performers have of coming out of the back of the circle "butt first." A tendency that is particularly noticeable when one becomes tense in the competitive situation.

## Sprint Out Drill

The sprint out drill is an excellent means of getting the feel of using torquing force. In this drill the athlete stands facing forward, the left, or pivot foot inside the periphery of the circle at the hypothetical center line. The driving right leg is outside the circle. The body angles slightly away from the direction of the throw.

Following one or two preliminary swings, the performer sprints to the power position. The extended left arm leads and the discus trails. The action sequence is more like a jump turn with the emphasis on rotation rather than linear motion. To capture torque both feet must come down quickly. The left leg sets the block, while the right leg and hip punch, to achieve maximum distance.

Discus throwers should also engage in a great deal of plyometric training, bounding, and sprint work. A typical single week's training work load for the off-season is to be found below:

3 days of weight training (see chapter 14)
2 days of plyometrics and bounding
2 days of short sprints, 50s-75s
2 days of drills on elements of the discus throw
1 day of full circle work with the discus
1 day of full circle work without the discus, using a trailing towel, or weighted object to hold the shoulder back

## Analysis of Performance

### A View from Directly Behind the Performer

First check the stance. Are the feet wider than shoulder width? Are the ankles, knees, and hips slightly flexed? Is the head erect, the eyes seeming to gaze out at the horizon?

Watch the preliminary swings. Are they relaxed, and smoothly coordinated? Is the discus carried back a full 180 degrees during the "windup"? If so, you should look directly at the point of the left shoulder. This also should be the high point as far as the center of gravity is concerned.

The turn back to the left is much like the downward spiral of a piano stool, the left shoulder and elbow leading the way. Watch for a complete shift to the left. Is the left arm extended forward off the pivot? It should be, for one wants a long upper body out of the back of the circle. This slows the torso down and permits the hips to rotate forward, creating separation between the upper and lower extremities.

**Figure 13.13.** To capture torque both feet must come down simultaneously. The left side sets the block, and the right leg and hip punch to achieve the appropriate flailing action where the right arm is concerned.

**Figure 13.14.** The flaillike action of the throwing arm across the face, following release of the discus, indicates that the implement has been released in an explosive manner.

**Figure 13.15.** (a) The turn out of the back of the circle is much like the downward spiral of a piano stool. (b) The weight is shifted from right to left as the performer pivots around the toe of the left foot. (c) The discus is trailed well behind the body during the pivot. (d) The free arm is extended forward to slow down the rotating torso and permit the hips to accelerate into the turn, creating essential separation between the upper and lower halves of the body.

# Training Activities Appropriate for the Beginning Discus Thrower

| Code | | | | | | |
|---|---|---|---|---|---|---|
| J | Jog | ( ⅓ speed ) | | SA | Short Approach ( ½ circle ) | |
| ST | Stride | ( ⅔ speed ) | | FA | Full Approach | |
| FS | Fast Stride | ( Relaxed sprint ) | | WT | Weight Training | |
| BU | Build Up | ( Jog to fast stride ) | | | | |

| Date | Warm Up | Running | Throwing | Recovery | Other |
|---|---|---|---|---|---|
| 1 | 440 J Stretch | 2 × 100 BU | 20 Min. shadow turns | | Finish with 15–20 step and throw |
| 2 | 440 J Stretch | 5 × 50 FS | | Walk back | WT 1 set, 10 reps |
| 3 | 440 J Stretch | 3 × 75 BU | 10–15 SA | | Concentrate on trailing the discus |
| 4 | 440 J Stretch | 5 × 50 FS | | Walk back | WT 1 set, 10 reps |
| 5 | 440 J Stretch | 4 × 100 BU | 20 Min. shadow turns | | Finish with 100 alternate-leg stair hops |
| 6 | 440 J Stretch | 5 × 50 FS | | Walk back | WT 1 set, 10 reps ( upper body ) Depth jumping |
| 7 | | Active rest | | | |
| 8 | 440 J Stretch | 2 × 150 ST | 10 SA 3 SA 25 FA | About 1 min. | To loosen up. For distance concentrate on shifting left |
| 9 | 440 J Stretch | | | | Wt. determine single maximum leg press Complete other lifts as scheduled |
| 10 | 440 J Stretch | 3 × 75 BU | 10–15 SA 25–30 FA | | Mark all FA throws and note difference between best FA today and best SA throw on Mon. |
| 11 | 440 J Stretch | 10 × 30 FS | | Walk back | WT 1 set, 10 reps |

## Training Activities Appropriate for the Beginning Discus Thrower—Continued

| Date | Warm Up | Running | Throwing | Recovery | Other |
|------|---------|---------|----------|----------|-------|
| 12 | 440 J Stretch | 2 × 150 ST | 10–15 SA 25–30 FA | | Concentrate on errors noted on Wed. |
| 13 | 440 J Stretch | | | | Wt. determine single best bench press Complete other lifts as scheduled |
| 14 | | Rest | | | |

## Fall Training Schedule for the Mature Discus Thrower

| Code | J | Jog | ( ⅓ speed ) | SA | Short Approach ( ½ circle ) |
|------|---|-----|-------------|-----|-----------------------------|
| | ST | Stride | ( ⅔ speed ) | FA | Full Approach |
| | FS | Fast Stride | ( Relaxed sprint ) | WT | Weight Training |
| | BU | Build Up | ( Jog to fast stride ) | | |

| Date | Warm Up | Running | Throwing | Recovery | Other |
|------|---------|---------|----------|----------|-------|
| 9/1 | 440 J Stretch | 4–6 × 50 BU | 10–15 SA | Walk back | WT 1 set, 10 reps |
| 9/2 | 440 J Stretch | 3 × 150 ST | 6–8 SA<br>15–20 FA | Walk back | Sprint out pulls Concentrate on "sticking" the left foot |
| 9/3 | 440 J Stretch | 10 sets of 20 stairs | | Walking | WT 1 set, 10 reps ( upper body ) |
| 9/4 | 440 J Stretch | 4–6 × 50 BU | 10–15 SA<br>15–20 FA | Walk back | Use 5-lb. weight plate Concentrate on rhythm |
| 9/5 | 440 J Stretch | 10 × 30 FS grass | | | WT 1 set, 10 reps |
| 9/6 | | Rest | | | |
| 9/7 | 440 J Stretch | 3 × 160 ST | 15 min. shadow drill | Walk back | Light WT workout |
| 9/8 | 440 J Stretch | 5 × 75 BU | 10–15 SA | Walk back | WT 2 sets, 8 reps |

| Date | Warm Up | Running | Throwing | Recovery | Other |
|---|---|---|---|---|---|
| 9/9 | 440 J Stretch | Several BU grass | 10–15 SA<br><br>20–25 FA | | Measure last 3 SA<br>Measure and compare with SA |
| 9/10 | 440 J Stretch | 5–8 × 50 FS | | Walk back | Light WT workout |
| 9/11 | 440 J Stretch | | | | WT determine maximum weight for 5–3 reps for lower body<br>Complete regular upper body workout |
| 9/12 | | Rest | | | |
| 9/13 | 440 J Stretch | 5 × 75 BU | | Walk back | WT determine maximum weight for 5–3 reps for upper body<br>Complete regular lower body workout |
| 9/14 | 440 J Stretch | 5 × 75 BU | 10–15 SA<br>15–20 FA | Walk back | "Blip" off the left foot |

## Spring Training Schedule for Mature Discus Throwers

| Code | J | Jog | ( ⅓ speed ) | SA | Short Approach ( ½ circle ) |
|---|---|---|---|---|---|
| | ST | Stride | ( ⅔ speed ) | FA | Full Approach |
| | FS | Fast Stride | (Relaxed sprint) | WT | Weight Training |
| | BU | Build Up | (Jog to fast stride) | | |

| Date | Warm Up | Running | Throwing | Recovery | Other |
|---|---|---|---|---|---|
| 3/1 | 440 J Stretch | 6–8 × 50 BU | 15 SA<br><br>25–35 FA | Use two discuses | Pull from the left shoulder; extend the lever |
| 3/2 | 440 J Stretch | 5–7 × 50 FS | 15 min. shadow turns | J easily | WT 3 sets, 5–3–1 reps |

## Spring Training Schedule for Mature Discus Throwers—Continued

| Date | Warm Up | Running | Throwing | Recovery | Other |
|------|---------|---------|----------|----------|-------|
| 3/3 | 440 J Stretch | 5–7 × 50 FS | 10–15 SA 25–35 FA | Throw two and recover | Concentrate on right foot plant-pull |
| 3/4 | 440 J Stretch | 3 × 100 BU grass | 10–12 SA | | WT 2 sets, 7–5 reps |
| 3/5 | 440 J Stretch | 3–5 × 50 BU | 6–8 SA 18 FA | Single discus J 440 between | Easy pulls to loosen up Target throws in sets of 6 |
| 3/6 | | Competition | | | WT 2 sets, 5–3 reps following competition |
| 3/7 | | Rest | | | |
| 3/8 | 440 J Stretch | 10 × 30 FS | 25 SA 25 FA | Use two discuses | Alternate SA-FA throws; emphasize left foot "stick" and lift |
| 3/9 | 440 J Stretch | | | J down | WT 3 sets, 5–3–1 reps |
| 3/10 | 440 J Stretch | 3 × 75 BU grass | 10 SA 30–40 FA | Use two discuses | Use 5-lb. weight plate Rhythm work; use the whole body |
| 3/11 | 440 J Stretch | 2 × 150 ST | | | WT 2 sets, 7–5 reps |
| 3/12 | 440 J Stretch | | | | Normal Fri. routine (see 3/5) |
| 3/13 | | Competition | | | WT 2 sets, 5–3 reps following competition |
| 3/14 | | Rest | | | |

Does the performer tend to drive off the left leg, losing balance at the center of the circle? One key to a smoothly coordinated turn is to desensitize the left leg while being active with the right leg.

Now check the landing of the right foot at the center of the circle. It should be on the toes, with continuous rotation as the left foot steps into place.

## What to Look for from the Side

First look for the blocking action of the front leg. The block must be solid and certain. A common problem here is for the beginner to unitize the throw with all body parts moving in the same direction at the same rate of speed. What you want again is separation, as much distance as possible between the lifting hip and the trailing discus. When this has occurred you will see the free left arm flail forward, the discus delay for an instant and then explode to the point of release.

Watch it all happen again, this time trying to sense the rhythm of the turn from backswing to power position. If a drummer were sounding the rhythm of a skillful turn, there would be a roll during the pivot out of the back of the circle and then a tap-tap as the feet come down. Commensurate with the second tap, the left side lifts and the right side continues to rotate, the throwing arm seeming to reach out, out, out to the point of release.

Next, time your performer from the instant the left foot leaves the throwing surface at the back of the circle until it strikes the throwing surface at the front. Quick feet are critical to effective discus throwing. A balanced turn, with quick feet, captures the torque put in during the backswing. A lethargic left foot, on the other hand, permits the body to unwind, forcing the performer to throw with the arm alone.

Carefully kept records seem to indicate that a time of 0.4 seconds from left lift to left plant is marginal for effective throwing. Good throwers get their left foot up and down again in from 0.2 to 0.4 seconds. Great discus throwers are so quick that one cannot start and stop a watch fast enough to accurately time this movement.

The discus throw has two lines of force, rotary and linear. Watch for these as they culminate in the ballistic fling of the discus. From the power position you should see the left shoulder and elbow drive up and around, stretching all of the chest muscles and imparting great tension to the pulling right arm. When the discus is released, the right arm whips across the performer's face, freed from the tension of the pull. A final recovery to accommodate all forces should be forward and around onto the right leg at the front of the circle. If your discus thrower is reversing back into the circle, chances are there has not been enough linear commitment.

# 14 Javelin

It seems strange that American athletes have not performed more effectively in the javelin since we tend to be an arm oriented people where sport and athletics are concerned. On closer examination, however, it may be this very tendency to throw things that has been a deterrent to the development of proper javelin technique. Though this section is entitled the Throwing Events, it has been noted that the two events heretofore described have been referred to with a specialized term. The shot put was called a "thrust," the discus a "fling," and now the javelin will be called a "flail."

A flail, it will be remembered, is an explosive, whiplike action stemming from the impartation of force to a trailing line at one end of a lever. When motion is suddenly checked the trailing line flails or snaps forward. In the javelin the athlete is the lever, the left or forward leg the check point, and the throwing arm and javelin the "trailing line." The keys to effective use of this system of levers and "trailing lines" are (1) the run up, (2) body torque or rotation, and (3) the force angle at which the javelin is released.

**Performance Techniques**

It is to be recognized that there are significant differences of opinion concerning all three issues. These include the speed of the run up, the extent of body rotation during the final cross steps, and the bent versus the straight front leg when checking forward motion. Recognizing that there are valid arguments for varying positions concerning these issues, the writer will nevertheless discuss only one point of view.

## Approach and Carry

Simply stated the speed of the approach should be controlled. It does one little good to accelerate during the run up, only to have to decelerate in order to get into the throwing position. For most athletes the run up will be from eighty to one hundred feet. The approach is relaxed, and the rate of acceleration is constant. The final three or four strides tend to be syncopated and are more rapid than those that precede.

**Figure 14.1.** The javelin is carried comfortable overhead.

While it makes little difference how the javelin is carried, i.e., tip up or tip down, the arm should be relaxed. The important factor here is carrying the javelin in a manner that will permit a smooth transition from the overhead, to the trailing position.

## Gather

To exert maximum force, the athlete must arrive at a position in which the left side is "facing" the intended flight of the javelin. This position puts the throwing muscles on stretch and provides for a maximum range of motion. Moreover, the side opposition stance permits a sudden breaking of the momentum by the forward leg and a transfer of this momentum to the javelin. Both the breaking action and the explosive transfer of momentum are imperative to the maximum javelin velocity. Numerous styles of footwork have been developed to put the athletes in this throwing position. These include the hop, the rear crossover, the glide, and the front crossover. All of these styles have something in their favor, and all have been used by successful javelin throwers. The front crossover seems to be used by most contemporary throwers, however, and this is the pattern that is discussed in detail here.

Figure 14.2                                Figure 14.3

**Figure 14.2.** The most critical part of the approach involves the last three steps. The first of these steps occurs when the left foot strikes the ground. Note that the shoulders are rotated rearward, the hand carrying the javelin is above the level of the shoulder, the point of the javelin along side the forehead.

**Figure 14.3.** The second step occurs by driving the right foot in front of the left to plant firmly with the toe rotated slightly outward. Note that the arms and shoulders are parallel to the line of approach.

## Crossover

The heart of the javelin throw is the final stage of the approach. For the front crossover, the critical period includes the last three steps. There is a period of relaxed acceleration between check marks one and two. As the foot strikes the ground at check mark two, the javelin is permitted to drift back and down so that it is being pulled along behind the performer. During this time, the tip of the javelin is carried alongside the cheek, the head and eyes are forward, the hips are held in the forward running position, and the right shoulder is turned so that is is parallel to the line of approach. The left arm is extended forward and it also is parallel to the line of approach.

The first of the critical steps involves placement of the left foot, with the toe turned slightly inward, or to the right. The next step is the cross step in which the right leg and the foot cross in front of the body in a normal running step. The right foot lands with only a slight turn outward, or to the right.

The last step must be exaggerated in order to get the checking or plant leg in front of the thrower as quickly as possible. The timing sequence is L—R-L. This will allow the upper body to remain behind the block so that one can take full advantage of the approach velocity. The

**Figure 14.4.**

a.          b.

**Figure 14.5.** The final step is taken by "sweeping" the plant leg beneath the body as quickly as possible. The straight leg block transfers all available force to the upper body and produces the explosive flailing action essential to the performance of this event.

a.                                                                    b.

**Figure 14.6.** The followthrough is initiated to absorb the violent expenditure of forces. It is a natural action which involves lowering the center of gravity and widening the base of support.

plant leg should be as straight as possible. The rigid left side thus becomes an axis of rotation about which the thrower can maximize torquing force.

In describing this critical action, Ken Shannon, USOC/TAC javelin coordinator stated "the plant foot must be moving as fast as possible underneath the body during the cross step. The best way to accomplish this is to keep it as close to the ground as possible. Sweeping it underneath the body while keeping it straight seems to be the most efficient method."

### Release of the Javelin

During the final three steps, the shoulders are parallel to the line of approach, right arm trailing, left arm extended. Both are on a plane with the shoulders, though the left arm is at ninety degrees to the line of approach. As the block is set the left arm swings across the body to facilitate the speed of rotation about the longitudinal axis. To avoid pulling the left shoulder down and lowering the angle of release, one must keep the nonthrowing arm high.

The throwing arm and hand are carried slightly above the level of the shoulders. As the block is set and rotation occurs, the arm is accelerated past the shoulder with the elbow rotated up and away from the body. (The key here is to keep the entire arm above the shoulder, with the elbow bend and flail action being delayed until the arm is accelerated by the torquing action of the body.)

The angle of release is determined both by the lifting action of the blocking leg and the bowed position of the upper body during the final stride. The latter places the trunk and shoulders at an angle of twenty to twenty-five degrees behind the perpendicular and occurs by actually running out from beneath the body during the cross over steps.

1. The distance the javelin will travel is determined by its velocity and trajectory at the time of release.
2. The velocity an individual is able to impart to the javelin is determined by the "captured speed of the approach," the muscular force which the athlete is capable of producing, and the range of motion through which these forces are applied.
3. The javelin throw is appropriately called a pull, terminated with an explosive expenditure of energy. The elbow must lead during the final stages of the pull, with the point of release high above the right shoulder.
4. There must be no loss of speed during the gather and crossover. These last five strides permit the athlete to maintain forward momentum while turning the upper body into the powerful throwing position.
5. The crossover step should place the body in a bowed position, the weight over the rear foot, the powerful throwing muscles on stretch. From this position muscular force is exerted sequentially from leg to hip to trunk to the throwing arm.
6. The crossover step actually occurs in the air. When properly executed, the heel of the right foot contacts the ground before the toe—and well ahead of the right shoulder. This action places the body in a lay-back or bowed position from which maximum force can be applied.
7. An instant before the left or forward foot contacts the ground, the right heel is rotated sharply outward, initiating the hip lift so essential to a good throw.
8. It is fundamental to success in the javelin event that the "work" be done behind the body. That is, the performer has the feeling of running up under, or away from, the javelin, then pulling ballistically through the shaft and into the throw. (Ineffective performers tend to pike away from the javelin, imparting most of their force above and in front of the body.)
9. Always select the appropriate distance-rated javelin. Nothing is more disheartening to the javelin thrower than to lose a good throw because the point failed to contact the ground ahead of the shaft.
10. When thrown into the wind, the javelin should be released at an angle of approximately twenty-five to thirty degrees, with an attack angle (point above the center of gravity) of not more than two to three degrees. When thrown with the wind, the javelin should be released at an angle of thirty-five to forty degrees, with an attack angle of three to four degrees.

Handhold

There are two commonly accepted techniques for gripping the javelin. The one which is advocated by the writer is noted in figure 14.7. In this grip the javelin is held in such a manner that the middle finger exerts the pulling force against the binding. The index finger lies along the shaft and provides some stability during the approach. The shaft itself lies diagonally across the hand, from a point on the soft pad just beneath the index finger to the soft pad at the juncture of the wrist and hand. Although there is latitude for choice with respect to the finger positions on the binding, the javelin *must* be held diagonally across the hand. Any deviation from this rule will result in a poor release and subsequent loss in distance.

Flight Control

Once the grip has been decided upon, the learner should begin immediately to develop control of the javelin itself. Perhaps this is best done by having the learner throw a distance of fifteen to twenty feet into a bank, into bales of hay, or at a target area on the ground. These throws should be relaxed and deliberate, with emphasis on control and accuracy. When the flight pattern can be controlled, the learner should move back a short

**Figure 14.7.** The Finnish javelin handhold.

distance and continue to throw. There should be no sense of pressure at this stage of learning, for the sole purpose of the activity is to develop a touch, a sense which often requires several days and hundreds of repetitions. (The writer has had considerable success in developing touch by having the learner walk around the field throwing the javelin short distances at weeds, a drill that is referred to as "daisy picking.")

When a sense of control has been developed, the learner should begin to extend the throws to distances of thirty, fifty, sixty, and perhaps seventy feet. These throws are made from a stand, although the base of support is extended to ensure balance and to permit a greater range of motion. The trajectory of the throws should be near thirty degrees, with great care being given to flight characteristics. All of the energy must be expended into the javelin so that there is a minimum of javelin flutter.

Since throwing from a run and throwing from a stand are two distinctly different motor skills, it is the strong belief of the writer that one should be introduced to the running throw as soon as they are able to control the flight of the javelin.

After studying the foot placement pattern, the learner should walk through the steps, javelin in the reach back position, verbalizing the sequence with the words step-cross-block. Later one can say step-cross-pull.

## Approach and Crossover

Setting the check marks is imperative to mastery of the javelin technique. The performer must be able to make the approach and crossover without direct attention to the details and mechanics of the event. Though the approach doubtless will be extended at a later date, seven strides seem to be adequate for the learner. To determine where the check marks will be set, the athlete stands with the feet side by side, the javelin extended in the carrying position overhead. The athlete simply steps forward onto the left foot, gradually accelerates for ten or more strides, and repeats this procedure several times. The coach or a manager marks the left foot placement at stride seven. The midpoint of these strides becomes the point from which the initial, seven step approach is measured. During the learning process, the scratch line is not used as this tends to force the learner into an unnatural stride pattern.

## Modifications for the Gym Class

In many areas, dangers associated with throwing the javelin have prevented its acceptance into the physical education program. The javelin is no more dangerous than the bow and arrow, however, and perhaps with the same restrictions would prove to be an exciting event for students. Some teachers have experimented with a blunt-nosed javelin. Blunting the javelin can be accomplished by drilling and then gluing a solid rubber ball to the tip, or perhaps a javelin handle could be cut off and a rubber ball affixed to either end for balance purposes. Other teachers have placed bindings on sticks or lengths of rubber hose and found that these could be adapted for the learner. Each of these implements serves as a substitute javelin and can be used in restricted areas with little chance of injury.

## Training Schedules for Javelin Throwers

Javelin throwing demands a well-conditioned body. While shot and discus performers might get by on strength alone, this is not so with javelin throwers. They must engage in long-term holistic preparation to avoid injury to soft tissue.

It now seems certain that the successful javelin thrower is an individual who participates in some form of throwing on a year-round basis. The head Russian javelin coach advocates a minimum of 8,000 javelin throws a year. (The recommended minimums for the discus and shot are 5,000 and 3,000, respectively.) Ed Tucker, an American authority on javelin throwing, agrees that extensive and continuous throwing is essential to success in this event.[1] Tucker noted that the Finns, who rank among the best javelin throwers in the world, throw weighted balls (two to four pounds) for months before engaging in technique work involving the javelin itself.

The younger and less mature a performer, the more important it is that one strnegthen the throwing mechanism. The schedules that follow reflect this position, advocating extensive general conditioning prior to full-approach technique work.

Training schedules for January and February would be similar to those for fall months. In areas where one cannot participate in outdoor training, general indoor throwing could be done with a football or basketball. Also, one could throw weighted objects (two to four pounds) into a tarpaulin or net. The indoor javelin can also be effectively used in the gymnasium.

A typical, off-season, single week work load for javelin throwers would include the following activities:

3 days of weight training
1 day of short sprints 50s, 75s, 100s
2 days of throwing activities including medicine balls, light weights, etc.
1 day of plyometrics and bounding activities
1 day of easy cross-country type running 2 to 3 miles

---

1. Ed. Tucker, "Why Are They So Good?" *Athletic Journal* (March 1968): pp. 28, 105-106.

## Activities Appropriate for the Beginning Javelin Thrower

| Code | | | | | | |
|------|---|---|---|---|---|---|
| | J | Jog | ( ⅓ speed) | SA | Short Approach ( ½ circle) | |
| | ST | Stride | ( ⅔ speed) | FA | Full Approach | |
| | FS | Fast Stride | (Relaxed sprint) | WT | Weight Training | |
| | BU | Build Up | (Jog to fast stride) | | | |

| Date | Warm Up | Running | Throwing | Recovery | Other |
|------|---------|---------|----------|----------|-------|
| 1 | 440 J Stretch | 5 × 50 BU | 20 min. (football) | J easily | WT 1 set, 10 reps |
| 2 | 440 J Stretch | 3 × 75 BU | 30 min. daisy pick | | Finish with 3 × 30 hills |
| 3 | 440 J Stretch | 2 × 150 ST | 15 min. medicine ball | J easily | WT 1 set, 10 reps |
| 4 | 440 J Stretch | Work with hurdlers | 15–20 SA | | Concentrate on straight-line pulls |
| 5 | 440 J Stretch | 1 × 220 ST | 20 min. 2-lb. weight | J easily | WT 1 set, 10 reps |
| 6 | 440 J Stretch | 6 × 30–40 cross-steps | 20–25 SA | | Work on javelin control |
| 7 | | Active rest | | | |
| 8 | 440 J Stretch | Stairs 6 × 25 | 20 min. (basketball) | | WT 2 sets, 8 reps |
| 9 | 440 J Stretch | Work with hurdlers | 20–25 SA (football) | | Work on long last stride; left foot plant-pull |
| 10 | 440 J Stretch | 5 × 50 FS | 20 min. 2-lb. weight | J easily | WT 2 sets, 8 reps |
| 11 | 440 J Stretch | 6 × 30–40 cross-steps | 20–25 SA | | Experiment with FA; work on steps |
| 12 | 440 J Stretch | 3 × 75 BU | 20 min. (football) | | WT 2 sets, 8 reps |
| 13 | 440 J Stretch | 5 × 50 FS | 15–20 SA | | Set a marker at 75–80 feet; work on alignment |
| | | | 5–7 FA | | Easy release from FA |
| 14 | | Active rest | | | |

## Fall Training Schedule for the Mature Javelin Thrower

| Code | J | Jog | ( ⅓ speed ) | SA | Short Approach ( ½ circle ) |
|------|-----|------|------|------|------|
| | ST | Stride | ( ⅔ speed ) | FA | Full Approach |
| | FS | Fast Stride | ( Relaxed sprint ) | WT | Weight Training |
| | BU | Build Up | ( Jog to fast stride ) | | |

| Date | Warm Up | Running | Throwing | Recovery | Other |
|------|---------|---------|----------|----------|-------|
| 9/1 | 440 J Stretch | 5 × 75 BU | 30 min. (football) | J easily | WT 1 set, 10 reps |
| 9/2 | 440 J Stretch | 5–7 × 30 cross-steps | 30 min. daisy pick | | 220 ST to finish |
| 9/3 | 440 J Stretch | | 30 min. quick arm (softball) | | 20 min. depth jumping WT 1 set, 10 reps |
| 9/4 | 440 J Stretch | 20 min. hurdle work | 15–20 SA | J down | Easy overhead pulls |
| 9/5 | 440 J Stretch | Several FS grass | 3-lb. weight work on hip punch | | WT 1 set, 10 reps |
| 9/6 | 440 J Stretch | 3 × 150 ST | 15–20 SA 8–10 FA | | Work on hip punch, 80% effort |
| 9/7 | | Active rest | | | |
| 9/8 | 440 J Stretch | 220 ST 150 BU 75 FS | 15 min. medicine ball | Walk 220 Walk 440 Walk 440 | Concentrate on "belly blast" WT 2 sets, 8 reps |
| 9/9 | 440 J Stretch | 20 min. hurdle work | 30 min. J and throw | | Continuous activity, 75% throwing effort |
| 9/10 | 440 J Stretch | 6 × 30 hills | 30 min. (football) | J easily | WT 2 sets, 8 reps ( upper body ) 1 set, 10 reps ( lower body ) |
| 9/11 | 440 J Stretch | 8 × 25 cross-steps sprints | 20–25 SA 8–10 FA | | Alignment drill Hip punch, 80% effort |
| 9/12 | 440 J Stretch | Several FS grass | 3-lb. weight work on hip punch | J easily | WT 2 sets, 8 reps |

| Date | Warm Up | Running | Throwing | Recovery | Other |
|---|---|---|---|---|---|
| 9/13 | 440 J<br>Stretch | 5 × 30 FS<br>with<br>javelin | 20–25 SA | | Set a marker at<br>100–115 feet;<br>work on<br>alignment |
| 9/14 | | Rest | | | |

## Spring Training Schedule for the Mature Javelin Thrower

| Code | J | Jog | ( ⅓ speed ) | SA | Short Approach ( ½ circle) |
|---|---|---|---|---|---|
| | ST | Stride | ( ⅔ speed ) | FA | Full Approach |
| | FS | Fast Stride | ( Relaxed sprint ) | WT | Weight Training |
| | BU | Build Up | ( Jog to fast stride ) | | |

| Date | Warm Up | Running | Throwing | Recovery | Other |
|---|---|---|---|---|---|
| 3/1 | 440 J<br>Stretch | 5 × 50 ST<br>with<br>javelin | 15 SA | Use two<br>javelins | Work up to<br>90% effort |
| | | | 8–12 FA | Use two<br>javelins | Concentrate on<br>left leg lift |
| 3/2 | 440 J<br>Stretch | Several FS<br>grass | | | WT 3 sets,<br>7–5–3 reps |
| 3/3 | 440 J<br>Stretch | 5 × 25<br>cross-steps<br><br>15 min.<br>hurdle<br>work | 8–10 SA<br>10–15 FA | | 3-lb. weight<br>Capture the<br>approach<br>speed |
| 3/4 | 440 J<br>Stretch | 5 × 50 FS | 10–12 SA | | All from 3-step<br>approach<br>WT 2 sets,<br>7–5 reps |
| 3/5 | 440 J<br>Stretch | Several FS<br>grass | 15 min.<br>daisy pick | | Check full-<br>approach<br>marks; run<br>through just<br>"letting the<br>javelin go" |
| 3/6 | | Competition | | | WT 2 sets, 5–3<br>reps following<br>competition |
| 3/7 | | Rest | | | |

| Date | Warm Up | Running | Throwing | Recovery | Other |
|------|---------|---------|----------|----------|-------|
| 3/8 | 440 J Stretch | 15 min. hurdle work | 10–12 SA | | Just loosen up Finish with several short hill sprints |
| 3/9 | 440 J Stretch | 5 × 25 cross-steps | Several SA 4 × 3 FA | J down | To loosen up. Throw each set of 3 to a different part of the sector, 100% effort |
| 3/10 | 440 J Stretch | Stairs 6 × 25 | 10 min. easy pulls | | WT 3 sets, 7–5–3 reps |
| 3/11 | 440 J Stretch | 220 ST with javelin | 10–12 SA 6 FA | 3–4 min. between throws | Form work as needed, 95% effort |
| 3/12 | 440 J Stretch | 20 min. ST | And throw easily | | Stretch well and J down |
| 3/13 | | Competition | | | WT 2 sets, 7–5 reps following competition |
| 3/14 | | Rest | | | |

**Analysis of Performance**

## Stand Behind the Performer

Check body and javelin alignment. This is a straight-line event. Thus from the first stride to the gather the performer should maintain a normal running posture. Check carefully to see if the point of the javelin "gets away" from the head during the draw-back. If it does, there is a subsequent tendency to deliver the javelin with a side-arm pull. The point of the javelin is controlled by applying pressure against the shaft with the little finger.

Another good viewing point is to step in behind the thrower during a full speed approach. One should be back approximately forty feet from the scratch line where it is possible to view the hips and shoulders during the last several strides. While some performers will rotate well past the midline of the runway during the cross steps, I am advocating controlled rotation wherein the arms and shoulders are parallel with the runway. The hips also rotate slightly rearward to get into position for the violent block and hip punch. The latter action takes place so explosively that it is difficult to follow with the naked eye.

a.                                                                              b.

**Figure 14.8.** During the final several strides, the performer endeavors to keep the hips forward to maximize approach speed. The shoulders are parallel to the runway to create separation between the upper and lower parts of the body, as well as produce the greatest possible range of motion during the flailing action.

## Move to the Side

Stand back twenty-five to thirty feet and opposite the second check mark. Watch the entire run up, trying to sense the rhythm of the approach. There should be continuous acceleration from the very first stride. Focus on the check mark. Does the performer's left foot contact the ground adjacent to the mark? Watch to see if the javelin has started to move down and back by the time the thrower is at the check mark. It should have.

Next watch the cross-step sequence from check mark to recovery. There should be no slowing down here, but rather controlled acceleration as the performer gathers for an explosive effort. Look for the keys to successful performance. First is the "armpit test." When the javelin drifts back, the arm becomes fully extended. The hand gripping the javelin is rotated strongly toward the thumb side so that the point of the elbow and the armpit are fully exposed.

a.            b.            c.

**Figure 14.9.** (a) During the final approach look for continuous acceleration through the cross steps and to the block. (b) The final cross step is an airborne gather during which the legs run out from beneath the body. (c) As the "throw" is initiated the hand is rotated toward the thumb side. This action tends to relieve strain at the elbow and places the arm in the most effective position for applying maximum flailing force.

**Figure 14.10.** The solid block and hip punch are two keys to skilled performance.

Now watch the hand from checkpoint to delivery of the javelin. The javelin must remain flat against the hand, which never falls lower than the throwing shoulder. Tail drag, a problem that occurs when the javelin is delivered at an attack angle which is too steep, frequently is caused by dropping the arm or letting the javelin get away from the hand. The diagonal line across the whole hand is the launching pad from which the javelin is sent flinging into space.

Next focus on the cross-step. This is an airborne gather during which the legs run out from beneath the body. With the trunk rotated toward the throwing arm, the right leg drives across the left and contact is made on the right heel. Look for the bow position as the left foot strikes well ahead of the right, indicating that the performer is in position for the so-called belly blast.

The action after the cross-step is so fast that one scarcely can follow the sequence with the naked eye. With practice, however, the important points can be seen. One of the most important is the action of the hip from left foot plant to left leg lift. Watch again for the bow position, the right side trailing as the left foot comes down. At that instant the right knee and hip are punched explosively forward. The combined forces of the hip punch, forward speed, and muscle power are so great that the throwing arm flails through to deliver the implement. The hip punch is the hallmark of the expert and should be the focus of attention during most preseason practice sessions.

Beginners tend to rush the javelin throw, delivering the implement before the left foot has come down (following the right cross-step). The result is a powerless pull against a javelin which likely is out of control. The correct rhythm for the final approach should be da-doo-da, with the javelin being delivered on the final da (that is, left-cross-pull). Having the beginner speak the words *left, cross, pull* during the final sequence is a great facilitator of learning.

Most javelin throwers cover from twenty-five to thirty feet during the final approach. They establish a wide throwing base and deliver the javelin at an angle of twenty-eight to thirty-eight degrees. (The angle of delivery is less into the wind than when the javelin is thrown with the wind.)

# part 5

# Multievent Training and Conditioning Activities

# 15 Multievent Training

Surely one of the most significant trends in track and field is the emergence of the multievent specialist. No longer are these performers merely highly skilled athletes who enter the decathlon or heptathlon on an occasional basis, but are specialists prepared both physically and mentally to engage in multievent competition. Commensurate with this trend is the emergence of the multievent coach. Perhaps most notable of these is Sam Adams, track and field coach at the University of California-Santa Barbara, a person who has committed much of his professional life to the development of multievent performers.

The decathlon for men consists of ten track and field "events" which are contested over a two day period. The events and the order in which they are contested on the first day, are: 100 meter dash, the long jump, the shot put, the high jump, and the 400 meter dash. The second day events and their order are: 100 meter hurdles, the discus throw, the pole vault, the javelin throw, and the 1500 meter dash.

The hepathlon, for women, consists of two day competition involving seven events. Four events are contested the first day. These are, in the order in which they are contested: the 100 meter hurdles, the shot put, the high jump, and the 200 meter dash. Three events are contested on the second day. They are, in order: the long jump, the javelin throw, and the 800 meter run.

A unique and highly significant aspect of multievent participation is that the athlete engages in both head to head competition and competition with an international scoring table. Indeed, it is the scoring table that dictates strategy concerning the selection and training of the multievent performer.

Although it is true that the great decathlete or heptathlete often scores "big" in an event or two, the best strategy is to select multievent athletes who have the potential for balanced performance in all events. Close scrutiny of the events in the decathlon make it plain that the decathlete must be a tall, powerful, well-coordinated athlete who is willing and able to train several hours each day. The heptathlete, on the other hand, may have a bias toward the tall, well-coordinated, sprint-jump type athlete.

## Developing the Multievent Performer

The best solution would be one similar to that practiced by the West German Track and Field Federation wherein all age group athletes are encouraged to be multievent participants. Under this program youngsters are tested during the early teens, and are thereafter guided into a specific event competition. It is believed that the early emphasis on general skill development has contributed to the success of most of West Germany's international performers.

Perhaps the best approach in this country is to first identify those youngsters who seem to have the physical and emotional characteristics essential to success in the heptathlon and decathlon and then encourge those, who so desire, to prepare for multievent competition on a long term basis. It is my strong belief that the learner should work on one event at a time. When the fundamentals have been mastered the athlete should then begin competing in this event in low level competition.

Initial competition in the decathlon or hepathlon should be aimed at the development of a sense of timing or rhythm. One must not get caught up emotionally in any part, to the detriment of the whole. Most multievent performers keep accurate records as they move from phase to phase, recognizing that points lost in one activity can be readily made up in another. This concept reemphasizes the fact that multievent athletes are not necessarily competing against other athletes, but are competing against themselves in an attempt to attain the highest possible number of points.

## Training Schedules for Multievent Performers

Where training is concerned the primary focus of attention is on the development of the skills and physical-emotional components essential to success in these events. The multieventer cannot spend as much time on any one event as the specialist. For this reason, all carry-over value from one event to another must be maximized. It is to be recognized that running is the basis of all track and field events, and thus running is the most important thing that a multievent performer can do. Recognize too that jump training complements sprinting as well as the throwing events. For this reason, one need not repeat the jump training, or sprint training, or other specific training activities for each different event.

Another thing to be remembered is that while an eighty percent stress load seems to be essential to the development of a specific fitness factor (strength, cardio-pulmonary endurance, etc.) a sixty percent stress load will maintain gains already achieved. Thus where off-season training might be primarily aimed at the development of performance components, training during the preseason and competitive season should be committed to the development of performance technique.

It is generally agreed that the multievent performer needs from three to four hours of training time each day. This would include warm up, flexibility training, weight training as dictated by the particular day, and technique work. With overwork one of the most significant problems faced by the multievent athlete the principle of hard day, easy day should be adhered to with care. It also must be recognized that rest is a formal part of the training program.

When referring to the principles of training for multievent performers, Sam Adams recently noted that "there are three primary types of training to be considered. All three are indispensible in the multievent program. The three are: running training, weight training, and technique work. The basic training cycles are formed by using running and weight training as a base. Insert the running and weight training sessions first and use these as the two cyclical components of training. Technique is then inserted into the program as needed, or desired."*

A typical, single week work load for the fall would be organized as follows:

*Monday*:
A morning run, low aerobic, 3 to 4 miles
Plyometric training, 20 to 30 minutes
Technique drills on one throwing event
Weights, upper body pulls and presses

*Tuesday*:
One mile warm up run, low aerobic
Hurdle drills
Technique work on one throwing event
Tempo running, 150s-220s-300s

*Wednesday*:
A morning run, aerobic, 2 to 3 miles
Technique work on one throwing event
Weight training, heavy on lower body, one set of high reps with upper body

*Thursday*:
Approach work on one jumping event
Technique work on one throwing event
Hill training, including hill bounding

*Friday*:
A morning run, low aerobic, 3 to 4 miles
Short sprints, 50s-75s
Technique work on one throwing event
Weights

*Saturday*:
Hurdle drills
Fartlek, aerobic-anaerobic-aerobic

---

*Sam Adams. Report to the TAC/USOC Development Committee, The University of Florida, Gainsville, Florida. January 8, 1981.

It should be noted that the throwing events are included in each day's training. This is because multievent performers have traditionally done less well in the throwing events than in the jumps and hurdles. Technically the throws, especially the discus and javelin, are difficult to master and require years of practice. The emphasis of all off-season training for the multievent performer should be in the development of correct fundamentals.

With a solid base of conditioning and running training there would be a shift in the training emphasis during the winter months. This is to be noted in the single week work load shown below:

*Monday*:
A morning run, aerobic, 3 to 4 miles
Short-approach, long jump training
Full circle work with the discus
High jump pops
Weights

*Tuesday*:
Short sprints with pole vault pole, 25s-30s
Pole vault training
Hurdle drills
Javelin work from short approach
Interval running, 220s-330s-440s at adjusted race pace

*Wednesday*:
A morning run, high aerobic, 1 to 2 miles
Full circle shot put training
Long jump runway work
Weight training

*Thursday*:
Full speed hurdle work over five hurdles
Discus training
Pole vault training
Tempo running, 550s-660s-800s

*Friday*:
A morning run, low aerobic, 3 to 5 miles
Full approach javelin work
Weight training

*Saturday*:
Bounding and plyometric activity, 20 minutes
Full circle work with shot put
Hurdle drills
Step down run, 500-400-300-200-150

During the competitive season it becomes increasingly difficult to follow a regular training cycle. Since most track and field meets do not have the decathlon or heptathlon on a regular basis, the multievent performer should use these meets for the purposes of training. One suggestion is that they participate in a strong event during each meet and one event in which they are not particularly proficient. They might also run a relay leg to work on speed or speed-endurance. The key to training for multievent performers during the competitive season is to work on each event at least once a week. And the key to ultimate success in these events is to see oneself, and be trained, as a multievent specialist.

All of the specific track and field events in the decathlon/hepathlon have heretofore been discussed. There is, therefore, no need in reviewing the technical aspect of skill performance. Rather, this final section will deal with strategy and other factors to be considered in multievent competition.

**Analysis of Performance**

Perhaps there is no other track and field event in which mental preparation is as important as it is in the decathlon/heptathlon. Prior to competition coach and athlete must appraise the forthcoming event in terms of, (1) the time of year, i.e., degree of readiness, (2) size of the competitive field, (3) the possible effects of weather conditions, (4) the trial during which one's best performance usually occurs, (5) the time necessary for warming up, and (6) the effect that heat selection has on performance, and the like.

The athlete should go into the meet with a performance plan and stated contingencies. The plan would list starting heights, factors which would dictate risking the "big" throw and those which would warrant playing it safe. Target times for the 800/1500 ought to be considered. The effect of points gained or lost during any phase of competition also must be reckoned with in terms of the effect on overall compeition.

A factor in this regard is the importance of sending the athlete on the field fully equipped to compete. This means having one's own tape measure, adequate clothing, shoes for each event, a copy of the international scoring table, heat sheets, the time schedule, etc. The athlete is then admonished to "play it cool," make each trial count, conserve one's energy between trials, and consider each contest an independent phase of the overall competition. The time between the first and second day of competition is used for rest, modifying one's strategy in lieu of the standings, rehydrating, forgetting today, and planning for tomorrow.

In the final analysis, remember that it takes time to become a multievent performer. Most top athletes in the United States have been at it for several years. Thus long term planning is indispensible. One should take joy in learning and competing, but also be realistic. This is no place to put the ego on the line until the work has been done. And even then, as noted earlier, the secret to success in the multievents is playing it cool, in being consistent.

# 16

# Conditioning Activities for Track and Field

It now seems certain that all participants in track and field would profit from an exercise regime aimed at the development of strength, flexibility, and endurance. Improvement in these factors likely would result in fewer injuries, facilitate the learning of skills, and markedly improve performance records. The wise teacher, therefore, ought to offer a unit on conditioning prior to the track and field unit, whereas coaches working with serious athletes surely would incorporate conditioning activities in the holistic preparation of such performers.

**General Conditioning Activities**

Holistic preparation includes both general and specific factors. General conditioning activities are aimed at building an adequate foundation for the development of more specific skills and abilities. Review of the materials covered under the heading Holistic Planning in chapter 1, as well as the training schedules for each event, will reveal that general conditioning activities are emphasized during preseason preparation. Thus for all track and field performers a part of each preseason training session includes jogging, stretching, weight training, gymnasium work, depth jumping, and the like. The possibilities for such activity are limited only by the imagination of the teacher.

**Specific Conditioning Activities**

The principle of specificity states that an activity performed in a specific manner will yield a specific result. Broadly interpreted, this means that to achieve ballistic, or explosive, strength one must engage in ballistic training. Or more precisely applied, this principle means that the acquisition of flexibility in the hamstring muscles is dependent upon careful and consistent stretching of the hamstring muscles.

Strength, flexibility, and endurance must be earned every day. While differences of opinion exist as to the best means of achieving gains in these areas, it is commonly agreed that to do so one must voluntarily push beyond present levels where these factors are concerned. It also is commonly agreed that measurable changes in these factors can be accrued by training at least twice a week for a period of six or seven weeks.

Resistance exercise constitutes a training program that seeks to produce gains in muscular strength and endurance through the systematic overloading of selected muscle groups. In its broadest sense this involves any type of resistance, though the particular emphasis of this discussion is the use of barbells, resistance-producing machines (such as the Universal Gym), wall pullies, and the like.

**Resistance Exercises**

Contrary to what some people believe, resistance exercises do not produce a condition that is referred to as "muscle-bound." Also, these kinds of exercises do not produce exaggerated muscle hypertrophy in female athletes. Mature women naturally posses nearly a third less muscle mass than do males. Too, the manner in which girls and women are affected by overloading of this kind is determined largely by their primary female hormone, estrogen; thus they could not modify their muscle masses even if they tried. Doctor Harmon Brown, hormone specialist and track coach, recently affirmed this fact in a speech to several hundred coaches and performers assembled at San Mateo, California.

Strength, endurance, and flexibility are specific adaptive responses to particular kinds of external demands. Optimum development of these fitness factors is dependent upon the wise selection and the careful application of overload principles. These are (1) gradually increase the total load, (2) gradually increase the speed of performance in a progressive manner, (3) progressively increase the total time that a given position can be held, and (4) with constant resistance, progressively increase the total number of performance bouts. Exercise programs having significant value must utilize one or more of these four principles.

**Principles of Progressive Resistance Activity**

Research has shown that strength gains occur when muscular tissue is called upon to resist force while lengthening as well as while shortening, or contracting. Thus eccentric activity can be utilized as well as concentric activity to produce the desired overload effect. This has important implications, for not only can an individual increase the work load in a given unit of time (by lifting up and resisting down), but one can also produce the margin of strength necessary to control one's own body weight when sufficient initial strength is lacking. (For example, the repeated resistance of gravity by lowering oneself from the extended arm to the chest resting position would eventually produce sufficient strength to perform the push-up from the resting position to the extended position.) Or, by resisting a weight while lowering oneself into the squat position, one actually is contributing to the development of sufficient strength to extend the legs upward again against that weight.

The second essential feature of the successful weight training program is that it must be *progressive in nature.* For continued gains in strength there must be a continued increase in the resistance applied. The rule usually followed in weight training is to increase the resistance against which one is working when a given exercise can be repeated more than twelve times. The practical rule is to start with a weight which can be moved through a particular range of motion (press, curl, etc.) eight times and to work repeatedly with such a weight until the exercise can be repeated twelve times. (Note here the principle of progression in the story of Milo and the bull.)

The *third* feature of the successful weight-training program is that it must be *consistent*. While there is no exact formula for attaining maximum results from an exercise program, the best evidence seems to indicate that an individual must train at least twice, and perhaps three times, each week for measureable gains to occur. It is probable that five bouts of activity each week are better than three, with alternate days of work varying in intensity and point of emphasis. The important idea here is that training must be consistent.

**Selected Resistance Exercises**

There are many weight-training exercises from which the serious performer can choose. Those which are shown here represent activities aimed at strengthening the muscle groups most frequently utilized in track and field. The reader is reminded, however, that the wise use of these exercises is dependent upon an understanding of the physioanatomical requirements of each track and field event. Strength is important. Strength development also is very specific, being determined by the quantity and quality of the demands imposed upon the body, with the greatest gains occurring at the site or through the range of motion where the stress is applied.

### Abdominal and Hip Flexor Exercises

The bent knee sit-up is probably the most common exercise for improving abdominal and hip flexor strength. This exercise can be performed either from a supine position on the floor or on an inclined board. For maximum benefit to the abdominal muscles the heels must be flexed tightly against the buttock while the performer curls the head upward toward the knees. A twisting action, flexing the right shoulder toward the left knee and the left shoulder toward the right knee, markedly improves the quality of this exercise.

Hanging leg lifts as demonstrated in figures 16.1 a and b are excellent exercises for improving abdominal and hip flexor strength. The advanced performer should attempt to torque the knees right and left from the bent leg position.

### Hip, Ankle, and Knee Extensor Exercises

Powerful antigravity muscles are essential to successful performance in nearly all track and field events. The double leg press (fig. 16.2) and the squat (fig. 16.3) are basic exercises for developing extensors of the ankles, knees, and hips.

a.                                                                          b.

**Figure 16.1.** Hanging leg lifts

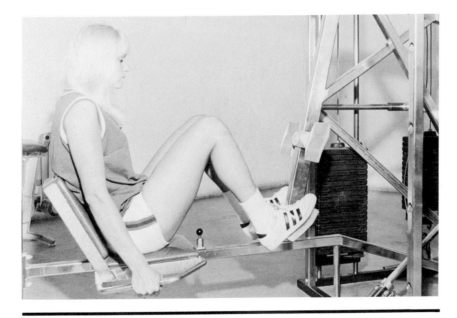

**Figure 16.2.** Double leg press

**Figure 16.3.** The squat position (the board beneath the heels helps the performer retain her balance).

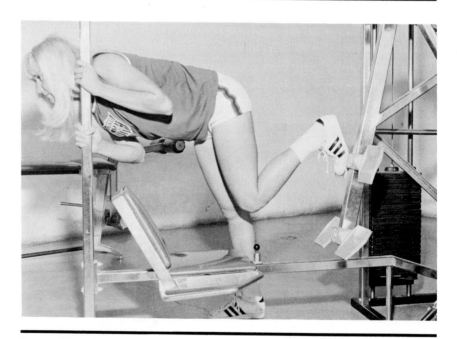

**Figure 16.4.** The single leg press

**Figure 16.5.** Beginning position for initiating the squat jump from a stride stand.

The single leg press demonstrated in figure 16.4 is an excellent means of developing strength essential to the sprint start, while the squat jump from a stride stand (fig. 16.5) is a basic exercise for jumpers.

## Exercises for the Knee Flexors

Since most athletes manifest a potentially hazardous differential between knee extensor and knee flexor strength, it is essential that the knee flexors be strengthened. (Anything more than a two-to-one advantage in extensor strength may predispose one to injury to the hamstring muscles during explosive sprinting or jumping.) In addition to the use of iron boots, or the Universal Knee flexion station, one can engage in the "buddy flex" for strengthening the knee flexors. To effect this exercise one member of a duo assumes a prone lying position, and the other kneels next to the ankle. Pressure is applied against the heel by the kneeling member while the lying member attempts to flex the knee. The pressure should be constant, but not so great that it cannot be overcome with effort.

The ingenious teacher who does not have the advantage of formal resistance-training equipment can use similar buddy exercises to strengthen most of the major muscles employed in track and field.

## Exercises for the Upper and Lower Back

Two types of so-called rowing exercises are to be found in the training schedules for throwers. One is upright rowing which involves a vertical pull from a standing position. This is primarily a shoulder exercise, though it does significantly overload the upper back muscles which elevate the shoulder girdle. Bent rowing, which is shown in figures 16.6 a and b demands powerful contraction of both posterior shoulder muscles and the adductors of the scapula.

The "back hypers" shown with and without the use of weights (figs. 16.7 and 16.8) are aimed at the development of the extensors of the spine. These exercises have particular significance to javelin throwers, who place great strain on the lower back when they assume the proper bow position for effecting the "belly blast" pull.

a.                                                                                                          b.

**Figure 16.6.** Bent rowing

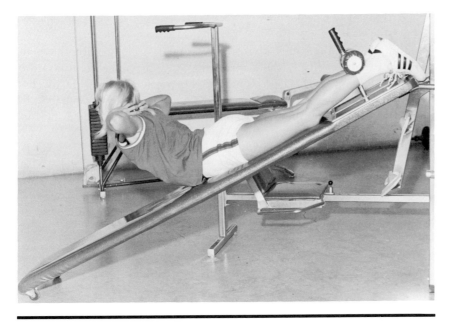

**Figure 16.7.** "Back hyper" without resistance

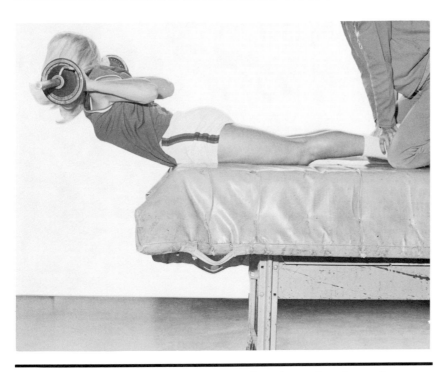

**Figure 16.8.** "Back hyper" with resistance (for advanced performers).

## Arm Depressor Exercises

The straight arm depressor (figs. 16.9 a and b), along with the bent arm pullover (figs. 16.10 a and b) and the javelin pull (fig. 16.11) are all aimed at improving the strength of the overhead throwing mechanism. The straight arm depressor also has a secondary effect on the abdominal muscles since they must stabilize the pelvis during the performance of this exercise.

a.                                                                          b.

**Figure 16.9.** Straight arm depressors

a.

b.

**Figure 16.10.** The bent arm pullover

**Figure 16.11.** The javelin pull

### Arm Flexor Exercises

The arm curl is the classic arm flexor exercise (figs. 16.12 and 16.13). When the curl is performed, the elbows ought to be held away from the side and the gluteal muscles should be contracted forcefully.

Other arm flexor and arm depressor exercises are the chin-up, the rope climb, and the pull down behind the neck.

### Exercises for the Arm Extensors, the Chest, and the Anterior Shoulder Girdle

The bench press is probably the most widely used exercise for developing the upper body (figs. 16.14 and 16.15). Shot-putters also use the snap press (figs 16.16 a and b) and the incline press (not shown) to develop strength through a very specific range of motion.

Two special exercises for discus throwers are shown in figures 16.17 a and b and 16.18 a and b. These are referred to as "flys" and constitute specific skill-related overloading of the pectoral muscles.

Figure 16.12          Figure 16.13

**Figure 16.12.**  The regular arm curl using the Universal Gym.

**Figure 16.13.**  The reverse arm curl (performed from a stride stand to improve balance).

Figure 16.14          Figure 16.15

**Figure 16.14.**  Beginning position for the bench press using the Universal Gym.

**Figure 16.15.**  The bench press using a barbell

a.                                                                        b.

**Figure 16.16.** The snap press

## Exercises for the Pelvic Girdle

In addition to the anterior-posterior movements of the pelvic girdle which are controlled by the abdominal and gluteal muscles, there are important lateral and torquing movements in the pelvic area as well. (Exercises for the abdominal wall already have been discussed. Uphill sprints are very effective for strengthening the gluteal muscles.)

The lateral lift shown in figures 16.19 a and b is an effective exercise for the lateral muscles in the pelvic area. Another is the torque twist which is initiated from the position shown in figure 16.20. The complete exercise involves a dipping of the right shoulder, coupled with a downward-upward twist as if one were throwing the discus. When sufficient strength is developed, the bar can be carried diagonally across the back, with the lower end in the right hand. The torque twist then more readily simulates the action preceding the discus fling.

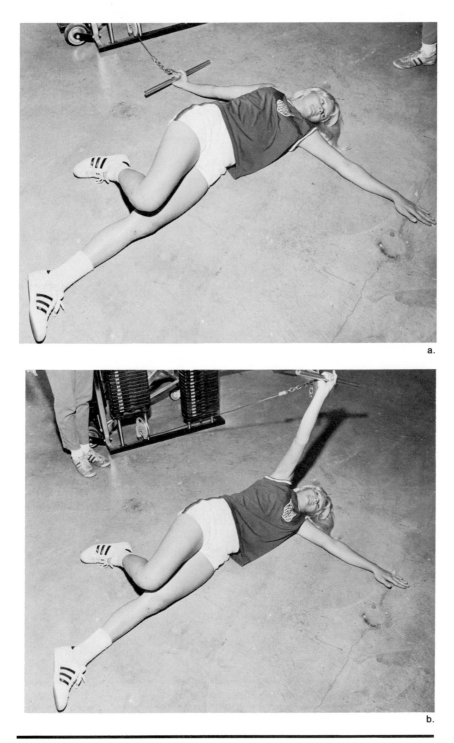

a.

b.

**Figure 16.17.** "Flys" using the Universal Gym

a.

b.

**Figure 16.18.** "Flys" using dumbbells for resistance.

a.                                                                                          b.

**Figure 16.19.** Lateral lifts.

**Figure 16.20.** Beginning position for the torque

**Exercises for Flexibility Development**

Flexibility is a modifiable factor, as are strength and endurance. The facts are that one achieves increased flexibility by following the overload principles previously applied to the development of strength. One must work against resistance (apply force) through an extended range of motion, progressively and continuously if flexibility is to be developed.

The importance of flexibility to the track and field performer cannot be stressed enough. Increased flexibility permits throwers and jumpers to apply force through the greatest possible range of motion. (Range of motion and velocity of release are the factors of primary importance to these events.) Research also has shown that flexibility, coupled with strength, constitutes a means of increasing sprint speed.

### Flexibility Exercises for the Back

The activities shown in figures 16.21 a and b, 16.22, and 16.23 represent the kinds of things that can be done to improve flexibility of the back. "Crossing the X" simulates the action initiated by the discus thrower out of the back of the circle and thus is a must exercise for participants in this event.

Grasping the hands behind the knees and rocking back and forth along the spine, in the "back stretcher" is an effective means of relieving low back pain (fig. 16.22). Widening the base in the "elbow touch" makes this an excellent activity for stretching the adductor muscles along the insides of the legs as well as the musculature of the low back (fig. 16.23).

### Stretching the Rotators and Adductors of the Leg

The "stride stretcher," as demonstrated, is primarily a means of stretching the groin (fig. 16.24). Shifting the support from the inner border of the right foot to the tops of the toes, then turning and facing forward, is an exercise that can be used to stretch the anterior, as well as the medial, musculature of the leg.

The "knee straddle" (fig. 16.25) is a classic stretch for high jumpers. Note that Pam Spencer is applying pressure against the knees by pressing outward with her elbows. This exercise can be improved by pulling the chest down toward the toes. A teammate also can apply pressure to the knees or the upper back to increase the range of motion. To effectively stretch the thigh rotators from the knee straddle position, the performer rotates one knee and then the other inward to touch the floor.

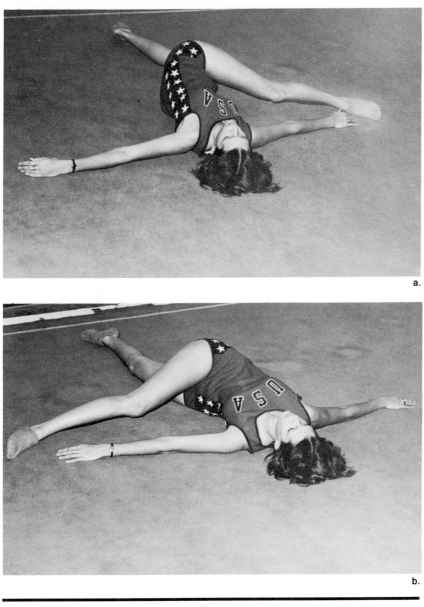

a.

b.

**Figure 16.21.** Crossing the X

**Figure 16.22.** The back stretcher

**Figure 16.23.** The elbow touch

**Figure 16.24.** The stride stretcher

**Figure 16.25.** The knee straddle

## Stretching the Hamstrings

The "hurdler's stretch," as shown (fig. 16.26), is an excellent means of improving flexibility in both the hamstring muscles and the low back. The performer ought to work toward touching the nose to both knees. Stretch well and then alternate forward and rearward legs.

To stretch the upper part of the hamstrings, place the bottom of the foot of the leg to be stretched on a bench or table and lean forward until the chest touches the thigh. Pressing the buttock forward will further increase the effectiveness of this stretch.

**Figure 16.26.** The hurdlers stretch

## Stretching the Quadriceps and Hip Flexors

The stretching exercise shown in figure 16.27 can be performed either standing or in a prone lying position. Pulling the knee back away from the body effectively stretches the hip flexors, as well as the anterior muscles of the thigh.

**Figure 16.27.** Stretching the quadriceps

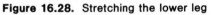

**Figure 16.28.** Stretching the lower leg

## Stretching the Posterior Muscles of the Lower Leg

It is particularly important that persons subject to Achilles tendon strain and/or shin splints carefully and consistently stretch the calf and adjoining muscles. The position demonstrated in figure 16.28 is an effective means of doing so. Standing with the toes on the edge of a stair step and lowering the heels as far as possible is another excellent means of stretching the posterior muscles of the lower leg.

Preparation for serious participation in track and field must be perceived as a year round proposition. Guidelines for the development of flexibility, aerobic endurance, and strength follow.

**Guidelines for the Holistic Conditioning Program**

## Flexibility Training

Stretching must be an integral part of the conditioning and preparation of all track and field athletes. When one recognizes the explosive nature of most track and field events, as well as the necessity of moving through a maximum range of motion, the need for flexibility becomes obvious.

Principles for initiating a sound flexibility program are:

Work through the full range of motion so long as the stretching is pain free.

Stretch "like a cat," i.e., long and slowly. Jerking tends to excite the antagonists, producing tension rather than relaxation.

Use your own body weight (gravity) to stretch your muscles. Hold the elongated position for an accumulative time of sixty seconds. This is to say that a particular exercise can be repeated several times, though the total time in the stretched position ought to be about sixty seconds.

Stretch daily.

**Aerobic Endurance**

It is my belief that all track and field athletes will profit from endurance training. For that reason we have all of our athletes engage in aerobic running during the preparatory (fall) season. As well as improving the cardiovascular system this kind of running is an excellent way to burn calories and help individuals lower their percentage of body fat.

The basic principle to which we adhere in this kind of training is to initiate the program for all but middle distance and distance runners by working at seventy percent of one's age adjusted maximum heart rate. This is achieved by subtracting the athlete's age from 225 to obtain the estimated age adjusted HRM, with the target work rate being seventy percent of the latter figure. Example: $225 - 17$ (age) $= 208 \times .70 = 145$. The beauty of using the heart rate to determine work loads is that this is a self adjusting factor. This is to say, as one adapts to the work load the resting heart rate goes down and greater demands must be imposed to reach the target rate. Using the heart rate as a measure of work loads thus utilizes the principle of progressive overloading which is so essential to continued improvement.

Although the aerobic threshold is currently under intense scrutiny by the exercise physiologist, it is safe to conclude that middle distance and distance runners would be well within their aerobic capacity when working at seventy-five percent of their age adjusted maximum heart rates. Initial conditioning loads for these runners would thus begin at the seventy-five percent level. Following four to six weeks of conditioning, the training threshold for middle distance and distance runners likely would be raised to eighty to eighty-five percent levels, with the thresholds for all other athletes being elevated to seventy-five percent levels.

The minimum time for target heart training each day is twenty minutes. The minimum number of such training sessions each week would be three. Six, thirty minute aerobic training sessions each week would be far more effective and a realistic goal for most track and field athletes.

**Strength Training**

When working with mature athletes it is recommended that weight training be done with free weights. The reason for this is that it is more likely one can simulate skilled performance with free weights than with machines. It also is true that the "guts" of track and field performance is explosive action. Thus every training program must include lifts such as the power clean and the snatch to dynamically overload the antigravity muscles.

The weight training recommended by the writer is holistic in nature, beginning with the first day of the fall season and continuing throughout the year. This program is oriented toward six week cycles and involves alternate days of lifting and resting, with a test day followed by a rest day concluding each cycle. The first six week cycle should be considered a conditioning program for the more serious training to follow. After selecting six lifts appropriate to the circumstances, each participant would be tested to determine their single repetition maximum for each lift (1RM). The work loads for the remainder of this cycle would be two sets, of eight repetitions, at sixty percent of the single repetition maximum for each lift ($2 \times 8 \times 60$ percent of 1RM). A suggested program involving the major muscle groups might be as follows:

| | |
|---|---|
| Bench press | $2 \times 8 \times 60$ percent of 1RM |
| Squats | $2 \times 8 \times 60$ percent of 1RM |
| Lat Pulls | $2 \times 8 \times 60$ percent of 1RM |
| Snatch | $2 \times 8 \times 60$ percent of 1RM |
| Leg Curls | $2 \times 8 \times 60$ percent of 1RM |
| Up Right Curls | $2 \times 8 \times 60$ percent of 1RM |

Following the day of testing to determine new single repetition maximums, and a day of rest, the second six week cycle would begin. During this cycle it is recommended that two additional exercises be added to the work load. These could be calisthenic type activities, such as the bent leg sit up and the back hyperextension to strengthen the abdominal and low back muscles, or additional lifting exercises. Whatever the case, during this cycle the lifter would work at seventy percent of his/her 1RM maximum, while performing three sets of five repetitions for each lift.

During the third six week cycle and thereafter, the work intensity would be eighty percent of the single repetition maximum for each lift, with five sets of five repetitions constituting the work load. As the performer accrues higher and higher levels of strength it might be wise to change one or two lifting activities during each six week cycle. This could involve subsituting the military press for the bench press, and/or bent over rowing for the upright pulls. Some mature performers find that they can achieve heavier work loads by lifting every day, with an emphasis on the upper body and an alternate days emphasis on the lower body. While following such a schedule the lifter would likely take one day of complete rest each week.

A comprehnsive program for the mature performer follows:

*Sprints and Hurdles*

| | |
|---|---|
| Double and single leg presses | Steep hill sprints |
| Arm curls | Upright rowing |
| Bench press | Leg curls |
| Starts against resistance | Calf raisers |
| Sprints against resistance | One-half squat jumps |
| Depth jumping | Sit-ups |

All flexibility exercises are aimed at stretching the musculature of the hips, the adductors, the flexors, and extensors of the thigh, the posterior muscles of the lower limb, and the back.

*High Jump and Long Jump*

| | |
|---|---|
| Double and single leg presses | Calf raisers |
| One-half squat jumps | Jump and reach |
| Depth jumping | Straight arm depressor |
| Stair hops | Sit-ups |
| Leg curls | Hanging leg lifts |
| Arm curls | Thigh flexors against resistance |

All flexibility exercises are aimed at stretching the musculature of the hips, the adductors, the flexors, and extensors of the thigh, the posterior muscles of the lower limb, and the back.

*Distance Runners*

| | |
|---|---|
| Double leg press | Sit-ups |
| Arm curls | Chin-ups |
| Leg curls | Push-ups |
| Bench press | Upright pulls |

All flexibility exercises are aimed at stretching the musculature of the hips, the adductors, the flexors and extensors of the thigh, the posterior muscles of the lower limb, and the back.

*Shot, Discus, and Javelin*
See Chapter 12

**Summary**

Fitness changes such as strength, flexibility, and endurance are produced by adhering to the overload principle. The latter involves working against resistance, working against progressively greater amounts of resistance, and doing so in a continuous manner. Although the kinds of resistance against which one works can vary, the use of weight is advocated since work loads can be quantified and the stress can be applied in a progressive manner. Beginners ought to engage in a six week, preconditioning program, involving stress loads amounting to sixty percent of one's single repetition maximum for a given lift. A holistic program for a mature individual would include eight different lifting activities, with five sets of five repetitions at eighty percent of one's single repetition maximum being achieved on alternate days. A symbolic description of such a program would read 5 x 5 x 80 percent of 1RM.

**Comprehensive Weight Training Program**

A comprehensive, year long program follows:

# Format for a Comprehensive Weight Training Program

| September Oct. 1-14 6 wk cycle | Oct. 15-30 November 6 wk cycle | Dec. 1-14 2 wk cycle | Dec. 15-30 January 6 wk cycle | February March 1-14 6 wk cycle | March 15-30 2 wk cycle | April May 1-14 6 wk cycle | May 15-30 June 6 wk cycle | July 1-14 2 wk cycle | July 15-30 August 6 wk cycle |
|---|---|---|---|---|---|---|---|---|---|
| 6 lifts 60% 1RM Bench Press Squats Lat Pulls Snatch Leg Curls Upright Pulls | 8 lifts 70% 1RM Bench Press Squats Lat Pulls Snatch Leg Curls Upright Pulls Flys French Curls | 8 lifts 60% 1RM Select any 8 lifts from the previous 2 cycles | 8 lifts 80% 1RM Incline Press Lat Pulls Power Clean Leg Curls Rowing Squat Jumps Flys French Curls | 8 lifts 80% 1RM Incline Press Pull Over Power Clean Leg Curls Rowing Squat Jumps Torque Twist French Curls | 8 lifts Pyramid Select any 8 lifts from the previous 2 cycles | 8 lifts 70% 1RM Bench Press Squats Lat Pulls Snatch Leg Curls Power Clean Upright Pulls Snap Press | 7 lifts 70% 1RM Incline Press Squat Jumps Snatch Flys Rowing Pull over Rowing | 7 lifts 60% 1RM | Active rest: Calisthenics, hiking, water skiing, volley ball and the like |
| 2 sets 8 reps Lift 3 days each week | 3 sets 5 reps Lift 3 days each week | 2 sets 12-15 reps Work upper body and lower body on alternate days | 5 sets 5 reps Lift 3 days each week | 5 sets 5 reps Lift 3 days each week | 3 sets 7-3-1 reps Work upper body and lower body on alternate days | 3 sets 5 reps Lift 3 days each week | 3 sets 5 reps Lift 3 days each week | 2 sets 12-15 reps Work upper body and lower body on alternate days | |
| Next to last day: test for 1RM Last day: rest | Next to last day: test for 1RM Last day: rest | Complete rest each 7th day | Next to last day: test for 1RM Last day: rest | Next to last day: test for 1RM Last day: rest | Complete rest each 7th day | Next to last day: test for 1RM Last day: rest | Next to last day: test for 1RM Last day: rest | Complete rest each 7th day | |

This program has been designed to parallel the school year. It is to be noted that the suggested program adheres to the principle of progressive overloading. Note also that the maintenance loads during the spring "competitive" season are less than the work loads during fall and winter. Too, the kinds of lifts suggested for the competitive season tend to be more explosive than those used to accomplish foundation work during the fall.

It is generally recognized by serious weight trainers that the percentage factors change during each cycle, i.e., if one achieves a 1RM of 200 lbs. for the bench press at the end of the first 6 week cycle, the work load of seventy percent for the second 6 week cycle would be 140 lbs. the first week, with an automatic increment of 5lbs. per week during the remainder of the cycle . . . and for each cycle thereafter.

# 17

# Planning and Conducting the Track and Field Meet

Track and field meets are fun. The excitement of keen competition seems to be contagious when athletes meet to test their various abilities in the running, the jumping, and the throwing events. There is a feeling about track and field meets that one seldom experiences in other athletic events— a feeling of anticipation, a sense of awe, a respect for the skill and dedication of an accomplished performance.

The successful track and field meet does not just happen, however; it represents hard work and cooperation on the part of many individuals other than the participants. Perhaps the director is most responsible for the success of a track and field meet, though all of the officials, maintenance personnel, recorders, equipment handlers, and, indeed, the spectators help to make a track meet a success. This chapter is an attempt to give the reader some idea of the work involved in organizing and conducting a track meet. It does not include a detailed accounting of every problem the meet director will face, but it does provide pertinent guidelines for one to follow in planning.

## Promoting Track and Field

Very probably a track and field meet will be little better than the publicity it receives. The finest of facilities and the best of performance records have little meaning without participants and spectators. Because this is so, the meet director should begin early to publicize the forthcoming event. The director should contact all potential participants well in advance, giving them pertinent information about the date, time, and location of the event. One should publicize in the available news media, highlighting all of the teams as well as the outstanding individuals and their performance records..

While it is never wise to exploit an individual, it is sound planning to tell the interested public what the better athletes have done, how they rank locally or nationally, and what they might be expected to do. People are interested in successful performance and are more likely to attend an event if they believe a record will be broken.

At the local level, promotion involves displaying pictures, posting names, and comparing times and distances. Short announcements in the school paper and skits in assembly also catch the eyes of potential participants and spectators.

In addition to public relations, there is considerable preplanning involved in organizing and conducting a track meet. This includes preparing and mailing entry forms, engaging officials, seeding performers, assigning heats and lanes, and preparing equipment and facilities.

**Planning for the Track and Field Meet**

## Preparation and Mailing of the Official Entry Form

The entry form is a vital communication link between the meet director and the participating schools. It should include such essential information as the schedule of events, the exact time and location of the meet, and space for the names of all participating athletes.

The entry form should be mailed to prospective participants at least three weeks prior to the track and field meet. To ensure adequate time for processing the entrants, seeding them, placing them in heats, and so forth, there should be a mandatory return deadline of several days.

## Obtaining Officials for the Track and Field Meet

The officials for a track and field meet include the referees, clerk of the course, starter, judges at the finish line, field event judges, timekeepers, and inspectors. (For a detailed description of the duties of all officials read the Division for Girls and Womens Sports Track and Field Guide or the Official National Collegiate Athletic Association Track and Field Rule Book, or the Official Track and Field Guide published by The Athletics Congress.)

To conduct a dual meet approximately twenty officials would be required, with ten or fifteen additional officials necessary for a meet having several participating teams. Acquiring a group of officials this large is no simple task. All must be contacted well in advance of the meet to make certain they will be available.

Two or three days ahead of the meet the wise director would send postal cards to all officials, reminding them of their responsibilities. These cards should include the time, place, and date of the meet as well as a word about appropriate dress, the specific duties of the recipients, and the person to whom they should report.

## Formation of Heats and Seeding of Participants

In a dual meet the number of participants in each event is usually agreed upon by the coaches beforehand. In the running events this number frequently is determined by the number of lanes available on the track.

In meets where several teams are participating, the entrants may be unlimited or minimum standards can be fixed to restrict the entry list. Whenever there are more entrants than lanes, it is necessary to run trial heats.

Heats are formed after all entries have been received and classified. To avoid eliminating the better contestants prior to the finals, times are compared and the fastest runners are scattered throughout the necessary heats for each event. (These times should be required on the entry form.) The fastest runners are called heat leaders or seeded participants. When all heats have been completed in writing, the meet committee draws a number for each contestant to determine the lane in which the participant will run.

The following table can be used to determine the number of trial heats necessary when six lanes are available. (Similar tables can easily be constructed for seven, eight, nine, or more lanes.)

| No. of Entries | No. Trial Heats | No. Qualifying (From Ea. Heat) | No. Semifinal Heats | No. Qualifying (From Ea. Heat) | No. in Final |
|---|---|---|---|---|---|
| 1 to 6 | 0 | 0 | 0 | 0 | 6 |
| 7 to 12 | 2 | 3 | 0 | 0 | 6 |
| 13 to 18 | 3 | 4 | 2 | 3 | 6 |
| 19 to 24 | 4 | 3 | 2 | 3 | 6 |

During the quarterfinals, semifinals, and finals of the sprints and hurdle races, it is customary to place together in the center lanes the runners who have the fastest times. This practice gives the timers and finish judges a better opportunity to determine accurately the winner of each race. It also helps the fastest performers to keep track of each other throughout the race.

## Equipment and Supplies

It is customary for the teams in a dual meet to supply their own shots, discs, javelins, and the like. In large meets, however, these items frequently are provided by the host school or team so all contestants will have standard equipment. The host school also supplies starting blocks, hurdles, crossbars, and many other items, some of which are listed following:

*Throwing Events*
Two to three each: discuses, shots, javelins
Clipboards and pencils
Event sheets
Numbered markers
Steel measuring tapes
Sector flags and makers

*Jumping Events*
Rake, broom
Standards and crossbars
Steel measuring tape
Clipboards and pencils
Event sheets

*General*
First-aid supplies                     Public-address system
Official badges                        Master score cards
Scorers' tables and chairs             Marking pens

*Running Events*
Starting blocks                        Two whistles
Hammers                                Starting pistol and blanks
Hurdles                                Clipboards and pencils
Finish yarn                            Heat sheets and final sheets
Batons                                 Timer's report cards
Stop watches                           Finsh judges' report cards
Stand for finish judges

## Preparation of the Track

Preparing the facilities for a meet is a long and tedious job. It requires watering, rolling, and marking the track and field, transport of hurdles and standards, setting of finish poles, and other similar jobs. All this work should be completed the day before the meet so that there is ample time to check facilities for accurary. It is especially important that the starting and finish lines be established, the baton exchange zones identified, and the throwing sectors for the shot, discus, and javelin visibly marked. While the markings of the track itself are determined by local conditions, markings for the three throwing events are fixed by the official rules governing strack and field. These are shown here to guide the reader in the preparation of the track and to assist one in measuring accurately for each of these events.

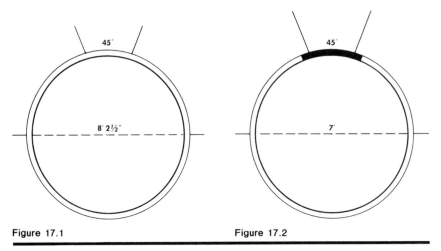

Figure 17.1

Figure 17.2

**Figure 17.1.** Discus ring and throwing sector. The discus ring is 8 feet 2½ inches in diameter. The throwing sector is designated by lines at an angle of 45 degrees radiating from the center of the circle.

**Figure 17.2.** Shot-put circle and throwing sector. The shot-put circle is 7 feet in diameter. A toeboard 4 feet long and 4 inches high is flush with the inside of the ring. The throwing sector is designated by lines at an angle of 45 degrees radiating from the center of the circle.

**Conducting the Track and Field Meet**

The day of the track and field meet will be filled with many last-minute details. To make certain that nothing is overlooked and that all is in readiness when the meet is supposed to begin, the director would be wise to prepare a checklist covering all of the known administrative details. This list should include the names and phone numbers of all officials, maintenance personnel, and other individuals having duties which are essential to the success of the meet. It should list all of the necessary equipment and supplies, the locker room assignments, and the names of the visiting coaches or team managers. This checklist should be both comprehensive and readily understandable, and it should be carefully reviewed before the meet has begun. (In two recent national meets embarrassing situations occurred which could have been averted had a premeet checklist been available and appropriately used. In one of these meets the measuring tapes were completely overlooked, and in the other the official entry forms were somehow left behind, making it impossible to run several trial heats when they were scheduled to go.)

A smoothly run track and field meet depends upon adequate pre-planning and the coordinated efforts of many responsible persons. At least one-half hour before the first event the officials should assemble for their final briefing. They should be given clipboards and packets containing the names of the participants, a summary of the rules governing the events they will officiate, a diagram of the exact procedure for

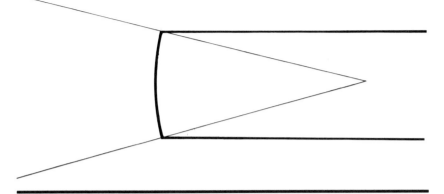

**Figure 17.3.** Javelin runway and throwing sector. The javelin runway is 13 feet 1½ inches wide and of indefinite length. The scratch mark is an arc 2¾ inches wide. This arc is of wood, metal, or white chalk. Each good throw is marked, and the best throw made by each contestant is measured by holding the 0 end of the tape in the field, stretching the tape through a point 26 feet and 3 inches behind the scratch line, and reading the distance on the runway side of the scratch line. The throwing sector is established by extending lines from the measurement point out through the ends of the scratch mark for an indefinite length.

**Figure 17.4.** Measuring the long jump. After the jump, a pencil, or some similar object is inserted in the sand at the point of contact nearest to the takeoff board. The loop end of the tape is placed over the pencil, and the tape drawn back to the takeoff board. The jumping distance is read at the pit side of the board.

measuring if the events for which they are responsible involves height or distance, and other materials pertinent to their job. Following this general briefing, the head field judge and the head timer should meet their respective assistants to give whatever final instructions they wish. With all their questions answered and with their watches, clipboards, markers, and tape measures in hand, the officials go to their stations and the meet is ready to begin.

It is customary for the referee to make a final inspection of all equipment and facilities prior to the start of the meet. Thereafter the clerk is in charge of the conduct of the event. The clerk checks individual athletes into their events and escorts all runners to the start of their race. The official starter takes over several minutes before each race is scheduled to start.

The starter makes certain that all performers know the rules pertaining to each race. Commands are given for removal of the warm ups, for getting into the starting blocks, and for starting. Working together in this manner the referee, clerk, starter, judges, and timers constitute an efficient team.

## Order of Events

Because many factors determine the events included in a track and field meet, it is not possible to state the exact order of participation. There are, on the other hand, certain guidelines which the meet director should follow.

1. The field events normally begin a half hour before the first running event. If there are four field events, it might be well to start and complete two of these before the second two are started. This procedure eliminates much of the confusion of running back and forth between events and permits two sets of officials to cover the four activities.
2. Because of the time involved in setting up the hurdles, it might be wise to run this race first, eliminating the problem of transporting, setting, and straightening the hurdles during the course of the meet.
3. The sprint races and the distance races should be well staggered so that a runner who wishes to participate in more than one race will have time to rest adequately between events.
4. Relay races are usually run last as a climax to the meet. The relay brings all of the teams together in face-to-face competition, giving the participants and the spectators a final exciting event to watch.

In meets where there are different divisions of competitions, the shorter sprint and hurdle races for the younger performer probably should precede the longer races for the more mature participants. The time factor also would be extended accordingly. In no instance should a runner be required to run more than two sprint races in less than one-half hour's time. For longer distances, an hour of rest should be permitted between races.

## Scoring the Track and Field Meet

Immediately after each event has been completed, the official entry forms should be taken to the scorer's table to be recorded on the master score sheet. Individual scores should be registered and a total score for each team posted. The revised total score should be readily available to the coaches and public-address announcer. By prompt and efficient reporting of scores, the place winners can be announced, helping to eliminate the time lapses so common in some track meets.

The scoring system for track and field meets varies with the number of participating teams as shown in the example following:

| Place Winners to Be Counted | 1st Place | 2nd Place | 3rd Place | 4th Place | 5th Place | 6th Place |
|---|---|---|---|---|---|---|
| 3 | 5 | 3 | 1 | | | |
| 4 | 5 | 3 | 2 | 1 | | |
| 5 | 5 | 4 | 3 | 2 | 1 | |
| 6 | 10 | 8 | 6 | 4 | 2 | 1 |

In the event of a tie by two or more competitors for a place that receives a score, the combined score for the places involved is divided equally among the competitors included in the tie. For example, if two athletes tie for second in a dual meet where three places receive scores, the points for second and third would be combined, with each competitor receiving half the total points. (In the illustration each of the compeitors would receive two points.)

The meet director has at least two additional responsibilities after the meet is over. The director should send a letter of appreciation to each of the officials for their willingness to serve without remuneration. One also should prepare a complete summary of the meet results, which includes the names of place winners, times, distances, and scores, and send it to all participating teams. These two courtesies will be rewarded by cooperation at future times and by an expanded interest in track and field.

1. Begin early. Planning and conducting a track and field meet is a time-consuming job.
2. Publicize the meet well. Send preliminary information to all prospective participants well in advance of the meet date.
3. Set realistic deadlines and then hold to them.
4. Contact the officials early; keep them posted; provide a training session for them if need be.
5. Prepare a detailed checklist (a tentative progress schedule) and follow it as carefully as possible.
6. Add "color" to the meet in every way possible. Announce each event; keep people posted on the progress of the participants where heights and distances are involved; present all awards with appropriate ceremony; provide programs which list all of the participants and the records for each event; use flags, banners, and bands wherever possible.
7. Keep coaches and spectators off the field at all times.
8. Provide adequate seating for coaches and competitors.
9. Extend sincere appreciation to all of the people who assisted in planning the meet and helped to make it a success.

**Promoting
Cross-country**

In some areas of the United States, cross-country running has become so popular that it is not uncommon to find hundreds of runners participating in a weekend event. That such a situation exists is to the credit of the teachers and coaches who have given of their time and energy to promote this worthwhile sport. The methods used by these successful teachers and coaches provide guidelines for those who are interested in initating cross-country programs in communities where they do not exist.

Perhaps the first prerequisite to success is the interest and enthusiasm of the coach. Cross-country requires little equipment, and the physical demands are those that can be imposed on almost any individual who is willing to work. Providing a measure of fun and excitement is of utmost importance to the successful program. This can be developed in part through attractive posters and other kinds of creative publicity. Many coaches have found that the bulletin board, with pictures, quotes from noted athletes, performance records, and other materials, is an excellent adjunct to promotion.

By initiating the program with tolerable overload demands and by nurturing the natural competitive interests of the performers, the teacher can develop a delight in running. The wearing of special tee shirts and membership in the 100-mile club, 200-mile club, and so on, are also excellent motivators. It is always true that where the program is related to the needs and interests of the participants with consistency and imagination success is likely to follow.

**Planning for the
Cross-country
Meet**

### Selection of the Course

Persons responsible for selecting a cross-country course would do well to remember that one of the most memorable parts of the cross-country race is the nature of the course itself. It has been my experience in more than thirty years of coaching that the conversation over long hours of returning from cross-country events usually centered on the "good sections" of the course just run. Indeed, our own Fort Casey Invitational race annually attracts nearly a thousand runners, many of whom drive for hours just to run the trails, beaches, and open spaces that our course offers.

For best results the course should be relatively open, free from dangerous obstacles, with terrain that varies from 50 to 150 feet in elevation. Better courses provide at least one-quarter mile of level, open ground at the start so that participants can establish their preliminary order without confusion. Better courses also finish uphill to minimize the wild rush that often occurs when the chute is on the level.

## Scoring the Meet

Perhaps the most tedious responsibility for the meet director is the compilation of information relative to scoring the meet. Numerous methods have been devised for this purpose, though one which currently is being used with success is the "chute and pen" method which utilizes some type of tag system to identfy individual finishers. Tags are secured prior to the race, filled in by indiivdual performers, and pinned to the shirt front.

The finish chute is a device constructed from rope stretched between stakes which have been driven into the ground over a distance of 75 to 100 feet. The end of the chute nearest the finish line is open like a funnel, narrowing to some 30 inches to avoid a shuffling of position after the finish line has been crossed. When this method is used, all runners are marshaled along the chute by "controllers" until their tags have been received by the official recorder. These tages are placed face down on a receiving spindle. When all runners have completed the course, the spindle is turned over, and the name and place of each performer are recorded on the official score sheet.

Another excellent system is to use gum back stickers that have the individual runner's name and affiliation printed on the face. These can be placed inside waterproof baggies and pinned to the performer's shirt. As the runners pass through the chute the baggies are removed and the stickers pasted to the master score sheet in the order of finish.

### Individual Score Tag

Name ...............................

Team ...............................

Event ..............................

Time ............. Place ...........

Following the recording of names, the official time for each participant is obtained from the master time sheet. Team scores are then figured by compiling the scores of the first five finishers from each team. In cross-country the team with the lowest score places first; the next lowest score, second; and so on. (For example, a team placing 2—3—4—7—9 for 25 total points would be victorious over a team placing 1—5—6—8—10 for 30 total points.)

# Appendix

## Conversion Table—Feet to Meters

| Feet | Meters and Centimeters | Feet | Meters and Centimeters |
|------|------------------------|------|------------------------|
| 1  | 0.305  | 37  | 11.278 |
| 2  | 0.610  | 38  | 11.582 |
| 3  | 0.915  | 39  | 11.887 |
| 4  | 1.219  | 40  | 12.192 |
| 5  | 1.524  | 41  | 12.497 |
| 6  | 1.828  | 42  | 12.801 |
| 7  | 2.133  | 43  | 13.106 |
| 8  | 2.438  | 44  | 13.411 |
| 9  | 2.743  | 45  | 13.761 |
| 10 | 3.048  | 46  | 14.020 |
| 11 | 3.352  | 47  | 14.325 |
| 12 | 3.657  | 48  | 14.630 |
| 13 | 3.962  | 49  | 14.935 |
| 14 | 4.267  | 50  | 15.240 |
| 15 | 4.572  | 100 | 30.480 |
| 16 | 4.876  | 110 | 33.527 |
| 17 | 5.181  | 120 | 36.575 |
| 18 | 5.486  | 130 | 39.623 |
| 19 | 5.791  | 140 | 42.672 |
| 20 | 6.096  | 150 | 45.720 |
| 21 | 6.400  | 160 | 48.768 |
| 22 | 6.705  | 170 | 51.816 |
| 23 | 7.010  | 180 | 54.864 |
| 24 | 7.315  | 190 | 57.912 |
| 25 | 7.620  | 200 | 60.960 |
| 26 | 7.024  | 210 | 64.008 |
| 27 | 8.229  | 220 | 67.056 |
| 28 | 8.534  | 230 | 70.104 |
| 29 | 8.839  | 240 | 73.152 |
| 30 | 9.144  | 250 | 76.200 |
| 31 | 9.449  | 260 | 79.248 |
| 32 | 9.754  | 270 | 82.270 |
| 33 | 10.058 | 280 | 85.344 |
| 34 | 10.363 | 290 | 88.392 |
| 35 | 10.668 | 300 | 91.440 |
| 36 | 10.972 |     |        |

## Conversion Table—Feet and Inches to Meters and Centimeters

| Inches | Centimeters | Inches | Centimeters |
|--------|-------------|--------|-------------|
| ¼ | 0.006 | 6 | 0.152 |
| ½ | 0.013 | 7 | 0.178 |
| ¾ | 0.019 | 8 | 0.203 |
| 1 | 0.025 | 9 | 0.229 |
| 2 | 0.051 | 10 | 0.254 |
| 3 | 0.076 | 11 | 0.273 |
| 4 | 0.101 | 12 | 0.305 |
| 5 | 0.127 | | |

## Hurdle Spacing and Stride Plan

| Distance of Race | No. of Hurdles | Hurdle Height | Distance to First | Steps to First | Distance Between | Steps Between |
|------------------|----------------|---------------|-------------------|----------------|------------------|---------------|
| **Men** | | | | | | |
| 110 meters | 10 | 3′6″ | 14 meters 15 yards | 8-9 | 9.1 meters 10 yards | 3 |
| 400 meters | 10 | 3′0″ | 45 meters 50 yards | 21-22 | 35 meters 38.3 yards | 13-15 |
| **Women** | | | | | | |
| 100 meters | 10 | 2′9″ | 13 meters 14.4 yards | 7-8 | 8.5 meters 9.3 yards | 3 |
| 400 meters | 10 | 2′6″ | 45 meters 50 yards | 23-26 | 35 meters 38.3 yards | 17-19 |

# Bibliography

Bowerman, William. *Coaching Track and Field*. Boston: Houghton Mifflin Company, 1974.

Bush, Jim and Weiskopf. *Dynamic Track and Field*. Boston: Allyn and Bacon, Inc., 1978.

Cooper, John M.; Lavery, James; and Perrin, William. *Track and Field for Coach and Athlete*. 2nd ed. Englewood Cliffs, N. J.: Prentice Hall, Inc. 1970.

Costill, David L. *What Research Tells the Coach About Distance Running*. Washington, D.C.: AAHPER, 1968.

Doherty, J. Kenneth. *Modern Track and Field*. Englewood Cliffs, N. J.: Prentice-Hall, Inc., 1963.

Dyson, Geoffrey. *The Mechanics of Athletics*. 6th ed., revised. London: University of London Press, 1973.

Ecker, Tom. *Track and Field Dynamics*. Los Altos, Calif.: Tafnews Press, 1974.

Ecker, Tom; Wilt, Fred; and Hay, Jim. *Olympic Track and Field Techniques*. West Nyack, N. Y.: Parker Publishing Company, 1974.

Fox, Edward L., and Matthews, Donald K. *Interval Training Conditioning for Sports and General Fitness*. Philadelphia: W. B. Saunders Company, 1974.

Jackson, Nell C. *Track and Field for Girls and Women*. Minneapolis, Minn.: Burgess Publishing Company, 1968.

Jorden, Payton, and Spencer, Bud. *Champions in the Making*. Englewood Cliffs, N. J.: Prentice-Hall, Inc., 1968.

Lydiard, Arthur, and Gilmour, Garth. *Run to the Top*. London: Herbert Jenkins, Ltd., 1962.

Powell, John T. *Track and Field Fundamentals for Teacher and Coach*. 3rd ed. Champaign, Ill.: Stipes Publishing Company, 1971.

Robinson, Clarence F., et al. *Modern Techniques of Track and Field*. Philadelphia: Lea & Febiger, 1974.

Thompson, Donnis H. *Modern Track and Field for Girls and Women*. Boston: Allyn & Bacon, Inc., 1973.

Wakefield, Frances; Harkins, Dorothy; and Cooper, John. *Track and Field Fundamentals for Girls and Women*. St. Louis: C. V. Mosby Company, 1966.

**Books**

**Journals**

*Runner's World.* P.O. Box 366, Mountain View, Calif. 94040

*Track and Field News.* P.O. Box 296. Los Altos, Cailf. 94022

*Track Technique* (published by Track and Field News). P.O. Box 296, Los Altos, Calif. 94022

**Audiovisual Aids**

Association Films, Inc. 25358 Cypress Avenue, Hayward, Calif. 94544

Cinema Associates, Inc. P.O. Box 9237, Seattle, Wa. 98109

Olympic Films, C/O The Sports Medicine Clinic, 1551 N.W. 54th, Seattle, Wa. 98107

Visual Track and Field Techniques. 292 South La Cienega, Suite 202, Beverly Hills, Calif. 90211

# Index